3RD EDITION

THE

"I DON'T KNOW HOW TO COOK" BOOK

300 GREAT RECIPES

You Can't Mess Up!

MARY-LANE KAMBERG

Adams Media

New York London Toronto Sydney New Delhi

For my daughters, Rebekka and Johanna
My gratitude to the Kansas City Writers Group

𝔔

Adams Media
An Imprint of Simon & Schuster, Inc.
100 Technology Center Drive
Stoughton, MA 02072

For information about special discounts for bulk purchases, please contact Simon & Schuster Special Sales at 1-866-506-1949 or business@simonandschuster.com.

The Simon & Schuster Speakers Bureau can bring authors to your live event. For more information or to book an event contact the Simon & Schuster Speakers Bureau at 1-866-248-3049 or visit our website at www.simonspeakers.com.

Manufactured in the United States of America

22 2023

Library of Congress Cataloging-in-Publication Data has been applied for.

ISBN 978-1-4405-8475-6
ISBN 978-1-4405-8476-3 (ebook)

Always follow safety and commonsense cooking protocol while using kitchen utensils, operating ovens and stoves, and handling uncooked food. If children are assisting in the preparation of any recipe, they should always be supervised by an adult.

Acknowledgments

From the first instant I shared the idea for a cookbook for people who can't cook, dozens of friends and family members encouraged and helped me in the effort. Special thanks to my mother and research assistant, Jessie Ladewig; my husband, Ken Kamberg; my daughters, Rebekka Rohrback and Johanna Falls; my siblings, Brock Ladewig, Amy Phillips, and Ann Nelson; and the rest of my extended family: cousins, in-laws, nieces, nephews, and my dear friends.

Particular thanks go to Michelle Langenberg, Lucy Lauer, Chalise Miner, Candy Schock, and Robin Silverman for their help. And to these friends and family who offered their favorite easy-to-make recipes: Melody Aldrich, Beth Bailey, Barbara Bartocci, Marsha Bartsch, Josh Baze, Nina Bertilsdotter, Deborah Bundy, Ginger Carter, Meri Carter, Judith Choice, Lance Clenard, Maril Crabtree, Alberta Daw, Ruth Ann Falls, Kerri Fivecoat-Campbell, Jeannine Fox, Brooke Fucille, Ricki Gilbert, Lisa Waterman Gray, Jacqueline Guidry, Madeline Guidry, Carolyn Hall, Greg Hockett, Ann Ingalls, Sally Jadlow, Judith Bader Jones, Ken Kamberg, Joe Karroll, Heather Kiepura, Tami Kohler, Betsy Krusen, Hank Krusen, Lindsey Krusen, Mary Ladewig, Julie Laird, Amelia Mendus, Sophia Myers, Joan Nietzchke, Jon Phillips, Jane Rogers, Nate Rogers, Rex Rogers, Larry Schilb, Marsha Schilb, Corrine Russell, Susan Shanaman, Niki Shepherd, Deborah Shouse, Patty Sullivan, Janet Sunderland, Polly Swafford, Vicki Swartz, Denise Tiller, Pat Walkenhorst, Toni Watson, and Bette Willmeth. Thanks, too, to my able, efficient agents, Mike and Susan Farris, and my editors, Danielle Chiotti, Chelsea King, Jacqueline Musser, and Katie Corcoran Lytle.

Contents

Introduction

Welcome to the kitchen! If you like to eat but think you can't cook, this book is for you. If you can read, you can make these dishes. Simply follow the easy directions.

The *"I Don't Know How to Cook" Book* is not a "teaching" workbook. The instructions don't use any fancy cooking terms that might scare you away. (You can look them up in the Glossary of Cooking Terms in Appendix B if you need to understand traditional cookbooks.) Instead, you'll create the dishes you want to eat without taking a cooking class.

For this third edition I focused on one question: If I couldn't cook but wanted to learn, which common foods could I try with the highest chance for success? I wanted to provide recipes so tasty and easy to make that new cooks would enjoy positive cooking experiences. The biggest change in this edition is the emphasis on healthy dishes. I tried to give new cooks something different to do with fruits and vegetables rather than just eating them plain. You'll find such new dishes as Watermelon-Raspberry Salad, Avocado-Cucumber Salad, Peas with Mint Butter, and Garlic Green Beans with Pecans.

But you'll find that I didn't ignore snacks and sweets. In Chapter 10: Snacks and Appetizers, you'll find delicious recipes for Popcorn and Fresh Tomato Salsa that belong in everyone's repertoire. In Chapter 11: Desserts, I included new recipes for such standards as Toll House Cookies, Lemon Bars, and Carrot Cake (with Cream Cheese Frosting), along with No-Bake Cheesecake and the best cookies in the world: Oatmeal Chocolate Chip. The cinnamon in this recipe makes these cookies irresistible!

In some cases I replaced old recipes with better ones. For example, Salmon Patties is gone, and Salmon-Potato Patties with Lemon-Basil Sauce stands in its place. Likewise, Beef Stroganoff replaces the less exciting Beef and Noodles from the second edition. I added some standard items like Pancakes the Old-Fashioned Way, Biscuits and Sausage Gravy, Baked Ham, Baked Beans, and Pan-Fried Chicken that should have been in earlier editions but were somehow overlooked. In Chapter 3: Soups and Stews you'll find the old standards Ham and Beans and French Onion Soup, along with the new and tasty Cheeseburger Soup with an unusual texture provided by shredded lettuce. (It's really good!)

Moving on from the basics, you'll find some fancy (but still easy!) recipes for French Toast Casserole, Layered Spinach Salad, Apple-Glazed Pork Chops, and Gorgonzola and Sage–Stuffed Chicken Breasts, to name a few. In short, there's enough variety in this new edition to make *The "I Don't Know How to Cook" Book* the only cookbook you'll need to get started in the kitchen.

All recipes in this cookbook—even those marked "hard"—were chosen because they're easy to make. The "hard" ones might use less common ingredients or take more steps than those marked "easy" or "medium." Trust me, they're still easy! The dishes are grouped according to difficulty within each chapter and are identified by these symbols:

LEVEL **E**
SERVINGS **4**

Easy: **E**
Medium: **M**
Hard: **H**

In addition, vegetarian recipes are identified with "**V**" after the recipe title.

Try the recipes marked "easy" first to ease into the cooking game. After that, challenge yourself with those marked "medium" and "hard." You'll gain cooking skills while you build your recipe stockpile, along with your confidence. I hope that after you succeed with some of these dishes, you'll venture out on your own culinary journey.

Enjoy!

Recipe for New Cooks

1. Before you begin, read the recipe all the way through. Assemble all ingredients. (The ingredients in *The "I Don't Know How to Cook" Book* are listed in the order of their appearance in the directions. If you like order, you can line them up in a row—but you don't have to!)

2. Always wash your hands before and after handling food, especially raw meats and poultry, which may contain harmful bacteria that proper cooking kills.

3. Ovens and microwaves vary, so many recipes give a range of cooking times. In recipes that give a range of cooking times, such as 15 to 20 minutes, check the food after the first time listed. If the dish is not done, return to the heat source for the additional time.

4. No recipe is carved in stone. After you try a recipe for the first time, make notes to yourself in the cookbook's margin. Note cooking times for your oven or microwave, as well as measurements you would like to adjust to your personal taste.

5. Sometimes you'll want to prepare fewer or more servings of a recipe. All you have to do is a little math. You can double a recipe by multiplying the measurement of each ingredient by two. You can cut a recipe in half by dividing the measurement of each ingredient by two. But be careful. Cooking times may vary—especially in microwaves that need more time to cook larger quantities of food. If you're doubling a recipe, do *not* double the cooking time. Cook it according to direc-

tions, but be aware that you may need a little more cooking time. The reverse may be true when cooking smaller amounts.

6. Plan menus. Eat different types of foods so you get a variety of nutrients. If you're new to meal planning, follow the school lunch menu, which often appears in local papers. Qualified dietitians plan the menus. Do what they do.

7. Nothing will dampen your enthusiasm for cooking more than a kitchen full of dirty pots, pans, and utensils when the food is done. Whenever possible, clean as you go. When you are finished with a pot, measuring cup, or mixing bowl, wash it while you're waiting for noodles to boil or during baking times. You can let the cooking utensils drip dry, or, if you're really a neat freak, you can dry them and put them away. (Nah!)

Bon Appétit!

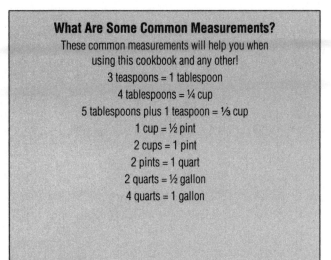

What Are Some Common Measurements?
These common measurements will help you when using this cookbook and any other!

3 teaspoons = 1 tablespoon
4 tablespoons = ¼ cup
5 tablespoons plus 1 teaspoon = ⅓ cup
1 cup = ½ pint
2 cups = 1 pint
2 pints = 1 quart
2 quarts = ½ gallon
4 quarts = 1 gallon

CHAPTER 1

Breakfasts and Breads

ORANGE-BANANA SMOOTHIE v

Wake up to this delicious breakfast in a glass, and get ready for a great day! Bananas are known to calm the mind and oranges are said to clear the mind. You'll be prepared to take on the world in just a few minutes. Use an electric blender or electric mixer.

What You Need:

1 banana

1 (6-ounce) can frozen orange juice concentrate

6 ounces water (use the orange juice can to measure)

Ice, as needed (about 2 cups)

What You Do:

1. Peel and slice banana. Place the orange juice, water, and banana in an electric blender. Blend until smooth.
2. Place ice in serving glasses. Pour the mixture over the ice.

POACHED EGG v

Poached eggs are cooked in steam. You can make them in a frying pan that has a lid, or you'll need a poaching pan, an electric egg poacher, or a microwave egg poacher. Poached eggs are especially good served on toast, with a somewhat runny yolk soaking into the bread. Yum.

What You Need:

About 1 teaspoon butter, margarine, vegetable oil, or nonstick cooking spray

1 egg

Water

What You Do:

1. Place the butter, margarine, or vegetable oil in a frying pan or spray with nonstick cooking spray. Heat the pan over medium heat until the shortening melts. (If using cooking spray, heat the pan for about 30 seconds.)
2. Break the egg into the pan. Add ½ teaspoon water (for each egg). Cover tightly.
3. Cook for about 5 minutes or until the egg is as firm as you like.

MAKIN' BACON

There's nothing like the sound and smell of bacon sizzling in the pan to start your day. Bacon is a favorite with eggs, pancakes, and French Toast (see recipe in this chapter). You can also use cooked bacon in tossed salads and on sandwiches.

Method 1: Pan-Fried

1. One at a time, lay strips of bacon side by side in a cold frying pan. Turn on heat to medium-high. As the bacon cooks, use a fork to move the slices often to avoid sticking. When each slice is brown on the first side, use a fork or tongs to turn it over.
2. Cook on the second side until the bacon is as crisp as you like it. Use a fork or tongs to remove each slice from the pan. Drain on several sheets of paper towels.

Method 2: Microwaved

1. Place 2 pieces of paper towels on a microwave-safe plate. Place strips of bacon on the paper towels in a single layer. Cover with another 2 pieces of paper towels.
2. Microwave on high for 4 to 6 minutes. Keep an eye on it. Check after 5 minutes and again every 2 minutes until done.

Method 3: Baked

Preheat oven to 400°F. Separate pieces of bacon and lay across the rack of a broiler pan. The slots in the broiler pan lid will let bacon fat drip into the lower part of the pan. If you don't have a broiler pan, use a shallow, ovenproof baking dish. Bake on a middle oven rack for about 10 minutes. No need to turn.

What Should I Do with the Bacon Fat?

Bacon fat is often used to add flavor to eggs, vegetables, or other foods. After cooking bacon, pour the fat into an ovenproof glass container. (The fat will be hot and could crack containers not designed to hold hot food.) Cool to room temperature. Cover and store in refrigerator until ready to use. If you don't plan to use it to add flavor to other foods, do not pour it down the sink. You'll clog your drain pipes. Instead, pour it into a used can, chill in refrigerator until solid, and discard.

FRIED EGG v

All you need to fry an egg is a frying pan—or a hot sidewalk—and some type of fat, like butter, margarine, vegetable oil, or nonstick cooking spray. For added flavor, use saved bacon grease or the drippings from freshly cooked breakfast sausage.

What You Need:

2–3 tablespoons butter, margarine, vegetable oil, or nonstick cooking spray

1 egg

What You Do:

1. Melt the butter (or alternative) in a frying pan over medium heat. When melted, crack the egg into the frying pan.
2. For "sunny-side up," cook until the yolk is done according to your preference. For "over easy," let cook until the white is almost done. Flip with a spatula. Immediately flip over onto serving plate. "Basted" eggs look like "over easy" eggs, but you don't flip them over. Instead, as the egg cooks, spoon hot fat from the frying pan on top of the egg. The top will cook, but you won't risk breaking the yolk during the flipping process.

VARIATION: **FRIED EGG AND CHEESE** v

When the egg white is cooked, or immediately after flipping over the egg, add a slice of your favorite cheese. Cook until the cheese melts.

LEVEL **E**

SERVINGS **1**

Both soft-boiled and hard-boiled eggs are cooked the same way. The only difference is the cooking time. Start with an egg at room temperature.

BOILED EGG v

What You Need:

1 egg

Water, as needed to cover the egg

What You Do:

1. Place the egg in a saucepan (for many eggs at once you can use a Dutch oven, but don't stack eggs on top of each other). Cover with water. Bring to a boil over medium-high to high heat.
2. When the water boils, cover tightly. Remove from heat. For a soft-boiled egg, let stand for 2 to 4 minutes, depending on your preferred firmness. For a hard-boiled egg, let stand for 20 minutes.
3. Rinse the egg in cold water to stop the cooking process and to make it easier to remove the shell.

How Do I Boil Water?

Boiling water means heating it enough that it turns to steam. All you do is pour the water into a saucepan or microwave-safe dish and heat over high heat on the stovetop or on high in a microwave until big bubbles break on the surface. Boiling water is an important cooking method used for cooking eggs, hot dogs, vegetables, and even some meat. Water boils faster if you cover the pan with a lid. Be careful not to let the pan boil dry. As water boils, it evaporates as steam. So if you heat it too long, all the water will disappear and your food will burn.

SCRAMBLED EGGS v

You can eat scrambled eggs alone or with cheese or other added ingredients, such as chopped bell pepper, chopped onion (or dried onion flakes), sliced olives, sliced mushrooms, bacon bits, diced cooked ham, or crumbled cooked sausage. You can use any type of milk from skim to whole. However, using water instead of milk makes the eggs fluffier.

What You Need:

1–2 tablespoons butter, margarine, vegetable oil, nonstick cooking spray, or bacon fat

2–3 eggs

2–3 tablespoons milk or water

What You Do:

1. Melt butter (or alternative) in a frying pan (any size) over medium heat. (If using butter, don't let it turn dark brown. Reduce heat if necessary.)
2. Crack the eggs into a small mixing bowl. Add 1 tablespoon milk for each egg. Quickly stir with a fork to break the yolks and blend in the milk. Add any optional ingredients. Pour into frying pan.
3. As the eggs cook, stir so they heat evenly for about 5 to 6 minutes. When the eggs are still a bit runnier than you like, remove from heat and let sit for 1 to 2 minutes. (Eggs will continue to cook.) Fluff with a fork.

Add a taste of Mexico to breakfast or brunch. You can mix the ingredients ahead of time and slip this dish into the oven when your guests arrive.

CHILI EGG PUFF v

What You Need:

1 tablespoon solid shortening, for greasing the pan

½ cup butter

10 eggs

3 cups shredded Monterey jack cheese

½ cup all-purpose flour

1 teaspoon baking powder

1 pint cottage cheese

2 (4-ounce) cans diced green chilies

What You Do:

1. Preheat oven to 350°F. Use the solid shortening to generously grease a 9" × 15" ovenproof baking pan. Melt the butter in a small frying pan or saucepan over low heat. Crack the eggs into a large mixing bowl. Beat until smooth and yellow.
2. Stir in the cheese, flour, baking powder, and cottage cheese. Beat again until well mixed.
3. Drain the chilies. Mix into the egg mixture by gently stirring the mixture from bottom to top.
4. Pour mixture into the baking pan. Bake for 35 minutes or until the mixture is puffy and no longer runny.

APPLE OATMEAL v

This is not your mother's oatmeal. With the fragrant aroma of apples and cinnamon, this oatmeal has the zing and spice of apple pie. Serve with cold milk to drink and/or stir into the cereal. Enjoy.

What You Need:

1 apple

⅓ cup oats (uncooked oatmeal—not instant)

¼ cup raisins (optional)

¼ teaspoon cinnamon

⅔ cup milk

About 2 tablespoons loosely packed brown sugar

What You Do:

1. Peel, core, and chop the apple. Place in a saucepan with the oats, raisins, and cinnamon. Stir in the milk and cook over medium heat until bubbly. Reduce heat to low. Simmer for 5 minutes, stirring occasionally.
2. Spoon into 4 serving bowls. Sprinkle each with about 1½ teaspoons brown sugar.

How Do I Use an Apple Corer?

If you like apples, you'll love a kitchen gadget called a corer. A corer is a circular tool with a round space in the middle and pie-shaped holes around the circle. The metal edges are sharp on the bottom side. To use, first rinse apple under cold, running water. Pat dry with a paper towel. Place apple on a cutting board, stem-side up. Place the circle of the corer over the stem. Push down in a single thrust. Lift tool. Apple slices will fall away, and the core will be removed.

You don't need a pancake mix for this all-you-can-eat breakfast. Double or triple the recipe if you need more than a dozen pancakes. For variety add 1 cup rinsed blueberries to the batter. Serve with butter and your favorite flavor of syrup or jam.

PANCAKES THE OLD-FASHIONED WAY v

What You Need:

1 cup all-purpose flour

2 tablespoons granulated sugar

2 teaspoons baking powder

½ teaspoon salt

1 large egg

1 cup milk

2 tablespoons vegetable oil, plus 1–2 tablespoons for cooking, divided

What You Do:

1. Place the flour, sugar, baking powder, and salt in a medium mixing bowl. Stir until well mixed. Set aside.
2. Crack the egg into a large mixing bowl. Add the milk and 2 tablespoons of the oil. Quickly stir it with a fork until well blended. Add the flour mixture. Gently stir until the batter is well mixed but still a little lumpy.
3. Place the remaining vegetable oil in a large frying pan or griddle. Use a paper towel to spread the oil to coat the entire surface. Heat over medium heat until a few drops of water sprinkled on the pan lightly dance on the surface.
4. For each pancake pour ¼ cup of the batter onto the frying pan. Cook for about 2 to 3 minutes until the edges look a bit hardened, the bubbles that form on the top of the pancake start to pop, and the bottom of the pancake is golden brown. The appearance of the pancake is more important than a specific cooking time. Use a spatula to flip to the other side for another 1 to 2 minutes, until golden brown.
5. Cook the remaining batter until it is all used up. Add more oil to the pan as needed to prevent batter from sticking.

(continued on next page)

PANCAKES THE OLD-FASHIONED WAY — CONTINUED

6. Optional: Serve as you go. Or, store the cooked pancakes on an ovenproof platter in a 200°F preheated oven until all the batter is used.

How Can I Sweeten Foods?

You can sweeten foods with corn syrup, honey, maple syrup, or molasses. But the most common sweetener used in home cooking is sugar. Sugar most commonly comes from sugar cane or sugar beet. However, some commercial sugars derive from sorghum, maple, or palm. The three types of sugar most often used in cooking are granulated sugar, brown sugar, and confectioners' sugar. Granulated sugar is the sugar you're used to seeing in a sugar bowl. Brown sugar is a mixture of granulated sugar and molasses. Brown sugar comes in light and dark varieties. Confectioners' sugar, also called powdered sugar, is fine granulated sugar mixed with cornstarch. Its texture resembles flour. When cooking, use the type of sugar the recipe specifies. Do not try to interchange them.

LEVEL **E**

SERVINGS **6**

Use the batter for Pancakes the Old-Fashioned Way (see recipe in this chapter) to make a sweet, baked breakfast dish. You can substitute ¾ cup of fresh blueberries for the apples. Serve warm with butter and maple syrup or confectioners' sugar.

VARIATION: BAKED APPLE (OR BLUEBERRY) AND SAUSAGE PANCAKES

What You Need:

1 tablespoon solid shortening or nonstick cooking spray, for greasing the pan
½ (12-ounce) package medium or hot spicy ground pork sausage
Batter for Pancakes the Old-Fashioned Way (see recipe in this chapter)
1 apple
1½ teaspoons cinnamon
1½ teaspoons granulated sugar

What You Do:

1. Preheat oven to 375°F. Use the solid shortening to grease an 8" × 8" ovenproof baking pan or generously spray with nonstick cooking spray.

(continued on next page)

VARIATION: **BAKED APPLE (OR BLUEBERRY) AND SAUSAGE PANCAKES** — CONTINUED

2. Brown the sausage in a large frying pan over medium-high heat. Drain off fat. Place in a large mixing bowl, stir in the pancake batter, and pour into the baking pan.
3. Peel, core, and slice the apple. Layer the slices on top of the batter. Sprinkle lightly with the cinnamon and sugar. Bake for 25 to 30 minutes, until puffy on the edges and golden brown on top. Cut it into squares and remove from pan with a spatula. Serve warm.

LEVEL **E**
SERVINGS **6**

If you feel like a nut—or a monkey—try this. Serve warm, with butter and maple syrup or confectioners' sugar.

VARIATION: **BAKED NUTTY BANANA PANCAKES** V

What You Need:

1 tablespoon solid shortening or nonstick cooking spray, for greasing the pan
Batter for Pancakes the Old-Fashioned Way (see recipe in this chapter)
1 teaspoon cinnamon
1 teaspoon vanilla extract
2 tablespoons chopped pecans
⅛ teaspoon salt
1 banana

What You Do:

1. Preheat oven to 375°F. Use the solid shortening to grease an 8" × 8" ovenproof baking pan or generously spray with nonstick cooking spray.
2. In a large mixing bowl stir together the pancake batter, cinnamon, vanilla extract, pecans, and salt. Pour the batter into the baking pan. Peel the banana, slice crosswise, and arrange in a layer on top of the batter. Bake for 20 to 25 minutes, until puffy on the edges and golden brown on top. Cut it into squares and remove from pan with a spatula.

FRENCH TOAST v

You can top this breakfast favorite with maple syrup, your favorite flavor of jam or jelly, honey, or confectioners' sugar. You can use slightly stale white or wheat bread that has become dry (but not moldy!) or 1"-thick slices of French bread left over from another meal.

What You Need:

2 eggs

½ cup milk

2 tablespoons butter or margarine

6 slices bread

What You Do:

1. Crack the eggs into a medium mixing bowl. Add the milk and stir with a fork until well blended.
2. Melt the butter (or margarine) in a large frying pan over medium heat. Dip each slice of bread into the egg mixture so it is coated on both sides. Place in the frying pan. Heat for 1 to 2 minutes until the bottom side is golden brown. The appearance of the bread is more important than the specific cooking time. Use a spatula to flip to the other side. Heat until golden brown. Serve immediately.

HONEY-BANANA BAGEL SPREAD v

What You Need:

3 ounces cream cheese

3 tablespoons butter or margarine

1 banana

3 tablespoons honey

What You Do:

1. Set out the cream cheese and butter (or margarine)
   to soften for 10 to 15 minutes. Place in a small mixing
   bowl.
2. Peel the banana and slice crosswise. Add to the mixing bowl. Add the honey. Use a potato masher or electric mixer to stir together until smooth.

PEACHES AND CREAM BAGEL SPREAD v

What You Need:

4 tablespoons cream cheese

2 tablespoons peach preserves

What You Do:

Set out the cream cheese to soften for 10 to 15 minutes.
In a small bowl, mash cream cheese until smooth. Stir
in preserves until well blended.

STRAWBERRY BAGEL SPREAD v

LEVEL E

SERVINGS 2

Strawberries and cream cheese on a toasted bagel—yum!

What You Need:

4 ounces cream cheese

½ cup fresh strawberries or 3 tablespoons strawberry jam

⅓ cup granulated sugar

1 tablespoon orange juice

What You Do:

Set out the cream cheese to soften for 10 to 15 minutes. Place in a small bowl. Clean the strawberries (see the "How Should I Clean Strawberries?" sidebar with the Fruit Pizza recipe in Chapter 11), and cut into slices. Mash with a fork. Add to the cream cheese. Stir in the sugar and orange juice. Use a spoon or electric mixer to blend until smooth.

HONEY BUTTER v

LEVEL E

SERVINGS 4

Try this melt-in-your-mouth spread on Biscuits or Easy Dinner Rolls (see recipes in this chapter).

What You Need:

½ cup butter or margarine

1 tablespoon honey

What You Do:

Set out butter (or margarine) to soften for 10 to 15 minutes. Place in a small mixing bowl. Use a fork or electric mixer to blend until smooth. Stir in the honey until well blended.

HUEVOS RANCHEROS v

LEVEL **M**

SERVINGS **4**

Here's a muy bien dish to give your breakfast a spicy flavor. Serve with sour cream and your favorite picante sauce or salsa—chunky salsa works well.

What You Need:

½ cup vegetable oil

4 (6") corn tortillas

⅔ cup shredded Monterey jack cheese

⅔ cup shredded sharp Cheddar cheese

4 eggs

What You Do:

1. Pour the oil into a large frying pan to about ⅛" deep. Heat the oil over medium-high heat.
2. One at a time, cook the tortillas in the oil for about 30 seconds until warm and just starting to brown. Turn and repeat on the other side. Add more oil if needed. Drain on paper towels or on a wire rack with a paper towel under it. Cover with paper or clean cloth towel to keep warm.
3. Mix the cheeses in a small mixing bowl and set aside.
4. Fry the eggs (see Fried Egg recipe in this chapter). Place each tortilla on a serving plate. Place a cooked egg on top of each tortilla. Top with the cheese mixture.

POPPY SEED HAM BISCUITS

LEVEL **M**

SERVINGS **24**

You can use refrigerated biscuits in this recipe or make your own Biscuits (see recipe in this chapter). Beware of eating poppy seeds if you are subject to drug testing at work. You may test positive for opiates for at least 48 hours after eating them!

What You Need:

¼ cup butter

3 cans of 8 refrigerated biscuits

1½ tablespoons finely chopped onion

1½ teaspoons poppy seeds

1½ teaspoons Dijon mustard

½ pound thin deli ham slices

What You Do:

1. Set out the butter to soften for 10 to 15 minutes.
2. Bake biscuits according to package directions. Let cool. Cut in half horizontally.
3. Preheat oven to 350°F.
4. In a small mixing bowl, stir together the butter, onion, poppy seeds, and Dijon mustard.
5. Spread the mixture on the bottom halves of the biscuits. Place in a shallow, ovenproof baking pan. Top each with one or two slices of ham and the biscuit tops.
6. Seal the pan with aluminum foil. Bake for 10 minutes or until warm.

BISCUITS AND SAUSAGE GRAVY

This hearty, stick-to-your-ribs breakfast is a traditional favorite. Use your choice of mild, medium, or hot sausage. You can use refrigerated biscuits in this recipe or make your own Biscuits (see recipe in this chapter). Serve with fruit.

What You Need:

1 can of 8 refrigerated biscuits

10 ounces ground pork sausage

¼ cup all-purpose flour

2½ cups milk

Salt and pepper, to taste

What You Do:

1. Bake the biscuits according to package directions.
2. Crumble the sausage into a large frying pan over medium heat as you would brown ground beef (see the "How Do I Brown Ground Beef? sidebar with the Chili Blue recipe in Chapter 3). Stir occasionally as it cooks until meat has no tinge of pink.
3. Stir in the flour a little at a time. Slowly add the milk, stirring constantly until the mixture boils and thickens. Keep stirring and reduce heat to medium-low for 2 more minutes. Sprinkle with salt and pepper.
4. Place the biscuits on serving plates. Spoon gravy over the top.

This recipe is an easy substitute for frozen hash browns. Serve with eggs or pancakes and some fruit, and add ketchup if you like.

ROASTED BREAKFAST POTATOES v

What You Need:

Nonstick cooking spray

2 pounds Yukon gold or new potatoes

5 teaspoons olive oil

½ to 1 teaspoon salt, or more to taste

What You Do:

1. Preheat the oven to 425°F. Generously spray a rimmed cookie sheet with nonstick cooking spray.
2. Wash and peel the potatoes. Cut into 1" to 1½" cubes. Place in a large mixing bowl. Sprinkle with the olive oil and salt. Use your hands to blend the mixture until well coated. Place in a single layer on the cookie sheet.
3. Bake 20 minutes. Remove from the oven. Stir and spread them out again. Leave any pieces that stick to the sheet in place. They'll be easier to move after they cook a little longer. Return to the oven for another 10 to 25 minutes until crisp and golden brown.

HOME-FRIED POTATOES v

Here's a way to enjoy cottage fries without the trouble of peeling and deep-frying. Serve with a Fried Egg (see recipe in this chapter).

What You Need:

1 tablespoon butter, margarine, or vegetable oil

1 (15-ounce) can sliced potatoes

¼ teaspoon garlic powder

¼ teaspoon onion powder

Salt and pepper, to taste

What You Do:

1. Melt the butter (or alternative) in a large frying pan over medium heat.
2. Drain the potatoes. Add to the frying pan. Gently stir until potatoes are well coated. Sprinkle with garlic powder, onion powder, salt, and pepper. Continue stirring until thoroughly heated and golden brown.

SAUSAGE SOUFFLÉ

A soufflé is a fluffy, baked egg dish with a wide variety of other ingredients. Prepare the night before. Some of the fat necessary in this recipe comes from the milk. So, if you use skim milk, add 1½ teaspoons of butter or margarine.

What You Need:

1 pound "hot" ground pork sausage

18 eggs

2½ cups whole milk

7 slices white bread

1½ cups shredded sharp Cheddar cheese

1½ teaspoons dry mustard

¾ teaspoon salt

What You Do:

1. In a medium or large frying pan, cook the sausage until browned. Drain off grease and set sausage aside.
2. In a medium mixing bowl, beat together the eggs and milk. Cut the bread (including crust) into 1" cubes. Stir into the egg mixture, along with the sausage, cheese, dry mustard, and salt until well mixed. Pour into an ungreased 9" × 13" ovenproof baking pan. Cover and refrigerate overnight so the bread can absorb the flavors.
3. Preheat oven to 325°F. Cover and bake for 45 minutes. Remove cover and bake for another 15 minutes.

¡Buenos días! Start your morning with a flavor from south of the border. Serve with salsa and sour cream.

BREAKFAST BURRITO

What You Need:

4 medium red russet potatoes
1 pound lean ground beef
8 eggs
¼ cup milk
10 (8") flour tortillas
2 cups shredded Cheddar cheese

What You Do:

1. Rinse the potatoes under cold, running water. Peel and cut into 1" cubes. Place the potatoes in a large frying pan with the ground beef. Brown the beef and potatoes (see the "How Do I Brown Ground Beef? sidebar with the Chili Blue recipe in Chapter 3). Drain off the fat and return to heat.
2. Preheat oven to 350°F. In a medium mixing bowl, beat together the eggs and milk with a fork, wire whisk, or electric mixer until well blended. Pour into the beef mixture and cook, stirring, until the eggs are done.
3. Place about ⅓ cup of the mixture onto the middle of a tortilla and sprinkle with cheese. Fold the bottom ¼ of the tortilla over the mixture. Fold one side over the mixture. Fold the other side over the first side. Gently roll the tortilla over and place seam-side down in a 9" × 13" ovenproof baking pan that has been sprayed with cooking spray. Repeat until all the tortillas are filled and in the baking pan.
4. Cover with aluminum foil and bake for 25 to 30 minutes or until heated through. Or, cover with a paper towel and microwave on high until hot. (Do not use aluminum foil in a microwave.)

What Do I Do If My Potatoes Sprout in Storage?

If your potatoes sprout while you're storing them, you can still use them. Just break off the sprouts before peeling the potatoes.

Quiche is basically an omelet in a pie crust. Serve it as an appetizer or a breakfast entrée.

QUICHE LORRAINE

What You Need:

1 (9") frozen pie crust

1 large onion

¼ pound bacon

1 cup grated Swiss cheese

4 eggs

¼ teaspoon salt

¼ teaspoon nutmeg

⅛ teaspoon cayenne pepper

2 cups milk

What You Do:

1. Preheat oven to 375°F. Bake the empty pie crust for 10 minutes or until lightly browned.
2. While the pie crust is baking, chop the onion and set aside. Fry the bacon (see Makin' Bacon recipe in this chapter). Remove the cooked bacon from the pan and drain the fat, leaving about 2 tablespoons in the frying pan. When the bacon has cooled, break the slices into crumbles and set aside.
3. Cook the onion in the bacon fat over medium-high heat, stirring constantly until tender.
4. Spread the cheese in an even layer in the bottom of the pie crust. Sprinkle the bacon and onion over the cheese.
5. In a medium mixing bowl, beat the eggs with a whisk or fork. Beat in the salt, nutmeg, and cayenne pepper until well mixed. Stir in the milk until well blended. Pour the egg mixture over the cheese, onions, and bacon in the pie crust. Bake for 30 minutes or until golden brown.

Here's a quiche for veggie lovers. You can use all one kind of mushroom or a combination of different varieties.

MUSHROOM QUICHE v

What You Need:

1 (9") frozen pie crust

1 pound fresh mushrooms

1 clove garlic (or ⅛ teaspoon dried minced garlic)

1 tablespoon butter

Salt and pepper, to taste

2 tablespoons chopped fresh parsley (or 2 teaspoons dried)

3 eggs

1½ cups whipping cream

½ cup grated Parmesan cheese

What You Do:

1. Preheat oven to 375°F. Bake empty pie crust for 10 minutes until lightly browned.
2. While the pie crust is baking, wipe the mushrooms with a damp paper towel and slice. Peel and slice the garlic (if using fresh).
3. Melt the butter in a medium or large frying pan over medium-high heat. Stir in the mushrooms and garlic. Season with salt and pepper. Cook, stirring constantly, until all the liquid is cooked out of the mushrooms. Stir in the parsley.
4. In a medium mixing bowl, beat together the eggs, whipping cream, and Parmesan cheese. Gently stir in the mushrooms and garlic. Pour the mixture into the baked pie crust. Bake for 30 minutes until golden brown.

BACON AND EGG CASSEROLE

Here's another casserole that you prepare the night before and pop into the oven in the morning. Some of the fat necessary in this recipe comes from the milk. So, if you use skim milk, add 1½ teaspoons of butter or margarine.

You can also serve this dish for dinner as an inexpensive main course; make it in the morning and cook it at dinnertime.

What You Need:

8 slices bacon

8 eggs

1 quart 2% or whole milk

1 cup shredded American cheese

1 teaspoon salt

1 (6-ounce) box herb-seasoned croutons

What You Do:

1. Fry the bacon (see Makin' Bacon recipe in this chapter). Remove the cooked bacon from the pan and drain on paper towels. When the bacon is cooked, crumble it with your hands. Place in a cup or small bowl. Cover and refrigerate overnight.
2. In a large mixing bowl, beat together the eggs and milk. Stir in the cheese, salt, and croutons. Pour into an ungreased 9" × 13" ovenproof baking pan. Cover and refrigerate overnight.
3. Preheat oven to 350°F. Sprinkle the crumbled bacon over the egg mixture. Cover with foil and bake for 45 minutes.

LEVEL **H**

SERVINGS **8-10**

This no-dough pizza is great for breakfast or brunch. For variety, substitute ham, sausage, mushrooms, peppers, or your own favorite toppings for the pepperoni. Do not use low-fat or fat-free cream cheese for this recipe. The fat in the cream cheese is a necessary ingredient.

EGG PIZZA

What You Need:

1 (8-ounce) box cream cheese

2 eggs

¼ teaspoon ground black pepper

1¼ teaspoons garlic powder, divided

¼ cup grated Parmesan cheese

½ cup pizza sauce

16–24 pepperoni slices, to your liking

1½ cups shredded mozzarella cheese

What You Do:

1. Unwrap the cream cheese and place in a medium mixing bowl to soften for 10 to 15 minutes. Preheat oven to 350°F. Spray a 9" × 13" ovenproof baking pan with cooking spray.
2. Add the eggs, pepper, 1 teaspoon garlic powder, and Parmesan cheese to the cream cheese. Mix well using an electric mixer.
3. Pour mixture into the baking dish. Bake for 12 to 15 minutes until golden brown. Cool for 10 minutes.
4. Spread the pizza sauce on the cooled crust. Place pepperoni slices on top of the sauce. Sprinkle with the mozzarella cheese and remaining ¼ teaspoon garlic powder.
5. Bake 8 to 10 minutes until cheese melts.

Prepare this dish the night before. In the morning pop it in the oven for a perk-me-up breakfast or brunch for a crowd. Serve with maple syrup.

FRENCH TOAST CASSEROLE v

What You Need:

CASSEROLE

Butter, as needed to coat the baking pan

1 loaf French bread

8 large eggs

2 cups half-and-half

1 cup 2% or whole milk

2 tablespoons granulated sugar

1 teaspoon vanilla extract

¼ teaspoon cinnamon

¼ teaspoon nutmeg

⅛ teaspoon salt

TOPPING

½ pound butter at room temperature

1 cup tightly packed light brown sugar

1 cup chopped pecans

2 tablespoons light corn syrup

½ teaspoon cinnamon

½ teaspoon nutmeg

(continued on next page)

FRENCH TOAST CASSEROLE

— CONTINUED

What You Do:

1. **For the Casserole:** Use butter to coat a 9" x 13" oven-proof baking pan.
2. Slice the French bread into 1" slices. (You'll need about 20 slices or whatever fits in your baking pan.) Place the bread in the baking pan in two rows, letting the slices overlap.
3. Crack the eggs into a large mixing bowl. Add the half-and-half, milk, sugar, vanilla, cinnamon, nutmeg, and salt. Beat together with an electric mixer until well blended.
4. Pour the egg mixture over and between the bread slices so all the bread is evenly soaked. Cover with aluminum foil. Refrigerate overnight.
5. **For the Topping:** In the morning, preheat the oven to 350°F.
6. In a medium mixing bowl stir together the butter, brown sugar, pecans, light corn syrup, cinnamon, and nutmeg. Spread the mixture over the top of the bread.
7. Bake 40 minutes until puffy and lightly browned.

ORANGE-GLAZED BISCUITS v

Sweet and tangy, these breakfast biscuits will start your day with sunshine. Make orange juice from the leftover orange juice concentrate. Measure remaining concentrate and add 3 times as much water, then stir.

What You Need:

½ cup butter or margarine

1 cup granulated sugar

3 tablespoons frozen orange juice concentrate

1 (12-ounce) can refrigerated biscuits

What You Do:

1. Preheat oven to 375°F. Melt the butter (or margarine) in a saucepan over low heat. Stir in the sugar and orange juice concentrate. Dip the top of each biscuit in this mixture and place glazed-side down, side by side and touching the other biscuits in a greased tube pan, bundt pan, or round cake pan.
2. Pour the remaining glaze over the biscuits in the pan. Bake, uncovered, for 15 minutes. During baking, the glaze works its way to the bottom of the pan, so when serving, turn biscuits upside down on serving plate so the glaze will drizzle over the top for an attractive presentation. Serve warm.

The aroma of cinnamon and freshly baked biscuit dough is an inviting way to start the day. You can substitute chopped walnuts for the pecans.

EASY COFFEE CAKE v

What You Need:

½ cup butter or margarine

½ cup firmly packed brown sugar

1 teaspoon cinnamon

Shortening or nonstick cooking spray, as needed

1 (12-ounce) can refrigerated biscuits

2 tablespoons chopped pecans

What You Do:

1. Preheat oven to 350°F. Melt the butter (or margarine) in a saucepan over low heat. Stir in the brown sugar and cinnamon.

2. Grease a 9" round cake pan with solid shortening or spray with nonstick cooking spray. Dip the top of each biscuit into the butter mixture. Place butter-side down in the pan, starting on the outer edge and overlapping the biscuits in a circle. Use remaining biscuits to fill the middle of the pan.

3. Add nuts to remaining butter mixture. Spoon the mixture onto the biscuits. Bake uncovered for 10 minutes.

For cheesy biscuits, add 1 cup shredded Cheddar cheese to the mix before baking.

BISCUITS v

What You Need:

Shortening, as needed

2 cups all-purpose flour

Pinch of salt

½ cup butter

½ cup ice-cold milk

What You Do:

1. Preheat oven to 400°F. Grease a baking sheet with shortening.
2. In a large mixing bowl, use a fork to mix together the flour, salt, and butter. Stir in the milk until well mixed.
3. Optional: Use your hands to knead in the cheese. Press the heel of your hand into the dough, then fold over the dough onto itself. Repeat until well mixed.
4. Drop heaping spoonsful of the dough onto the prepared baking sheet in rows. Bake for 10 to 12 minutes, until golden brown.

LEVEL **E**

SERVINGS **6**

You can't serve ham and beans without corn bread. This crumbly bread goes well with other pork dishes, too. Serve warm with lots of butter. If you like your corn bread sweeter, add an additional tablespoon of sugar to the batter.

CORN BREAD v

What You Need:

1½ cups cornmeal

½ cup all-purpose flour

1 tablespoon granulated sugar

1½ teaspoons baking powder

½ teaspoon salt

¼ cup butter

1½ cups plain yogurt

1 large egg

What You Do:

1. Preheat the oven to 375°F. Spray an 8" round cake pan (or square baking pan) with nonstick cooking spray.
2. In a medium mixing bowl, mix together the cornmeal, flour, sugar, baking powder, and salt. Set aside.
3. Melt the butter in a small frying pan over low heat. Pour into a small mixing bowl. Stir in the yogurt and egg until well blended. Slowly add to the cornmeal mixture just until the dry ingredients are moistened.
4. Pour the batter into the pan. Bake for 25 to 30 minutes. The corn bread is done when the edges are golden brown and the top is puffy and cracked. Cut into wedges or squares to serve.

Is Corn a Vegetable?

Many people think of corn as a "yellow vegetable." Don't let the color fool you. Although it is sold in the produce department, corn is a grain, not a vegetable. Corn is a staple in many cultures, and it's a good source of vitamin C. In some American Indian cultures, corn is used for ritual and healing.

BLUEBERRY MUFFINS v

Don't pay for a box of muffin mix. You'll be proud to serve these muffins you made from scratch! You'll need paper muffin cups, or you can grease 9 cups of a muffin tin for baking.
For a different flavor, replace the blueberries with 1 cup cranberries or ¾ cup raisins or chopped nuts

What You Need:

1¾ cups all-purpose flour

¼ cup granulated sugar

2½ teaspoons baking powder

1 egg

¾ cup milk

⅓ cup vegetable oil

1 cup blueberries

What You Do:

1. Preheat the oven to 400°F. In a medium mixing bowl, combine the flour, sugar, and baking powder. Set aside.
2. In a separate, small bowl, use a fork to beat the egg. Still using the fork, stir in the milk and vegetable oil.
3. Pour the egg mixture into the flour mixture. Stir slowly just until blended into a slightly lumpy mixture. Stir in the blueberries.
4. Place paper muffin cups into a muffin tin, and pour the batter almost to the top. Bake 20 to 25 minutes. Test for doneness by inserting a toothpick into the center of one of the muffins. Muffins are done when the toothpick comes out clean.

MEXICAN CORN BREAD v

Spice up ordinary corn bread to make a tasty snack that you can eat by itself or serve with soups or stews. This is especially good with pork.

What You Need:

2 eggs

1 (4-ounce) can diced green chilies

1 cup yellow cornmeal

¾ cup vegetable oil

1 (14.75-ounce) can creamed corn

½ teaspoon baking soda

1 teaspoon salt

Shortening, as needed

1½ cups shredded Cheddar cheese

What You Do:

1. Preheat oven to 400°F. Crack the eggs into a large mixing bowl. Beat with a fork until smooth. Drain the chilies and add to the bowl. Stir in the cornmeal, vegetable oil, creamed corn, baking soda, and salt. Pour into a 9" × 12" ovenproof baking pan that has been lightly greased with shortening.
2. Top with the cheese. Bake for 45 minutes until the top is golden brown.

What's an Easy Way to Drain Canned Foods?

If you need to drain a can of beans, fruits, or vegetables, you can open the can and dump the contents into a sieve or colander. An easier way is simply to open the can, but leave the separated lid in place. Hold it in place with your fingers as you invert the can until the liquid drains out.

SPINACH BREAD v

Spinach for breakfast? This bread is a good way to get a dark green, leafy vegetable in an unusual way. Serve warm with whipped butter.

What You Need:

1 (10-ounce) package frozen spinach, thawed

½ stick butter or margarine

2 eggs

1 cup all-purpose flour

¾ teaspoon salt

1 teaspoon baking powder

1 cup milk

1 pound Monterey jack cheese, grated

What You Do:

1. Place a paper towel in the bottom of a colander. Place the spinach on top to thaw. When thawed, cover with another paper towel. Press to drain the spinach well.
2. Melt the butter (or margarine) in a small saucepan. Pour into an 8" × 11" baking pan, tipping the pan until well coated. Return remaining melted butter to the saucepan. Preheat oven to 350°F.
3. In a large mixing bowl, beat the eggs. In a medium mixing bowl, stir together the flour, salt, and baking powder. Alternately add milk and the flour mixture to the eggs, stirring until well blended. Add the melted butter, drained spinach, and cheese. Mix well. Pour into the greased baking pan. Bake for 35 minutes.
4. Remove from oven. Cut into serving squares.

This tasty bread brings the pumpkin flavor of fall holidays to the breakfast table any time of year. You can omit the nuts if you prefer.

PUMPKIN-NUT BREAD v

What You Need:

Shortening, as needed
2 cups all-purpose flour
2 teaspoons baking powder
½ teaspoon salt
½ teaspoon pumpkin pie spice
¼ teaspoon baking soda
1 cup firmly packed brown sugar
⅓ cup vegetable oil
2 eggs
1 cup canned pumpkin
¼ cup milk
½ cup chopped walnuts

What You Do:

1. Preheat oven to 350°F. Use solid shortening to grease the bottom (not the sides) of a loaf pan.
2. Combine the flour, baking powder, salt, pumpkin pie spice, and baking soda in a medium mixing bowl; stir until well mixed.
3. In a separate, large mixing bowl, use an electric mixer to beat together the brown sugar, vegetable oil, and eggs until well blended. With a spoon, stir in the pumpkin and milk.
4. Add the flour mixture about ¼ cup at a time, stirring until the batter is just smooth. Gently stir in the nuts. Pour the batter into the loaf pan. Bake for 1 hour. Let cool for 10 minutes; then remove from pan and place on a wire rack until cooled.

How Do I Measure Brown Sugar?

Some recipes that call for brown sugar specify that the measurement should be "firmly packed." To measure that way, put the brown sugar in the measuring cup and use the back of a spoon to pack it down. Keep tightly pressing it into the measuring cup until you have the amount asked for. This method results in more brown sugar than you would get using the usual measuring method—and that's what the recipe writer intends.

BANANA BREAD v

Moist and aromatic, this banana bread will become a family tradition. When serving, sprinkle with confectioners' sugar. If you're going to make 1 loaf, why not make 3 loaves at once? Purchase foil loaf pans you can give away. Let loaves cool in the pans. Then cover with plastic wrap and tie with ribbons to give as gifts.

What You Need:

1 cup solid vegetable shortening, plus extra for greasing
2½ cups cake flour, plus 3 tablespoons for dusting
2 cups granulated sugar
4 eggs
6 ripe bananas
1 teaspoon baking soda
1 teaspoon salt

What You Do:

1. Grease 3 loaf pans with shortening. Add about 1 tablespoon flour to each. Tilt in all directions, tapping gently until the pans are lightly coated. Preheat oven to 350°F.

2. In a large mixing bowl, use a spoon or electric mixer to beat together 1 cup shortening and sugar until soft and smooth; set aside.

3. In a separate, medium mixing bowl, use a potato masher or electric mixer to combine the eggs and bananas; set aside.

4. Combine 2½ cups flour, baking soda, and salt in a sifter or strainer. Sift 3 times over waxed paper or into another large mixing bowl. If using a strainer, shake the dry ingredients through the strainer 9 times.

5. Add about ½ cup of the egg-banana mixture to the sugar-shortening mixture; beat. Add about ½ cup of the flour mixture; beat. Continue alternating the banana and flour mixtures until well blended. Do not overbeat.

6. Pour into the greased and floured loaf pans. Bake for 45 minutes. Let cool in the pans. To freeze, wrap loaves in waxed paper, then wrap again in aluminum foil. Use directly from the freezer, thawed, slicing off ¾" slices as needed.

Fresh-baked rolls add a homey aroma and flavor to any meal. Make these in a muffin tin for attractive puffy rolls.

EASY DINNER ROLLS v

What You Need:

1 (0.25-ounce) packet active dry yeast

1 cup warm tap water

2 tablespoons granulated sugar

1 teaspoon salt

2¼ cups all-purpose flour

1 egg

2 tablespoons solid shortening, plus more for greasing the pan

What You Do:

1. Dissolve the yeast in the water in a large mixing bowl. Stir in the sugar, salt, and ½ of the flour. Beat until smooth. Stir in the egg and shortening, then add the remaining flour. Beat until smooth. Cover with a clean kitchen towel. Set aside at room temperature until it rises to twice its original size (at least 30 minutes).

2. Grease a muffin tin with the solid shortening. Punch down the dough until it reduces in size. Fill the muffin tin cups about ½ full. Set aside for another 20 to 30 minutes. The dough will rise again to the top of the cups. Preheat oven to 400°F. Bake for 15 to 20 minutes, until browned.

CHAPTER 2
Sandwiches

GRILLED CHEESE SANDWICH v

Golden brown bread and melted cheese is a well-known kid favorite that adults like, too. For variety, add a slice of a different type of cheese before grilling. Serve with cream of tomato soup.

What You Need:

2 tablespoons butter or margarine, divided

2 slices bread

1 slice American cheese

What You Do:

1. In a large frying pan or on a griddle, melt 1 tablespoon of the butter (or margarine) over medium heat.
2. Butter one side of one piece of bread and place in the frying pan, buttered-side down. Place a slice of cheese on top. Butter one side of the remaining slice of bread and place on top of the cheese, buttered-side up.
3. Cook for 2 to 3 minutes, until the bottom is golden brown. Use a spatula to flip the sandwich. Cook another 1 to 2 minutes or until the second side is golden brown. Serve warm.

Here's a traditional American favorite. You can use freshly cooked bacon or leftover bacon that you have covered and stored in the refrigerator. If you like, add a slice of your favorite cheese.

BLT

What You Need:

2 slices bacon

1 leaf lettuce

2 slices bread

1–2 tablespoons mayonnaise or mayonnaise-like salad dressing

1–2 slices tomato

What You Do:

1. Fry bacon (see Makin' Bacon recipe in Chapter 1). Drain on paper towels. When cool, break each slice in half crosswise to make 4 strips about the width of the bread.
2. Rinse the lettuce under cold, running water and pat dry with a paper towel.
3. Toast the bread. Spread mayonnaise on one side of each slice. On one slice, stack lettuce, bacon, and tomato. Top with second slice of bread (mayonnaise-side down).

GRILLED PB&J v

Here's a new twist on an old favorite. Try it with other peanut butter sandwich variations, such as pickles, raisins, bananas, or other ingredients. Serve with fresh fruit or sliced raw carrots.

What You Need:

2 tablespoons peanut butter

2 slices bread

2 tablespoons jam or jelly (any flavor)

2 tablespoons butter or margarine, divided

What You Do:

1. Spread the peanut butter on a slice of bread. Spread jam or jelly on the other. Put the 2 slices together. Spread 1½ teaspoons of the butter (or margarine) on the top of the sandwich.

2. Melt 1 tablespoon of the butter in a large frying pan or griddle. Place the sandwich in the frying pan, butter-side down. Spread the remaining 1½ teaspoons of butter on the side of the sandwich that is now facing up. Cook until the bottom slice is slightly browned and crusty. Use a spatula to flip once. Cook until the second side is slightly browned.

LEVEL **E**

SERVINGS **1**

BACON, ONION, AND CHEESE SANDWICH

This sandwich is quite tasty, especially when the bacon is freshly fried. You can make this with toast, but also try it on untoasted bread, which soaks up the bacon fat and melted cheese. Yum!

What You Need:

2 slices bacon

1 slice white onion

1 slice American cheese

Mayonnaise or mayonnaise-like salad dressing, as needed (about 1 tablespoon)

2 slices bread

What You Do:

1. Cut the bacon slices in half horizontally and fry (see Makin' Bacon recipe in Chapter 1). When you have turned the bacon the final time, arrange the 4 halves of bacon slices in a row so that the pieces are touching in the bottom of the frying pan. Reduce heat to low.
2. While the bacon continues to cook, place the onion slice on top. Place the cheese on top of the onion. Heat until the cheese melts.
3. Spread the mayonnaise on one side of each slice of bread. Use a spatula to remove the bacon, onion, and cheese from the pan as one unit. Place on bottom slice of bread, on top of the mayonnaise. Top with the second slice, mayonnaise-side down.

Egg sandwiches aren't just for breakfast. You can eat them for lunch—or even for dinner. Here are a couple of versions.

EGG SANDWICH v

What You Need:

1 egg

2 tablespoons butter, margarine, or bacon fat, plus 1 pat butter or margarine

1 slice American cheese (or your favorite cheese)

2 slices bread

What You Do:

1. Fry the egg (see Fried Egg recipe in Chapter 1) in the 2 tablespoons butter (or alternative). Break the yolk in the pan. Flip the egg once.
2. While the egg is cooking on the second side, place the cheese on top. Heat until the cheese melts.
3. Butter one side of each slice of bread. Use a spatula to remove the egg from the pan and place on buttered side of one piece of bread. Top with the second slice of bread (buttered-side down).

VARIATION:

OPEN-FACE EGG SANDWICH v

Soft-boil the egg (see Boiled Egg recipe in Chapter 1). Toast and butter a slice of bread. When the egg is done, gently crack the shell. Use a knife or spoon to scoop the egg onto the toast. Use a knife to cut up the egg and spread it in an even layer on the toast. Eat with a knife and fork.

Here's a quick way to serve a hot lunch in the time it takes to make a sandwich. Hot and yummy.

OPEN-FACE HOT HAM AND TURKEY SANDWICH

What You Need:

1 slice dark rye bread

1 slice deli-style turkey

1 slice deli-style ham

1 slice tomato

½ cup shredded mozzarella cheese

What You Do:

1. Preheat the broiler. Toast the bread in a toaster. Stack the turkey, ham, tomato, and cheese on top. Place on an ungreased baking sheet.
2. Broil 4" to 6" from the heat until the cheese melts.

FRIED BOLOGNA SANDWICH

Here's a new twist on bologna and cheese that will remind you of a hot ham and cheese sandwich. Serve with a fresh apple or Waldorf salad (see recipe in Chapter 4).

What You Need:

1 tablespoon butter

1 slice bologna

1 slice American or Swiss cheese

2 slices bread

1 tablespoon mayonnaise

1½ teaspoons prepared mustard

1 slice tomato

What You Do:

1. Melt butter in a medium or large frying pan over medium heat. Add bologna and heat until it puffs up. Leave the bologna in the pan, but remove from heat. Place cheese on top until it melts.

2. While cheese is melting, toast bread in a toaster. Spread mayonnaise on one side of one piece of toast and mustard on one side of the other piece of toast. When bologna and cheese are ready, place on one piece of toast. Add tomato slice. Top with second piece of toast with the condiments on the inside of the sandwich

This adult grilled cheese has more flavor and nutrition than the traditional sandwich. Hint: Get the sliced mushrooms and artichoke hearts at the salad bar in the grocery store deli section instead of buying a large can with more than you need.

TURKEY GRILLED CHEESE

What You Need:

1–2 tablespoons butter, divided

1 tablespoon sliced mushrooms

2–3 artichoke hearts marinated or canned in water

2 slices white, whole wheat, or rye bread

1–2 slices deli-style turkey

2 slices provolone cheese

What You Do:

1. Set out the butter to soften. Place the mushrooms on small microwave-safe plate with about 1 teaspoon of the butter. Microwave for 10 to 15 seconds or until cooked just a little. Place in a small bowl. Add the artichoke hearts. Use paper towels and press down on the mushroom mixture to absorb as much liquid as possible.

2. Spray a small frying pan with nonstick cooking spray and place over medium heat. Butter one side of 1 piece of bread and place buttered-side down in the pan. Layer one slice of the cheese, the turkey, artichoke hearts, and mushrooms on top. Add the second slice of cheese. Butter one side of the other piece of bread and place butter-side up on top of the sandwich.

3. Cook until the bottom is toasty brown. Use a spatula and carefully flip the sandwich so the top can cook. (If any ingredients fall out, just stick them back in.) Cook until the second side is toasty brown.

TUNA SALAD SANDWICH

Recipes for tuna salad abound. Eat the salad by itself, or serve on bread or toast with a leaf of lettuce. Because tuna salad contains mayonnaise, you should keep it cold until ready to eat. It's not a good choice for a trip to the beach on a hot day. For a slightly different flavor, you can substitute mayonnaise-like salad dressing for the mayonnaise.

What You Need:

2 eggs (optional)
1 (12-ounce) can tuna
1 stalk celery
⅔ cup mayonnaise or mayonnaise-like salad dressing
2 slices bread or 1 hamburger bun

What You Do:

1. Hard-boil the eggs (see Boiled Egg recipe in Chapter 1). Remove the shells. Chop the eggs and place them in a medium mixing bowl.
2. Drain the tuna. Use a fork to flake it into the bowl.
3. Chop the celery and add it to the bowl.
4. Stir in the mayonnaise until well blended. Chill for at least 1 hour before serving.
5. Spread on bread or bun.

VARIATION: CHICKEN SALAD SANDWICH

Follow the directions for the Tuna Salad Sandwich, but substitute 1½ cups of precooked chicken (see the "How Should I Save Cooked Chicken for Other Recipes?" sidebar with the Chicken and Rice Casserole recipe in Chapter 6) or 1 (10-ounce) can drained chunk chicken for the tuna.

How Do I Use an Egg Slicer?

An egg slicer is a handy kitchen tool that makes slicing and chopping eggs easier than it is with a knife. For slices, open the slicer, and place a peeled hard-boiled egg lengthwise in the bottom. Pull down the top. Remove the slices. For chopped eggs, carefully lift the sliced egg, holding the slices together as if the egg were still whole. Lift the top of the slicer. Lay the sliced egg crosswise in the slicer. Pull down the top. Voilà! Chopped egg.

LEVEL **M**

SERVINGS **2**

Serve egg salad by itself or as a sandwich filling. Keep cold until ready to eat.

EGG SALAD SANDWICHES v

What You Need:

4 eggs

1½ stalks celery

2 tablespoons mayonnaise or mayonnaise-like salad dressing

½ teaspoon prepared mustard

1 teaspoon granulated sugar

Salt and pepper, to taste

4 slices bread or 2 hamburger buns

What You Do:

1. Hard-boil the eggs (see Boiled Egg recipe in Chapter 1). Gently crack the shell and remove the shell from each egg. Chop the eggs and place them in a medium mixing bowl.
2. Chop the celery and add it to the bowl. Add the mayonnaise, mustard, sugar, salt, and pepper; stir until well blended. Cover and refrigerate until ready to serve.
3. Spread on bread or buns.

What Does "To Taste" Mean?

Recipes sometimes include ingredients without specific measurements followed by the words "to taste." Most often this phrase applies to salt and/or pepper. It means to add an amount that tastes good to you. Just pretend you are adding the ingredient to your own serving plate.

GRILLED REUBEN SANDWICH

This grilled sandwich is a deli favorite. Use slices of corned beef left over from Boiled Corned Beef and Cabbage (see recipe in Chapter 5). Serve with a dill pickle and frozen French fries cooked according to package directions.

What You Need:

2 tablespoons bottled Thousand Island salad dressing

2 slices pumpernickel rye bread

2–4 thin slices corned beef

1 slice Swiss cheese

¼ cup canned sauerkraut

1 tablespoon butter or margarine

What You Do:

1. Spread ½ of the salad dressing on one side of each slice of bread.
2. Stack the thinly sliced corned beef on the bread. Add the Swiss cheese on top. Drain the sauerkraut and use a fork to scoop it on top of the cheese. Top with the other piece of bread.
3. Melt the butter (or margarine) in a medium or large frying pan over medium heat. Place the sandwich in the frying pan. Cook for about 1 minute, until the bottom side of the bread is browned. (It will be hard and crisp.) Use a spatula to flip the sandwich to the other side; cook until the second side is browned.

VARIATION: **GRILLED RACHEL SANDWICH**

Follow the directions for Grilled Reuben Sandwich, but substitute pastrami for the corned beef, and coleslaw for the sauerkraut.

BROILED TUNA PUFFS

Bubbly and cheesy, this yummy open-face tuna sandwich with a slightly tangy flavor will satisfy your hunger. The ingredients list may seem long, but this tasty recipe is easy to prepare—and worth the effort. You can substitute hamburger buns for the English muffins.

What You Need:

2 English muffins
1 tomato
½ fresh green bell pepper (optional)
1 (6-ounce) can tuna
1½ teaspoons prepared mustard
¼ teaspoon Worcestershire sauce
½ teaspoon dried minced onion
¾ cup mayonnaise, divided
½ cup shredded Cheddar cheese

What You Do:

1. Preheat oven broiler. Cut the English muffins in half horizontally.
2. Slice the tomato into 4 slices about ¼" thick. Set aside. Clean the green pepper and remove the seeds. Cut the pepper in half. Cover and store 1 half in the refrigerator for another use. Chop the remaining half and place in a medium mixing bowl. (Depending on your preference, you may want to limit the amount of this ingredient to about 2 tablespoons or less.)
3. Drain the tuna and add to the bowl. Add the mustard, Worcestershire sauce, onion, and just ¼ cup of the mayonnaise. (You'll use the rest in the last step.) Stir until well blended.
4. Toast the English muffins in a toaster. Remove from the toaster and place on a baking sheet. Heap ¼ of the tuna mixture on each muffin half. Spread the mixture all the way to the edges of the muffin to prevent burning. Place a tomato slice on each muffin half.
5. In a separate bowl, mix the remaining ½ cup mayonnaise with the cheese. Top each muffin half with ¼ of the cheese mixture. Broil in the oven on the second rack from the top for 3 to 5 minutes until mixture "puffs" and the sandwich is heated through.

HUMMUS POCKET SANDWICH v

Tired of ordinary sandwiches on ordinary white bread? Try this high-protein vegetarian sandwich instead. Serve with spicy pickles.

What You Need:

12 ripe cherry tomatoes

4 (7") pita bread rounds

2 cups Hummus (see recipe in Chapter 10)

1 (0.75-ounce) package alfalfa sprouts

Olive oil, as needed

What You Do:

1. Rinse the cherry tomatoes under cold, running water and cut into halves.
2. Slice an opening at the top of each pita. Spread the hummus on the inside of each side. Stuff alfalfa sprouts and 6 cherry tomato halves into the opening of each pita.
3. Drizzle olive oil over the sandwich filling. Serve.

HOAGIES FOR A CROWD

Serve a crowd in the time it takes to make a sandwich! After heating and slicing, reassemble on a serving tray and let guests serve themselves. Place any remaining salad dressing and mustard mixture in a small serving bowl for guests who want more.

What You Need:

1–1½ cups mayonnaise-like salad dressing

1–3 teaspoons prepared mustard

1 loaf French bread

½ head iceberg lettuce

2 tomatoes

1 red onion (about 3½" diameter)

3 types of deli-style sliced meat to total about 12 ounces

2 types sliced cheese to total about 6 ounces

What You Do:

1. Start with 1 cup salad dressing and ½ teaspoon mustard. Add mustard as needed to make a golden color. (If it gets too yellow, add more salad dressing.) Set aside.
2. Cut bread in half horizontally (as if it were a hamburger bun). Spread mustard mixture on each half. Shred lettuce using the large holes on a grater or by cutting into thin strips.
3. Rinse tomatoes under cold running water. Pat dry with paper towels. Thinly slice tomatoes and onion. Alternate layers of meat, cheese, shredded lettuce, onion slices, and tomato slices on the bottom half of the bread. Replace top of loaf, and cover entire sandwich in aluminum foil. Store in refrigerator until about an hour before ready to serve.
4. Preheat oven to 350°F. Remove sandwich from refrigerator. Heat in the wrapper for 30 to 40 minutes or until warm. Unwrap and place on cutting board. Cut slices about 2" wide, or let guests cut their own. Serve warm.

CUCUMBER SANDWICHES v

These are especially great for summer, while the cucumbers are fresh. Serve as a sandwich or snack, or use party rye or crackers topped with 1 cucumber slice and serve as an appetizer. Refrigerate leftovers.

What You Need:

1 (8-ounce) package cream cheese

½ cup mayonnaise

1 (0.7- to 1-ounce) packet dry Italian salad dressing mix

1 cucumber

8 slices bread

What You Do:

1. Place the cream cheese and mayonnaise in a small mixing bowl. Stir together until well blended.
2. Sprinkle the dry Italian salad dressing mix into the bowl, stirring until well blended.
3. Rinse the cucumber. Peel and slice crosswise about ¼" thick.
4. Spread the cream cheese mixture on a slice of bread. Top with cucumber slices. Add another piece of bread.

Make this restaurant favorite at home. Serve with potato chips and your favorite pickles and condiments. Be sure to wash your hands with soap after handling the raw meat.

PATTY MELT SANDWICHES

What You Need:

4–5 tablespoons butter, as needed

¾ pound ground chuck or round beef

Salt and pepper, to taste

¼–½ medium yellow onion

2 tablespoons olive oil, divided

1 tablespoon fresh parsley leaves

⅛ teaspoon red pepper flakes

4 slices rye bread

4 slices Swiss cheese

What You Do:

1. Set out the butter to soften.
2. Place the ground chuck in a large mixing bowl. Season with salt and pepper. Use your hands to form into two patties about the size and shape of the rye bread. Set aside.
3. Slice the onion into thin half-moon shapes. Pour 1 tablespoon of the olive oil into a large frying pan over medium-high heat. When the oil is hot, cook the onion slices for about 8 minutes until lightly browned, stirring as they cook.
4. Chop the parsley leaves and add to the cooked onion. Sprinkle with the red pepper flakes, salt, and pepper. Transfer the onion mixture to a small bowl.
5. To the same frying pan add the second tablespoon of olive oil over medium-high heat. When the oil is hot, cook the patties on one side for 3 to 4 minutes until blood appears on the top of the patty and the cooked side is well browned. Use a spatula to flip the patties. Cook for another 2 to 3 minutes until the second side

(continued on next page)

is well browned. Remove from heat. Discard the beef fat, and wash out the frying pan.

6. Melt about 1 tablespoon of butter in the frying pan over low heat. Spread 1 tablespoon butter on one side of each slice of rye bread. Place 2 of the slices, buttered-side down, in the frying pan. Increase heat to medium-high. Place 1 slice of cheese on each of 2 pieces of rye bread. Top with the onions. Place each patty on top of the onions. Add another slice of cheese and the remaining pieces of rye bread, butter-side up.

7. Grill each side of the sandwiches for 3 to 4 minutes until the cheese melts and the bread is golden brown.

Here's hot ham and cheese with extra flair and flavor. For a spicy variation, substitute your favorite bottled barbecue sauce for the Mustard Sauce (see sidebar).

SAUCY HOT HAM AND CHEESE SANDWICHES

What You Need:

½ pound precooked ham

1 (½-pound) block processed cheese

1 recipe Mustard Sauce (see sidebar)

4 hamburger buns

What You Do:

1. Preheat oven to 400°F. Cut the ham and cheese into ¾" cubes and place in a medium mixing bowl. Add the Mustard Sauce and stir until well coated.
2. Spoon the mixture onto the hamburger bun bottoms. Replace the bun tops. Tightly wrap each sandwich in aluminum foil.
3. Bake for 10 to 15 minutes or until heated through.

How Do I Make Mustard Sauce?

For mustard sauce that goes well with Saucy Hot Ham and Cheese Sandwiches and other ham recipes, combine ¼ cup chopped green bell pepper; 2 sweet pickles, chopped; and 3 hard-boiled eggs (see Boiled Egg recipe in Chapter 1), chopped, in a small mixing bowl. Add 1½ teaspoons minced onion, ¼ cup mayonnaise, and 2 tablespoons prepared mustard. Stir until well blended. For extra zip, substitute prepared horseradish mustard for the prepared mustard. You can omit the green bell pepper from the sauce, if you prefer.

SLOPPY JOES

Here's an easy, make-ahead dinner for a crowd. To serve, spoon about ⅓ cup of the beef mixture onto hamburger buns. Or, for an open-face version, spoon onto buttered English muffin halves. Top with some shredded Cheddar and broil until the cheese bubbles.

What You Need:

¼ medium white or yellow onion
1 tablespoon vegetable oil
2 pounds ground beef
2 stalks celery
⅔ cup ketchup
½ cup water
2 tablespoons lemon juice
1 tablespoon loosely packed brown sugar
1½ teaspoons Worcestershire sauce
1½ teaspoons salt
1 teaspoon vinegar
¼ teaspoon dry mustard

What You Do:

1. Chop the onion. Heat the vegetable oil in a large frying pan over medium-high heat. Add the onion. Stir until the onion is tender. Crumble in the ground beef and brown (see the "How Do I Brown Ground Beef?" sidebar with the Chili Blue recipe in Chapter 3). Drain off fat.
2. Rinse the celery under cold, running water. Chop the celery and add it to the beef mixture. Reduce heat to low. Stir in the ketchup, water, lemon juice, brown sugar, Worcestershire sauce, salt, vinegar, and dry mustard until well mixed. Cover. Cook for 30 minutes, stirring occasionally. Serve hot.

VARIATION: **VEGETARIAN SLOPPY JOE SANDWICH** v

Follow the directions for Sloppy Joes, except substitute 2 pounds of veggie burgers for the beef.

CHAPTER 3
Soups and Stews

THE BEST CHILI EVER

If you like spicy chili, this recipe is for you! Serve with saltine crackers, shredded Cheddar cheese, and sour cream if you can't take the "heat."

What You Need:

2 pounds ground beef

1 (1.25-ounce) packet chili seasoning mix

¼ teaspoon garlic salt

Salt and pepper, to taste

Chili powder, to taste (about 1–3 teaspoons)

1 (15.5-ounce) can kidney beans

2 (15.75-ounce) cans hot chili beans

1 (15-ounce) can tomato sauce for chili

1 (12-ounce) can tomato paste

What You Do:

1. In a large frying pan, brown the ground beef (see the "How Do I Brown Ground Beef?" sidebar with the Chili Blue recipe in this chapter) along with chili seasoning mix, garlic salt, salt, pepper, and chili powder. Drain off the fat. Place the mixture in a Dutch oven, stew pot, or 2-quart slow cooker.
2. Drain the kidney beans and chili beans. Stir into the ground beef mixture. Stir in the tomato sauce and tomato paste. Cover and cook over low heat on the stovetop or high heat in a slow cooker until warmed through. For best flavor, cook at least 1 hour—longer to let seasonings mingle.

FRENCH ONION SOUP

If you like, place a slice of toasted French bread into each serving bowl. Top with a slice of provolone, shredded mozzarella, or grated Parmesan cheese. Let the cheese melt before serving.

What You Need:

3 yellow onions

2 tablespoons butter or margarine

2 (10.5-ounce) cans condensed beef broth (do not dilute)

½ cup water

1 teaspoon Worcestershire sauce

⅛ teaspoon pepper

What You Do:

1. Remove and discard the outer skin of the onions. Cut the onions into thin slices. Melt the butter (or margarine) in a large frying pan over medium heat. Stir in the onions. Cook for about 5 to 7 minutes or until tender. Scoop the onions and butter into a slow cooker or Dutch oven.
2. Stir in the beef broth, water, Worcestershire sauce, and pepper. Cover. In a slow cooker, cook on low for 4 to 6 hours (or 2 to 3 hours on high). In a Dutch oven, cook over low heat for 30 minutes until heated through.

How Do I Prevent Tears When I Chop an Onion?

Some people are quite sensitive to the tear-producing quality in onions. If your eyes water when you slice or chop onions, refrigerate them first. To cut down on onion odors in the kitchen, store leftover cut onions in a sealed container and refrigerate immediately. And, immediately discard unused pieces of onion in your outside garbage. To remove odor, wash your hands with soap after handling.

MINERS' STEW

You can serve this dish by itself or place a piece of toast on the serving plate. Place a slice of American cheese on top, and spoon Miners' Stew over it.

What You Need:

½ small onion

1 pound ground beef

1 (15-ounce) can pork and beans

¼ cup ketchup

What You Do:

1. Chop the onion. Add to the ground beef in a large frying pan. Brown over medium-high heat. Drain.
2. Return beef and onion to the frying pan. Reduce heat to low.
3. Stir in pork and beans and ketchup. Warm, stirring occasionally, until heated through.

What If I Can't Find the Right Ingredient Size?

What if your recipe calls for a 10.75-ounce can of mushroom soup, but you get to the store and find only a 10.5-ounce can? Do you buy two 10.5-ounce cans and try to measure out 0.25 ounces from the second? No. Can sizes may vary by brand. If a recipe calls for a certain size can, choose the size closest to the one the recipe calls for. For example, canned vegetables come in sizes that are roughly 8 ounces and 15 ounces. If your recipe calls for 2 cups of green beans, use the 15-ounce can.

Here's an easy soup using different vegetables and full-of-fiber beans. Serve with saltine crackers.

FIESTA BEAN SOUP v

What You Need:

¼ red bell pepper

½ cup canned red kidney beans, drained

½ cup canned chickpeas (also called garbanzo beans), drained

½ (8-ounce) can cut green beans, drained (or ½ cup frozen cut green beans)

½ cup frozen chopped broccoli

½ cup frozen cut carrots

1 (14.5-ounce) can stewed tomatoes, with juice

2 vegetable bouillon cubes (or substitute chicken bouillon cubes for non-vegetarian soup)

¼ teaspoon celery salt

¼ teaspoon garlic salt

2 teaspoons dried parsley flakes

¼ teaspoon salt

⅛ teaspoon pepper

Water, as needed (about 1 quart)

What You Do:

1. Chop the red bell pepper. Place in a slow cooker, Dutch oven, or stew pot. Add the drained kidney beans, chickpeas, and green beans to the pot, along with the broccoli, carrots, and tomatoes.
2. Unwrap the bouillon cubes and add to the pot. Sprinkle with celery salt, garlic salt, parsley flakes, salt, and pepper. Add water to the Dutch oven to just cover all the ingredients; stir. In a slow cooker, cover and cook on low for 10 to 12 hours or on high for 5 to 6 hours. In a Dutch oven or stew pot, cover and simmer over low heat for 1 to 2 hours.

When it's hot outside, you can enjoy this nutritious soup served cold. Gazpacho is most often served as an appetizer in place of salad.

GAZPACHO

What You Need:

½ cucumber

¼ green bell pepper

1 tomato

¼ small white or yellow onion

¼ cup beef broth

¼ cup tomato juice

1 tablespoon vegetable oil

2 tablespoons red wine vinegar

½ teaspoon salt

Hot pepper sauce, to taste

Worcestershire sauce, to taste

What You Do:

1. Rinse the cucumber, bell pepper, and tomato under cold, running water. Peel the cucumber. Remove the seeds from the bell pepper. Chop the cucumber, green pepper, tomato, and onion and place in large mixing bowl.
2. Gently stir in the beef broth, tomato juice, vegetable oil, wine vinegar, and salt. Add the hot pepper sauce and Worcestershire sauce a few drops at a time, to taste. Cover and chill for at least 1 hour in the refrigerator before serving.

Each serving of this tasty vegetarian chili provides approximately 19 grams of protein and 18 grams of fiber. Serve with saltine crackers.

VEGGIE LOVERS' CHILI v

What You Need:

½ large white or yellow onion

2 tablespoons vegetable oil

1 (15-ounce) can red kidney beans

1 (8.5-ounce) can corn

1 medium zucchini (about 8" long)

1 (14.5-ounce) can stewed tomatoes, with juice

¼ teaspoon dried minced garlic

1 tablespoon chili powder

2 teaspoons dried oregano

What You Do:

1. Chop the onion. In a small frying pan, cook the onion in the vegetable oil over medium-high heat, stirring constantly until tender. Transfer the onion and oil to a Dutch oven, stew pot, or 2-quart slow cooker.
2. Drain the beans and corn. Add to the pot.
3. Rinse the zucchini under cold, running water. Chop the zucchini and add to the pot.
4. Stir in the tomatoes, with the juice. Add the garlic, chili powder, and oregano. In a Dutch oven or stew pot, cover and bring to a boil over medium-high heat. Reduce heat to low. Cook for about 15 minutes or until the zucchini is tender. Uncover for the last 5 minutes. In a slow cooker, cover and cook for 1 hour on high. Reduce heat to low until ready to serve. Uncover for the last 5 minutes.

CURRIED VEGETABLE STEW v

You don't have to be a vegetarian to enjoy this spicy and colorful stew. Serve with saltine crackers or Easy Dinner Rolls (see recipe in Chapter 1). You can use the other half of the sweet potato for another meal such as Stir-Fry Parsnip Medley (see recipe in Chapter 9).

What You Need:

1 (10-ounce) package frozen lima beans or 1¼ cups canned lima beans

1 cup frozen cut green beans or 1 cup canned cut green beans

½ sweet potato

3 (6"–8"-long) zucchini

1 large white or yellow onion

1 red bell pepper

2 tablespoons olive oil

1 teaspoon curry powder

Salt and pepper, to taste

2 cups water

What You Do:

1. Thaw the lima beans if using frozen, or drain canned lima beans. Let the green beans thaw if using frozen, or drain canned green beans. Place the lima beans and green beans in a Dutch oven, stew pot, or 2-quart slow cooker. Set aside.

2. Cut the sweet potato in half lengthwise. Wrap ½ and store in the refrigerator for another use. Peel the remaining half. Cut in half lengthwise again. Slice crosswise. Place in a large mixing bowl. Cut the zucchini in half lengthwise; then slice crosswise. Chop the onion and red bell pepper. Add to the mixing bowl.

(continued on next page)

CURRIED VEGETABLE STEW

— CONTINUED

3. Heat the olive oil in a large frying pan over medium-high heat. Fry the sweet potato, zucchini, onion, and red bell pepper, stirring constantly until tender but still firm. Sprinkle with curry powder, salt, and pepper. Add the mixture to the Dutch oven, stew pot, or slow cooker. Add the water. (If 2 cups is not enough to cover the ingredients, add more.)

4. In a slow cooker, cover and cook on high for 1 hour. Reduce heat to low and cook until the sweet potato is tender (about 15 to 20 minutes more). In a Dutch oven or stew pot, cover and bring to a boil. Reduce heat to low. Keep covered. Simmer for 30 minutes. Keep warm until ready to serve.

How Do I Know Which Types of Olive Oil to Use?

If you've tried to buy olive oil, you've likely stared at the labels wondering which type to choose. The three main types are pure, virgin, and extra-virgin. These labels pertain to the olive oil's grade, which is determined by the amount of oleic acid. The less acid, the better. So extra-virgin, which has the least acid—as well as the strongest smell and flavor—is the best quality. If you see "light" olive oil, don't think it's a diet food. The term applies to the pale color and bland flavor, not the calorie count.

This soup is flavorful, and it's good for you, too. It's loaded with vitamins A and C, but you don't have to tell! The bouillon cubes have lots of salt, so add extra salt sparingly to taste, rather than all at once.

BEEF BARLEY SOUP

What You Need:

1 small white or yellow onion

2 tablespoons vegetable oil

1 pound ground beef

2 raw carrots

2 stalks celery

1 (8-ounce) can diced or crushed tomatoes, with juice

⅓ cup barley

1 tablespoon dried parsley flakes

2 beef bouillon cubes

½–1 teaspoon salt, to taste

¼ teaspoon pepper

¼ teaspoon basil

2½ cups water

What You Do:

1. Thinly slice the onion. Pour the vegetable oil into a large frying pan over medium-high heat. Stir in the onion. Crumble the ground beef into the pan. Stir often until the beef browns (see the "How Do I Brown Ground Beef?" sidebar with the Chili Blue recipe in this chapter). Drain off the fat. Transfer the mixture to a slow cooker or Dutch oven.

2. Rinse the carrots and celery under cold, running water. Peel the carrots. Thinly slice the carrots and celery crosswise. Add to the pot. Stir in the tomatoes, barley, parsley, bouillon cubes, salt, pepper, basil, and water. Cover. In a slow cooker, cook on high for 5 to 6 hours (or on low for 10 to 12 hours). In a Dutch oven, bring the mixture to a boil over medium-high heat. Reduce heat to low. Cook, covered, for 1 hour, stirring occasionally.

TACO SOUP

What You Need:

1 small white or yellow onion

1 clove garlic (or ⅛ teaspoon dried minced garlic)

1 pound ground beef

1 (4-ounce) can diced green chilies

1 (16-ounce) can Mexican-flavored stewed tomatoes, with liquid

1 (15-ounce) can tomato sauce

2 cups water

1 cup bottled or fresh salsa

1 (15-ounce) can pinto beans, with liquid

1 (15-ounce) can kidney beans, with liquid

1 (2.25-ounce) packet taco seasoning or 2 tablespoons chili powder

What You Do:

1. Chop the onion and garlic. Place the ground beef in a large frying pan. Add the onion and garlic. Brown the beef (see the "How Do I Brown Ground Beef?" sidebar with the Chili Blue recipe in this chapter). Drain off the fat. Place the beef mixture in a Dutch oven or stew pot.

2. Drain the chilies. Add to the pot. Stir in the stewed tomatoes, tomato sauce, water, salsa, pinto beans, kidney beans, and taco seasoning (or chili powder). Bring to a boil over medium-high heat, stirring occasionally. Reduce heat to low. Cover and cook for 30 minutes.

HAM AND BEANS

Serve Corn Bread (see recipe in Chapter 1) with this hearty dish. You can substitute ½ pound leftover cooked ham for the ham hock in this recipe.

What You Need:

1 ham hock

2 quarts chicken stock

2–3 cups water, divided

1 medium onion

2 medium carrots

3 medium stalks celery

2 tablespoons vegetable oil

3 (15-ounce) cans navy beans

Salt and pepper, to taste

What You Do:

1. Place the ham hock in a Dutch oven. Cover with the chicken stock and 2 cups of the water. Bring to a boil over high heat. Turn heat to low. Let simmer.
2. Chop the onion, carrots, and celery. Pour the vegetable oil into a large saucepan over medium heat. Stir in the onion, carrots, and celery, and cook until the vegetables are soft. Add to the ham hock in the Dutch oven.
3. Drain the navy beans into a colander, and rinse with cold water. Add to the soup. Sprinkle with salt and pepper.
4. Let soup simmer on low for 30 minutes. After 15 minutes taste the soup. If it tastes too salty, add the rest of the water. (Otherwise, omit the last cup of water.)

CHEESEBURGER SOUP

You might be surprised by the nice texture the cooked lettuce adds to this all-American favorite in soup form. Serve with potato chips or fresh fruit.

What You Need:

2 pounds ground beef

Salt and pepper, to taste

3 medium tomatoes

1 head of lettuce

1 large onion

1 tablespoon butter

32 ounces chicken broth

1½ pounds processed cheese product (like Velveeta)

1½ pints half-and-half

1 tablespoon all-purpose flour

1–2 tablespoons water, divided

What You Do:

1. Brown the ground beef in a large frying pan (see the "How Do I Brown Ground Beef?" sidebar with the Chili Blue recipe in this chapter). Season with salt and pepper. Drain and set aside.
2. Cut the tomatoes into bite-sized pieces and set aside. Cut the head of lettuce into fourths. Save one of the quarters for another salad. Shred the other three pieces by slicing parallel to the cuts to make stringy pieces of lettuce. Set aside.
3. Peel and chop the onion into bite-sized pieces. Place the butter in a Dutch oven over medium heat. Add the onion. Stir until the onion pieces are translucent.
4. Pour the chicken broth into the Dutch oven with the onion. Cut the cheese into 1" cubes, and add to the pot. Stir in the half-and-half. Stir until the cheese melts.

(continued on next page)

5. In a small mixing bowl or coffee cup, stir the flour and 1 tablespoon of the water until the mixture is smooth and thin, but not watery. If it's too thick, add a little more of the water. Stir into the cheese mixture. Increase the heat to medium-high and bring to a boil, stirring constantly to keep the cheese from sticking to the bottom of the pot.
6. Add the ground beef to the soup. Turn the heat to medium-low. Stir in the tomatoes and lettuce. Reduce heat to low until ready to serve.

LEVEL **M**

SERVINGS **6**

Rich and creamy, this potato soup is a winter favorite. To prevent scorching, be sure to add the milk just before serving.

POTATO SOUP v

What You Need:

3 medium potatoes

½ small white or yellow onion

2 tablespoons butter

1 teaspoon salt

⅛ teaspoon pepper

1 teaspoon caraway seed

3–4 cups water

2 cups milk

What You Do:

1. Peel and chop the potatoes. Chop the onion. Add the potatoes and onion to a Dutch oven or stew pot. Add the butter, salt, pepper, and caraway seed. Cover with water. Stir. Cook over medium-high heat for about 10 minutes or until the potatoes are tender.
2. Reduce heat to low. Stir in the milk. Cook until heated through. (Do not boil.)

YOU-CAN-DO-THIS CLAM CHOWDER

This recipe is a version of New England clam chowder (the white soup), rather than Manhattan clam chowder (the red soup, with tomatoes). Serve with oyster crackers.

What You Need:

1 medium onion

2 slices bacon

1 medium potato

1 (7-ounce) can minced clams, with juice

Water, as needed

3 cups milk

Salt and pepper, to taste

3–4 tablespoons butter

Fresh parsley leaves, as needed

What You Do:

1. Peel and chop the onion. Chop the raw bacon. Fry the onion and bacon together in a medium saucepan over medium-high heat until the onion is tender. (The bacon fat will cook the onion.) Remove from the heat.
2. Wash and peel the potato. Chop into ½" cubes. Add the potato to the saucepan. Use the lid of the canned clams to drain the clam juice into the saucepan, leaving the clams in the can. Add enough water to cover the potato. Cook over medium-high heat, stirring occasionally, for 10 to 15 minutes or until the potato is tender.
3. Stir in the clams and milk. Sprinkle with salt and pepper, to taste. Continue cooking until the soup is warm.
4. To serve, pour into soup bowls or mugs. Top each with 1 tablespoon of the butter. Place a few leaves of parsley on top of the butter.

QUICK & EASY CHICKEN NOODLE SOUP

This soup is great anytime, especially if you're feeling under the weather. It's almost as quick and easy as opening a can—but much tastier. Serve with saltine or oyster crackers and a bowl of fruit if you feel up to it.

What You Need:

1 pound boneless, skinless chicken (any parts)

2 medium carrots

1 medium onion

2 stalks celery

2 tablespoons extra-virgin olive oil

2 bay leaves

½ teaspoon salt

½ teaspoon pepper

½ teaspoon poultry seasoning

6 cups chicken stock

½ pound uncooked wide egg noodles

¼ cup fresh parsley leaves

¼ cup fresh dill leaves

What You Do:

1. Cut the raw chicken into small cubes. Set aside. Wash your hands, knife, and cutting board with soap and water after handling raw chicken.
2. Peel and chop the carrots and onion. Chop the celery. Place the olive oil in a large stew pot or Dutch oven over medium heat. Stir in the carrots, onion, and celery. Add the bay leaves, and sprinkle with the salt, pepper, and poultry seasoning. Stir in the chicken stock. Increase heat to medium-high and bring to a boil.
3. Stir the chicken into the pot, and bring to a boil again. Boil for 5 minutes, stirring occasionally.
4. Stir in the uncooked noodles. Boil for another 7 minutes. Remove from the heat. Remove the bay leaves.
5. Stir the parsley and dill into the soup and serve.

This aromatic blend of spices makes a delicious homemade soup to warm a cold winter night. Serve with Hot Cheese Toast (see recipe in Chapter 8) or Easy Dinner Rolls with Honey Butter (see recipes in Chapter 1). This soup is easy to make in a slow cooker.

VEGETABLE-BEEF SOUP

What You Need:

1 pound cubed beef for stew (or ask your butcher to cube round steak for you)

½ (10-ounce) package frozen mixed vegetables (carrots, peas, potatoes, and green beans)

1 (14.5-ounce) can crushed or stewed tomatoes, with juice

1 baking potato (or 2–3 russet potatoes smaller than baseballs)

1½ large stalks celery

½ small white or yellow onion (or substitute 1 tablespoon dried minced onion)

½ teaspoon salt

⅛ teaspoon pepper

1 bay leaf

⅛ teaspoon garlic powder

⅛ teaspoon basil

⅛ teaspoon rosemary

Pinch of thyme

¼ teaspoon dried parsley flakes

2 beef bouillon cubes

Water, as needed (about 1 quart)

What You Do:

1. Place the beef, mixed vegetables, and tomatoes with juice in a Dutch oven, stew pot, or slow cooker. Rinse the potato and celery under cold, running water. Peel the potato. Cut in half lengthwise; then cut crosswise to make 1½" cubes. Add to the pot.

(continued on next page)

VEGETABLE-BEEF SOUP – CONTINUED

2. Chop the celery and onion. Add to the pot. Sprinkle with salt, pepper, bay leaf, garlic powder, basil, rosemary, thyme, and parsley. Unwrap the bouillon cubes and add to the pot.
3. Add enough water to cover all the ingredients; stir. In a slow cooker, cover and cook on low for 10 to 12 hours or on high for 5 to 6 hours. In a stew pot, cover and simmer over low heat for 3 to 4 hours, until the meat is tender and cooked through. Remove the bay leaf before serving.

LEVEL **H**

SERVINGS **4**

VARIATION:
VEGETARIAN VEGGIE SOUP v

For a vegetarian variation, substitute 1 eggplant for the beef. Rinse the eggplant under cold, running water. Peel and remove the seeds. Cut the eggplant into ½" cubes. Substitute vegetable bouillon cubes or granules for the beef bouillon.

What Do I Do with the Leftover Frozen Vegetables?

When a recipe calls for a portion of a 10-ounce package of frozen vegetables (which come in a frozen block), just place the package on a cutting board and cut it crosswise with a sharp knife. Wrap the part you won't use in aluminum foil and replace in the freezer for later use. Or, purchase the vegetables in a 16-ounce bag and simply pour out the amount you need.

You'll need to start this soup the night before you plan to serve it, but it is worth the effort. Serve with Mexican Corn Bread (see recipe in Chapter 1).

BLACK BEAN SOUP v

What You Need:

2 cups dried black beans

6 cups plus 2 quarts water

½ small white or yellow onion

2 stalks celery

2 teaspoons salt

⅛ teaspoon pepper

1 tablespoon butter

2 tablespoons all-purpose flour

1 lemon

2 hard-boiled eggs (see Boiled Egg recipe in Chapter 1)

What You Do:

1. Place the beans and the 6 cups water in a Dutch oven or stew pot. Bring to a boil over high heat. Cover and reduce heat to low. Simmer for 1½ hours. Remove from heat and let cool. Refrigerate overnight.
2. Drain the beans in a colander. Rinse under cold, running water. Drain. Return to the Dutch oven.
3. Chop the onion and celery. Add to the pot. Stir in the 2 quarts water, salt, and pepper. Cook over low heat for 3 to 4 hours.
4. In a small saucepan, melt the butter over low heat. Stir in the flour until well blended. Gradually add in a few tablespoons of the soup liquid from the Dutch oven, stirring until thickened. Pour the thickened liquid back into the Dutch oven with the beans.
5. Rinse the lemon under cold running water and thinly slice (do not peel). Remove the shell from the hard-boiled eggs and slice (an egg slicer makes this step easy). When ready to serve, place 1 egg slice and 1 lemon slice on top of each serving.

Here's an old favorite from Girl Scout camp. The chili has a sweet flavor that tastes almost as good cooked indoors as it does over an open fire in the woods. You'll find chili sauce in the ketchup aisle. Serve with French bread (see the "How Do I Prepare French Bread?" sidebar with the Baked Spaghetti recipe in Chapter 5) or Mexican Corn Bread (see recipe in Chapter 1).

CHILI BLUE

What You Need:

3 slices bacon

1 pound ground beef

¾ cup bottled chili sauce

¼ cup loosely packed brown sugar

2 teaspoons prepared mustard

2 (15-ounce) cans pork and beans

What You Do:

1. Preheat oven to 350°F. Fry the bacon (see Makin' Bacon recipe in Chapter 1) until crisp. Remove the bacon from the pan and set it aside on paper towels; cool and crumble. Brown the ground beef in the bacon drippings (see the "How Do I Brown Ground Beef?" sidebar with this recipe). Use a slotted spoon to remove the meat from the frying pan and place into an ungreased 9" × 13" ovenproof baking pan.

2. Stir in the chili sauce, brown sugar, mustard, bacon, and pork and beans until well mixed. Cover with aluminum foil and bake for 30 to 45 minutes, until thoroughly heated. Or, place all the ingredients in a slow cooker. Cover and cook on high for 1 to 3 hours or on low for 2 to 6 hours, until heated through.

How Do I Brown Ground Beef?

Ground beef is a versatile meat for casseroles and other dishes. Use your hands to crumble the meat into a frying pan over medium-high heat. Stir occasionally as meat cooks. Heat until juices run clear and there is no tinge of pink in the meat. Drain. You can brown ground pork sausage using the same method. (Note: Do not pour fat down the sink. Discard by pouring into an empty can with a plastic lid. Cover and store in refrigerator until fat turns solid. Throw away.)

BLACK-EYED PEAS

What You Need:
4–6 cups water
1¼ cups dry black-eyed peas
½ medium white or yellow onion
1½ stalks celery
1½ pounds smoked ham hocks
2 bay leaves
⅛ teaspoon cayenne pepper

Method 1: On a Stovetop

1. In a covered Dutch oven, bring 4 cups water and the black-eyed peas to a boil over high heat. Boil for 2 minutes. Keeping the cover in place, remove from heat. Let sit for 1 hour.
2. Chop the onion and celery. Add to the pot along with the ham hocks, bay leaves, and cayenne pepper. Stir until well mixed. Bring to a boil. Cover and reduce heat to low. Simmer for 1 hour, stirring occasionally.
3. Uncover and cook for 1 more hour. Remove ham hocks and cut the meat from the bone. Discard the bones, and add the meat to the pot and stir. Remove bay leaves before serving.

Method 2: In a Slow Cooker

1. In a covered Dutch oven over high heat, bring 6 cups water and the black-eyed peas to a boil. Cover. Reduce heat to low. Cook for 1½ hours. Remove from heat. Uncover and cool at room temperature. Cover and refrigerate overnight. (The peas will absorb most of the water.)
2. In the morning, chop the onion and celery. Add to slow cooker along with the peas and any remaining water, ham hocks, bay leaves, and cayenne pepper. Stir until well mixed. Cover, and cook on low for 10 to 12 hours or on high for 5 to 6 hours. Stir occasionally. Remove bay leaves before serving.

ITALIAN SAUSAGE SOUP

A taste of Italy in a bowl. The aroma of this soup cooking will make you imagine yourself in a villa in Venice. If you prefer to use fresh herbs, use ¾ teaspoon each of oregano, basil, and thyme and 3 tablespoons fresh parsley.

What You Need:

¾ pound mild or hot ground Italian sausage

½ medium white or yellow onion

3 stalks celery

1 clove garlic

2 tablespoons olive oil

1 (8-ounce) can diced or crushed tomatoes, with liquid

½ cup tomato purée

2 (10.5-ounce) cans chicken broth

¼ cup water

¼ teaspoon dried oregano

¼ teaspoon dried basil

¼ teaspoon dried thyme

1 tablespoon dried parsley flakes

½–¾ cup uncooked macaroni

Grated Parmesan cheese, as needed

What You Do:

1. Remove the sausage casing with a sharp knife and place the meat in a frying pan. Use a wooden spoon to break up the meat. Brown the sausage as you would ground beef (see the "How Do I Brown Ground Beef?" sidebar with the Chili Blue recipe in this chapter). Drain off the fat. Set the meat aside.
2. Chop the onion and celery. Mince the garlic. Pour the oil into a Dutch oven over medium-high heat. Stir in the onion and celery; cook, stirring constantly, for about 1 to 2 minutes until tender.

(continued on next page)

3. Stir in the sausage, tomatoes, tomato purée, chicken broth, water, oregano, basil, thyme, and parsley. Reduce heat to low. Cover and cook for 1 hour, stirring occasionally.
4. Add the macaroni. Cook for another 30 minutes, stirring occasionally. To serve, top each bowlful with grated Parmesan cheese.

How Do I Grate Cheese?

To grate hard cheese, start with a block of cheese rather than cheese slices. Place a grater across the top of a small mixing bowl (or stand it on one end in the bottom of the bowl) with the sharp-edged bumps facing up. If using a box grater, set it on a cutting board or flat plate and firmly grasp the handle. Choose the side you want to use. Unwrap the cheese and hold it by one end. Pull across the grater so the sharp edges on the bumps "grab" the cheese and cut it into strings. Continue until you have the amount you need. Watch your fingers so you don't accidentally cut them.

MULLIGATAWNY SOUP

Curry gives this heavily spiced, flavorful soup an East Indian flavor. You can cook this soup on a stovetop or in a slow cooker. (If using a slow cooker, melt the butter in a small frying pan and cook the onion, stirring constantly, until tender. Then add it to the slow cooker along with the remaining ingredients.)

What You Need:

1 carrot
1 stalk celery
1 green bell pepper
1 apple
1 medium white or yellow onion
¼ cup butter
1 cup precooked chicken (see the "How Should I Save Cooked Chicken for Other Recipes?" sidebar with the Chicken and Rice Casserole recipe in Chapter 6)
2 (10.5-ounce) cans chicken broth
⅓ cup all-purpose flour
1 teaspoon curry powder
1 teaspoon lemon juice
½ teaspoon granulated sugar
2 whole cloves
1 teaspoon dried parsley flakes
1 (8-ounce) can crushed tomatoes
Salt and pepper, to taste

What You Do:

1. Rinse the carrot, celery, bell pepper, and apple under cold, running water. Peel the carrot. Chop the carrot, celery, and green bell pepper. Peel and core the apple. Slice vertically. Slice the onion.
2. Melt the butter in the bottom of a Dutch oven over medium heat. Add the onion, stirring constantly until the onion is tender, about 5 to 7 minutes. Reduce heat to low. Stir in the carrot, celery, bell pepper, apple, chicken, and chicken broth.
3. Transfer some of the liquid to a small mixing bowl and stir in flour a little at a time until well blended. Return to the pot. Stir in the curry powder, lemon juice, sugar, cloves, parsley, tomatoes, salt, and pepper. Cover and cook for 30 minutes. (In a slow cooker, cook on low for 8 to 10 hours.) Remove the cloves before serving.

If you like Italian food, this soup is for you. If you don't have time to cook the dried beans, you can substitute 1 (15.5-ounce) can of beans (drained) and reduce the cooking time to 45 minutes total.

MINESTRONE

What You Need:

½ cup dried kidney beans or great northern beans

1 cup beef stock

3 cups water

1 carrot

1 stalk celery

1 medium potato

½ large white or yellow onion

1 tablespoon olive oil

⅛ teaspoon dried minced garlic

¼ cup uncooked macaroni

½ (8-ounce) can crushed tomatoes

1½ teaspoons salt

⅛ teaspoon pepper

What You Do:

1. In a Dutch oven, bring the beans, beef stock, and water to a boil. Cover and reduce heat to low. Cook for 3 to 4 hours. Stir once or twice per hour.
2. During the last half-hour of cooking time, prepare the vegetables. Rinse the carrot, celery, and potato under cold, running water. Peel the carrot, potato, and onion. Chop the carrot, celery, potato, and onion. Place the olive oil in a large frying pan over medium-high heat. Cook the chopped vegetables in the olive oil, stirring constantly, until tender but still firm.
3. Stir the vegetables and garlic into the beans. Cover and continue cooking for 30 minutes. Stir often.
4. Stir in the macaroni, tomatoes, salt, and pepper. Cook for 15 minutes more.

CHAPTER 4
Salads

TOSSED SALAD v

Tossed salads accompany almost any meal, so here's one to get your meal started. All ingredients except the greens are optional. Add your own choices of vegetables, meats, or cheeses. Serve with bottled salad dressing, or see the recipes in this chapter to make your own.

What You Need:

3-4 cups mixed greens (iceberg lettuce, romaine lettuce, Bibb lettuce, spinach)

1 cucumber (optional)

1 small red or white onion (optional)

4 radishes (optional)

1 cup cherry tomatoes (optional)

What You Do:

1. Rinse the lettuce and other greens under cold, running water. Drain on paper towels. Tear into bite-sized pieces and place in a large salad bowl.
2. Rinse the cucumber and slice crosswise. Add to the bowl.
3. Peel and slice the onion and radishes, and add to the bowl.
4. Slice the cherry tomatoes in half (or leave whole), and add to the bowl.
5. Toss all ingredients until well mixed. If you like, add about ½ cup of salad dressing and toss again. Or, serve without dressing and let guests apply their own.

VINAIGRETTE v

What You Need:

½ cup extra-virgin olive oil

½ cup total of two types of vinegar (see recipe message for more information)

1–2 teaspoons Dijon mustard, to taste

¼ –½ teaspoon salt, to taste

Freshly ground black pepper, to taste

What You Do:

1. Place the olive oil, vinegar, 1 teaspoon of the Dijon mustard, and ¼ teaspoon of the salt into a small plastic storage container with a lid. Shake well. Taste.
2. Add more mustard and/or salt, to taste. Add pepper, to taste. Shake well.

HONEY-MUSTARD DRESSING   v

What You Need:

¼ cup white wine vinegar

1 tablespoon honey

1 tablespoon Dijon mustard

½ cup olive oil

¼ cup vegetable oil

Salt and pepper, to taste

What You Do:

In a small mixing bowl, stir together all ingredients until well blended.

CAESAR SALAD v

Serve this classic salad plain or add cut-up grilled or fried chicken for an entrée salad. Use packaged classic seasoned croutons (not garlic or other flavors). You can use bottled salad dressing, or make your own (see recipe in this chapter). You can cut the total amount of Parmesan cheese in half if you prefer.

What You Need:

1 head romaine lettuce

½ cup croutons, divided

½ cup freshly grated Parmesan cheese, divided

Creamy Caesar Salad Dressing (use bottled dressing or see recipe in this chapter)

What You Do:

1. Separate the romaine lettuce leaves, rinse them under cold, running water, and pat dry with a paper towel. Wrap in dry paper towels and chill in the refrigerator for at least 30 minutes.
2. Tear 4 cups of the chilled lettuce into a large salad bowl. Add ¼ cup of the croutons and ¼ cup of the Parmesan cheese. Toss until well mixed. Add the rest of the croutons and cheese, and toss again. Chill in the refrigerator until ready to serve.
3. Just before serving, add the salad dressing 1 tablespoon at a time. Toss with salad utensils or 2 large spoons. Continue adding dressing and tossing salad until the romaine is lightly coated.

How Do I Prepare Head Lettuce for a Salad?

To prepare head lettuce for salad, find the bottom of the core (a round, white circle about 1" in diameter). Face the core toward your (clean) counter. Hold the head of lettuce like a basketball and whack it on the counter. Turn over the head and use your fingers to twist out the core; discard it. Hold the lettuce upside down under cold, running water, letting it run into the hole where the core was. Turn the lettuce right-side up and let water drain. Repeat several times under the water. Place hole-side down in a colander set in the sink. Drain. Pat dry with paper towels. Tear off a section of lettuce leaves about the size of your palm and about ¼" thick. Tear the leaves into bite-sized pieces and place them in a salad bowl.

CREAMY CAESAR SALAD DRESSING V

The dressing makes the salad, and that's especially true with the popular Caesar Salad (see recipe in this chapter). You can use bottled dressing, but it's so easy to make your own. Give it a try!

What You Need:

2 large cloves garlic

1 cup extra-virgin olive oil

½ teaspoon Worcestershire sauce

1½ teaspoons lemon juice

1 tablespoon red wine vinegar

⅓ cup heavy cream

¼ teaspoon salt

¼ teaspoon pepper

What You Do:

1. Mince the garlic by chopping it into very small pieces. Place in a small mixing bowl.
2. Stir in the olive oil, Worcestershire sauce, lemon juice, vinegar, cream, salt, and pepper until well blended. When ready to serve, spoon 1 or 2 tablespoons at a time onto the salad. Toss until lightly coated.

LAYERED SPINACH SALAD

This salad is great for entertaining, but you have to make it the night before to give it time to chill properly for the best serving temperature and texture.

What You Need:

DRESSING

2 cups mayonnaise

1 cup sour cream

1 (0.7- to 1-ounce) packet dry ranch salad dressing mix

SALAD

1½ cups frozen peas

6 eggs

1 pound bacon

1 head iceberg lettuce

1 (10-ounce) package fresh spinach

1 bunch scallions (about 3.5 ounces)

What You Do:

1. **For the Dressing:** Stir together the mayonnaise, sour cream, and dressing mix until well blended.
2. **For the Salad:** Set out the peas to thaw. Hard-boil the eggs (see Boiled Egg recipe in Chapter 1). Cook the bacon (see Makin' Bacon recipe in Chapter 1), and drain on paper towels. Crumble. Set aside.
3. Rinse the lettuce. Drain and pat dry with paper towels. Tear into bite-sized pieces. Place in the bottom of a large mixing bowl or salad serving bowl. Rinse the spinach under cold, running water, and drain. Pat dry with paper towels. Place in a layer over the lettuce.
4. Rinse the scallions under cold running water and remove outer skin and "tassels." Slice crosswise, including the green tops. Layer on top of the spinach. Pour the thawed peas on top of the onions.
5. Peel the eggs and use an egg slicer to slice them. Arrange on top of the salad. Top with the crumbled bacon. Cover the entire top of the salad with the dressing. Cover with plastic wrap and refrigerate overnight. Toss when ready to serve.

This salad with an Asian flair is a nice break from "everyday" tossed salads.

ROMAINE AND MANDARIN ORANGE SALAD v

What You Need:

2 cups romaine lettuce

½ cup slivered almonds

2 scallions (also called green onions)

½ (4-ounce) can mandarin oranges

4–6 tablespoons bottled poppy seed salad dressing

2 tablespoons grated Parmesan cheese

What You Do:

1. Rinse romaine, drain, and blot dry with paper towel. Tear into bite-sized pieces and place in a large mixing bowl. Cover and refrigerate at least 1 hour.
2. Preheat oven to 400°F. Place almonds on an ungreased cookie sheet or pie plate. Roast until golden brown (about 6 minutes). Set aside until ready to serve.
3. When ready to serve, rinse the scallions under cold running water and remove outer skin and "tassels" and slice, including about 2" of the dark green tops. Drain oranges. Add scallions, oranges, and almonds to the romaine.
4. Add dressing one tablespoon at a time. Toss lightly using salad utensils until ingredients are lightly coated. Place on serving plates. Sprinkle ½ of the grated Parmesan cheese on each salad.

Serve this salad for breakfast, brunch, or lunch—or even for a midday snack. If you like, top it with 1 to 2 tablespoons fruit-flavored yogurt.

WATERMELON-RASPBERRY SALAD v

What You Need:

1 pound whole watermelon

1 cup raspberries

½ cup cranberry juice

¼ cup fresh mint leaves

What You Do:

1. Remove the watermelon seeds and cut the fruit into 1" cubes. Place in a medium mixing bowl or salad serving bowl.
2. Rinse the raspberries under cold, running water just before using. Drain on paper towels. Add to the watermelon.
3. Add the cranberry juice and mint leaves. Gently stir to mix well. Chill in the refrigerator for at least 15 minutes before serving.

NUTTY BANANA-STRAWBERRIES ∨

You can substitute sliced almonds for the chopped pecans. You can also substitute mandarin oranges (drained) for the strawberries. For a lower-calorie, vegan variation, substitute frozen nondairy whipped topping for the whipped cream.

What You Need:
½ cup sliced strawberries
½ teaspoon granulated sugar
1 banana
Lemon juice, as needed (a few drops)
¼ cup chopped pecans
Pressurized, canned whipped cream, as needed

What You Do:

1. Clean and slice the strawberries (see the "How Should I Clean Strawberries?" sidebar with the Fruit Pizza recipe in Chapter 11). Sprinkle with sugar.
2. Peel and slice the banana. Sprinkle the slices with a few drops of lemon juice to help prevent browning.
3. Gently stir together the banana, strawberries, and pecans. Place in serving dishes. Top each serving with whipped cream.

GRAPE SALAD v

If you'd like to add color and flavor, use ½ bunch of each color of seedless grapes for this cool fruit salad. For a vegan variation, substitute tofu sour cream (see the "How Do I Make Tofu Sour Cream?" sidebar with the Quick Vegan Enchiladas recipe in Chapter 8).

What You Need:
½ cup slivered almonds
1½ pounds red and/or green seedless grapes
½ cup sour cream
1 teaspoon firmly packed brown sugar

What You Do:

1. Preheat oven to 400°F. Place the almonds in a single layer on a baking sheet. Bake for 4 to 5 minutes until brown. (Watch carefully so they don't burn!) Remove from oven. Set aside.
2. Rinse the grapes under cold, running water. Drain. Remove from stems.
3. In a large mixing bowl, stir together the sour cream and brown sugar. Add the grapes and stir until coated. When ready to serve, spoon into serving dishes and top with toasted almonds.

FRUIT AND COCONUT SALAD v

LEVEL E

SERVINGS 4

You can eat this salad right away if you like, but if you make it the day before and chill it in the refrigerator overnight, the flavors will blend for an even more delicious result.

What You Need:

1 cup canned mandarin oranges

1 cup canned pineapple tidbits

1 cup unsweetened, flaked coconut

1 cup sour cream or plain yogurt

What You Do:

1. Pre-chill the mandarin oranges and pineapple tidbits in the cans. Drain and place in a medium mixing bowl.
2. Stir in the coconut and sour cream or yogurt. Cover and refrigerate for at least 1 hour before serving.

ORANGE-BANANA SALAD v

LEVEL E

SERVINGS 4

Fresh bananas and sweet mandarin oranges blend for a mellow flavor in this treat you can eat as a snack, salad, or light dessert. Bananas are tropical fruits, so do not refrigerate until after they are cut. You can substitute chopped walnuts for the chopped pecans.

What You Need:

2 bananas

Lemon juice, as needed (a few drops)

1 (8-ounce) can mandarin oranges

¼ cup chopped pecans

What You Do:

1. Peel the bananas. Slice crosswise into circles about ¼" thick and place in a medium mixing bowl.
2. Sprinkle the bananas with a few drops of lemon juice to help prevent browning. Drain the oranges and add them to the bowl.
3. Add the pecans, stirring gently until well mixed. Chill in the refrigerator until ready to serve.

QUICK COTTAGE CHEESE SALAD v

Low in fat and chock-full of vegetables, this satisfying salad is a great midday pick-me-up. Keep covered in the refrigerator until ready to eat.

What You Need:

2 scallions (also called green onions)

1 green bell pepper

2 carrots

½ bunch radishes

1 (24-ounce) carton small-curd cottage cheese

What You Do:

1. Rinse the scallions, green bell pepper, carrots, and radishes under cold, running water.
2. Remove outer skin and "tassels" from the scallions. Slice the scallions (including the dark green tops) and place in a medium mixing bowl. Chop the green bell pepper and add to the bowl. Peel the carrots. Use the large holes on a grater to grate the carrots into the bowl. Slice the radishes and add to the bowl.
3. Gently stir in the cottage cheese until all the ingredients are well mixed. Cover and chill in the refrigerator for at least 1 hour before serving.

AVOCADO AND SHRIMP SALAD

LEVEL **E**

SERVINGS **2**

The avocado peel creates a decorative serving bowl for this salad. To eat, spoon the avocado and shrimp from the peeling. The shrimp in this recipe is also called baby shrimp or cocktail shrimp. You can serve this dish for lunch or as an appetizer.

What You Need:

1 ripe avocado

¾ cup frozen salad shrimp

2 teaspoons minced red onion

½ cup sour cream

⅛ teaspoon garlic powder

¼ teaspoon pepper

¼ teaspoon celery salt

Lemon juice, as needed (a few drops)

What You Do:

1. Pre-chill the avocado. Set out the shrimp to thaw for about 15 to 20 minutes. Place the onion in a medium mixing bowl. Add the sour cream, shrimp, garlic powder, pepper, and celery salt. Stir together until well blended. Cover and chill in refrigerator.
2. Cut the avocado in half lengthwise and remove the seed (see the "How Do I Remove Avocado Seeds?" sidebar with the Avocado-Cucumber Salad recipe in this chapter). Place halves on serving plates. Sprinkle lemon juice on the avocado to help prevent browning. Spoon chilled shrimp mixture on top of the avocado halves.

LEVEL **E**

SERVINGS **4**

VARIATION: SLICED AVOCADO & SHRIMP SALAD

Prepare Avocado and Shrimp Salad as directed, except peel and slice the avocado. Sprinkle with a few drops of lemon juice to help prevent browning. Arrange the slices on top of a bed of about 1 cup of salad greens on each of four salad plates. Top with the shrimp mixture.

CUCUMBER SALAD v

This cool, crisp salad makes a refreshing contrast to main courses with heavy sauce. If the dressing is too tart for your taste, add sugar. If it's too sweet, add a little vinegar.

What You Need:

2 cucumbers

2 scallions (also called green onions)

Water, as needed (about 1 quart)

1 teaspoon salt

¼ cup white vinegar

5 teaspoons granulated sugar

⅛ teaspoon pepper

What You Do:

1. Rinse the cucumbers under cold, running water. Peel and thinly slice the cucumbers crosswise. Place in a medium mixing bowl. Rinse the scallions and remove outer skin and "tassels." Slice the scallions, including the dark green tops. Add to the cucumbers. Add enough water to the bowl to cover the cucumbers and onions. Stir in the salt until it dissolves. Soak in the refrigerator for 2 to 3 hours. The cucumber slices will soften.

2. In a small mixing bowl, stir together the vinegar and sugar until the sugar dissolves. Set aside.

3. Drain the cucumbers and scallions. Gently squeeze the cucumbers with your hands to remove excess salt water (do not rinse). Place in a serving bowl and sprinkle with pepper. Stir in the vinegar and sugar mixture. (There will be extra liquid in the serving bowl.) Serve with a slotted spoon.

How Do I Know What Type of Vinegar to Choose?

Vinegar can be distilled from almost any food that contains sugar. Examples include cider vinegar, white vinegar, red wine vinegar, and rice vinegar. Unless you're adventurous (and willing to risk disaster), it's best not to substitute one type of vinegar for another in a recipe.

Black olives accent the bright red, deep green, and white vegetables that make this salad colorful as well as delicious. A clear glass serving bowl makes an attractive presentation. You can substitute grape tomatoes for the cherry tomatoes.

BROCCOLI-CAULIFLOWER SALAD v

What You Need:

1 pint cherry tomatoes

½ head cauliflower

½ head broccoli

1 (8-ounce) can pitted black olives

¼–½ cup bottled Italian salad dressing

What You Do:

1. Rinse the cherry tomatoes, cauliflower, and broccoli under cold, running water. Drain.
2. Remove the stems from the cauliflower and broccoli, and cut the florets into bite-sized pieces.
3. In a serving bowl, gently stir together the cherry tomatoes, cauliflower, and broccoli. Drain the olives and add to the serving bowl. Gently stir to mix the ingredients. Cover with plastic wrap and chill in the refrigerator for at least an hour or overnight. When ready to serve, sprinkle with Italian salad dressing. Gently stir until all the ingredients are lightly coated.

How Can I Use Broccoli Stems?

After cutting broccoli florets (the "treetops") from a bunch of broccoli, save the stems. Cover and store in the refrigerator for another use. You can eat them raw with veggie dip, or cut them into bite-sized pieces and add to a soup or tossed salad. You can also steam them for a side dish. Or, place them on a piece of toast and cover with melted cheese for an easy, hot lunch.

COLD MIXED VEGGIES SALAD v

This crisp, cold salad is a nice accompaniment to creamy casserole dishes. Try it with Mac 'n' Cheese (see recipe in Chapter 8). If you prefer to use fresh basil, use ¾ teaspoon.

What You Need:

1 green bell pepper

1 carrot

2 stalks celery

1 cucumber

1 medium red onion

1 teaspoon lemon juice

3 tablespoons vegetable oil

½ teaspoon water

¼ teaspoon dried basil

¼ teaspoon salt

What You Do:

1. Rinse the green bell pepper, carrot, celery, and cucumber under cold, running water. Peel the carrot and cucumber. Chop all the vegetables and place in a large mixing bowl. Chop the onion and add it to the bowl.

2. In a small mixing bowl, stir together the lemon juice, vegetable oil, water, basil, and salt until well mixed. Pour the mixture over the chopped vegetables. Stir until the vegetables are well coated. Cover and refrigerate at least 1 hour until ready to serve.

Here's a popular dish for potlucks and picnics. Prepare it the night before, as it needs several hours to chill. Chickpeas are also known as garbanzo beans. If you like, substitute lima beans for any of the other beans in this recipe.

FOUR-BEAN SALAD v

What You Need:

1 medium onion

¾ cup sugar

½ teaspoon black pepper

⅓ cup corn oil

⅓ cup white vinegar

1 (15-ounce) can red kidney beans

1 (15-ounce) can chickpeas

1 (15-ounce) can cut green beans

1 (15-ounce) can yellow wax beans

What You Do:

1. Peel and chop the onion into small pieces. Place in a large mixing bowl. Stir in the sugar, black pepper, corn oil, and vinegar until well blended.
2. Place a colander in the sink. Open the red kidney beans, chickpeas, green beans, and yellow wax beans and pour into the colander. Rinse with cold water. Stir a few times to let the liquid drain.
3. Add the drained beans to the bowl. Stir until the beans are well coated with the dressing. Cover and refrigerate at least 3 hours. Stir before serving.

WALDORF SALAD v

This cold salad has been a favorite for generations. The lemon juice helps keep the apples from turning brown. Serve in a bowl or on a lettuce leaf on a salad plate.

What You Need:

3 medium apples (about ¾ pound total)

4 stalks celery

½ cup chopped walnuts

¼ cup mayonnaise

1 tablespoon granulated sugar

½ teaspoon lemon juice

⅛ teaspoon salt

½ cup frozen nondairy whipped topping (or canned whipped cream)

What You Do:

1. Rinse the apples and celery under cold, running water. (Do not peel the apples.) Remove the cores of the apples with a knife or apple corer (see "How Do I Use an Apple Corer?" sidebar with the Apple Oatmeal recipe in Chapter 1). Cut the apples into 1" cubes. Chop the celery. Place apples and celery in a medium mixing bowl. Stir in the walnuts.
2. In a large mixing bowl, stir together the mayonnaise, sugar, lemon juice, and salt until well blended. Stir in the frozen nondairy whipped topping or whipped cream.
3. Add about ⅓ of the apple mixture to the mayonnaise mixture and stir to coat the fruit. Continue adding about ⅓ of the mixture at a time until the ingredients are well coated.

How Should I Store Celery?

Save the sleeve packaging and use it to cover celery when you store it in the refrigerator. If left uncovered, it will become dehydrated. If that happens, don't throw it out. Place it in a large container of ice water. The celery will absorb the moisture. Celery is a good source of vitamin C, and 2 stalks contain only 25 calories.

Bright green and red ingredients give this salad a festive look. You can use canned peas (drained), but frozen peas look and taste much better. For a vegan variation, omit the egg and substitute your choice of nondairy bottled salad dressing for the mayonnaise.

CHILLED PEA SALAD v

What You Need:

1 egg

1 cup frozen peas

1 tomato

½ stalk celery

2 tablespoons mayonnaise

What You Do:

1. Hard-boil the egg (see Boiled Egg recipe in Chapter 1).
2. Rinse the peas in cold water, drain, and let thaw.
3. Chop the tomato, celery, and egg, and place in a bowl.
4. Gently stir in the peas. Stir in the mayonnaise until all the ingredients are lightly coated. Chill in the refrigerator for at least 1 hour before serving.

How Can I Use Peas in Recipes?

Today, peas are eaten raw, added to salads, steamed, and stir-fried, as well as used in soups and stews. A ½ cup serving provides 30 percent of the recommended daily allowance of vitamin C. Peas originated in Middle Asia as far back as 5,000 years ago. Ancient Greeks and Romans cultivated them for their dried seeds. In Athens, Greek street vendors commonly sold hot pea soup. And in ancient Rome, fried peas were a common snack at the theater—much the way popcorn is in America today. The first mention of green peas occurred after the Norman Conquest of England in 1066. By the seventeenth century in France, green peas were used raw or cooked in the pod and considered quite a delicacy.

THREE-COLOR PASTA SALAD v

For best results, you'll need to start early (or the day before) to give the flavors a chance to mingle in this popular cold salad.

What You Need:

½ head broccoli

½ head cauliflower

2 carrots

2 scallions (also called green onions)

¼ cup sliced black olives

1–1½ cups bottled or homemade Italian salad dressing, divided

8 ounces uncooked tri-color spiral pasta

½ cup cubed Cheddar cheese

⅓ cup shredded Gouda

⅓ cup grated Parmesan cheese

Salt and pepper, to taste

What You Do:

1. Rinse the broccoli, cauliflower, and carrots under cold, running water. Peel the carrots. Chop broccoli, cauliflower, and carrots and place together in a medium mixing bowl. Rinse the scallions in cold, running water and remove outer skin and "tassels." Slice them crosswise into circles. Add to the bowl. Drain the black olives. Add to the bowl. Stir in ½ cup of the salad dressing until the veggies are well coated. Set aside for 30 minutes at room temperature, stirring occasionally.

2. Cook the pasta according to package directions. Drain. Transfer to a large mixing bowl and add ¼ cup of the salad dressing. Add additional dressing to taste. Save remainder for another salad. Cool to room temperature, stirring occasionally. Cover both bowls and refrigerate for at least 6 hours (or overnight).

(continued on next page)

THREE-COLOR PASTA SALAD

— CONTINUED

3. When almost ready to serve, add the Cheddar, Gouda, and Parmesan to the bowl of vegetables and toss. Then add the vegetables to the bowl of pasta and toss. Sprinkle with salt and pepper.

LEVEL **M**

SERVINGS **4-6**

Feeling a little blue? This salad with blueberries, blue cheese, and sweet, tangy dressing will chase those blues away.

BLUE-ON-BLUE SALAD v

What You Need:

2 tablespoons olive oil

½ cup pecan halves

1 head Bibb lettuce

½ cup blueberries

½ cup crumbled blue cheese

Bottled raspberry vinaigrette, as needed

What You Do:

1. Pour the olive oil into a small frying pan over medium-high heat. Stir in the pecans. Cook 2 to 3 minutes until warm. Drain on a paper towel. Set aside.
2. Rinse the lettuce under cold water. Tear apart the leaves and drain on a paper towel. Arrange on salad plates.
3. Top lettuce with the blueberries, and pecans. Sprinkle with the blue cheese. Serve with bottled raspberry vinaigrette.

OLD-FASHIONED COLESLAW v

Coleslaw is a favorite summertime side dish. You can also spoon it onto a sandwich to add flavor and crunch. Use it on the Grilled Rachel Sandwich (see recipe in Chapter 2) or on a turkey, ham, or bologna and cheese sandwich.

What You Need:

½ head cabbage

4 carrots

3 tablespoons white vinegar

½ teaspoon salt

¼ teaspoon paprika

3 tablespoons granulated sugar

½ cup sour cream

What You Do:

1. Remove the outer leaves of the cabbage. Cut in half lengthwise. Store the other half tightly wrapped in the refrigerator for another use within a day or two. Cut the remaining half crosswise into 2 pieces. Use the large holes on a grater to grate both halves of the cabbage into a colander. (Grate only the amount you need. Do not store grated or shredded cabbage for future use. It spoils faster and quickly loses its vitamin content once it's been cut.)

2. Peel the carrots and rinse under cold, running water. Grate the carrots, using the large holes on the grater, into the bowl with the shredded cabbage. Use two forks to toss together. Cover and refrigerate for at least 2 hours.

3. In a small mixing bowl, stir together the vinegar, salt, paprika, sugar, and sour cream until well blended.

4. Remove the cabbage mixture from the refrigerator. Add the dressing 1 tablespoon at a time, to taste, using two table forks to toss until the cabbage and carrots are lightly coated. Chill about 1 hour and serve.

If you'd like to try something a bit different, consider this flavorful, cold salad. Couscous is a North African dish made from a rice-like steamed, crushed grain. You'll find instant couscous in the rice aisle of your supermarket.

EXOTIC (YET SIMPLE) COUSCOUS SALAD v

What You Need:

1 (10-ounce) box instant couscous

1 cucumber

3 tomatoes

3 roasted red peppers (from a jar)

2 scallions (also called green onions)

1 (4.25-ounce) can chopped black olives

2 cloves fresh garlic (or ¼ teaspoon dried minced garlic)

¼ cup olive oil

¼ cup lemon juice

1 teaspoon ground cumin

¼ teaspoon salt

⅛ teaspoon black pepper

⅛ teaspoon cayenne pepper (optional)

What You Do:

1. Cook the couscous according to package directions.
2. Peel and chop the cucumber. Chop the tomatoes and roasted red peppers. Rinse the scallions in cold, running water and remove outer skin and "tassels." Slice. Stir the cucumber, tomatoes, red peppers, and scallions together in a medium mixing bowl. When the couscous is done, fluff with a fork. Stir in the cucumber, scallions, tomatoes, and peppers. Drain the chopped olives. Add to the salad and stir. Set aside.
3. Finely chop the garlic and place in a small mixing bowl. Stir in the olive oil, lemon juice, cumin, salt, black pepper, and cayenne pepper (if using). Pour over the salad. Toss with two forks until well mixed. Chill for about 1 hour or until cool.

You can make this lemony salad with either bulgur wheat or couscous. And you can use either flat-leaf or curly parsley.

TABBOULEH SALAD v

What You Need:

1 small cucumber

2 medium tomatoes

1 cup fresh parsley

2 tablespoons chopped fresh chives

3 scallions (also called green onions)

1 cup uncooked cracked instant bulgur wheat (or instant couscous)

½ cup olive oil

½ cup lemon juice

Salt and pepper, to taste

What You Do:

1. Rinse the cucumber, tomatoes, and parsley under cold, running water. Drain, chop, and place in a large mixing bowl. Add chopped chives to the bowl. Rinse the scallions in cold, running water and remove outer skin and "tassels." Slice scallions and add to the bowl.
2. Cook the bulgur wheat or couscous according to package directions. While it's cooking, stir together the olive oil, lemon juice, salt, and pepper until well mixed. When the bulgur wheat is done, add it to the vegetables in the large mixing bowl.
3. Pour the dressing over the ingredients in the mixing bowl. Gently toss until well coated. Cover and refrigerate for 2 to 3 hours to allow the flavors to mingle.

Serve this refreshing salad with unbuttered, sliced French bread to soak up the delicious dressing (see the "How Do I Prepare French Bread?" sidebar with the Baked Spaghetti recipe in Chapter 5). Wait until the fresh local tomato crop is in for best results, or use cherry tomatoes instead of the wedges. You can also use canola oil instead of the olive oil.

MARINATED TOMATO SALAD v

What You Need:

3 tablespoons chopped fresh parsley

2 tablespoons chopped fresh basil

3 scallions (also called green onions)

1 tablespoon granulated sugar

1½ teaspoons garlic salt

1½ teaspoons seasoned salt (like Lawry's)

¾ teaspoon dried thyme

½ teaspoon ground black pepper

¾ cup extra-virgin olive oil

½ cup red wine vinegar

6 whole tomatoes

What You Do:

1. Place the chopped parsley and basil in a medium mixing bowl. Rinse the scallions in cold, running water and remove outer skin and "tassels." Slice the scallions and add to the bowl.

2. Stir in the sugar, garlic salt, seasoned salt, thyme, pepper, olive oil, and vinegar. Mix well.

3. Rinse the tomatoes under cold, running water and cut into wedges. Place in a large mixing bowl.

4. Pour the dressing over the tomatoes. Gently stir to coat the tomatoes. Set aside at room temperature for 2 hours. Gently stir every half-hour. Eat warm or chill before serving.

This fresh summer salad goes well with any kind of grilled meat and French bread (see the "How Do I Prepare French Bread?" sidebar with the Baked Spaghetti recipe in Chapter 5). You can substitute grape tomatoes for the cherry tomatoes, and you can omit the olive oil from the dressing if you like.

AVOCADO-CUCUMBER SALAD v

What You Need:

SALAD

4 avocados
2 cups cherry tomatoes
2 cups cucumbers
¾ cup chopped red onion

DRESSING

4 tablespoons chopped fresh cilantro
2 teaspoons chopped fresh garlic
2 tablespoons lime juice
¼ cup virgin or extra virgin olive oil
Salt and pepper, to taste

What You Do:

1. **For the Salad:** Slice the avocados in half lengthwise and remove the seeds. Use a spoon to remove the flesh. Cut into 1" cubes. Place in a large mixing bowl.
2. Slice the tomatoes in half, and add to the bowl.
3. Peel the cucumbers and slice crosswise into circles. Add to the bowl.
4. Add the onion to the bowl.
5. **For the Dressing:** Combine the cilantro, garlic, lime juice, olive oil, salt, and pepper in a small mixing bowl and mix well.
6. Pour the dressing over the avocados, tomatoes, cucumbers, and onions. Gently stir until lightly coated. Chill before serving.

How Do I Remove Avocado Seeds?

Here's an easy way to remove the seed from an avocado: Slice through the avocado lengthwise, deep enough to touch the seed. Cut all the way around the fruit. With one hand on each half, gently twist to separate. Plunge the knife into the seed with a quick thrust. Twist the seed, and lift out.

Serve this lunch salad with your favorite muffin or Mexican Corn Bread (see recipe in Chapter 1).

SPINACH, BACON, AND EGG SALAD

What You Need:

4 eggs

8 slices bacon

4 ounces baby spinach

⅓ cup bottled Italian salad dressing

What You Do:

1. Hard-boil the eggs (see Boiled Egg recipe in Chapter 1). Cool. Peel and slice with an egg slicer.
2. Cook the bacon until crisp (see Makin' Bacon recipe in Chapter 1). Drain on paper towels. When cool, break into pieces 1–1½" long.
3. Rinse the spinach and drain. Pat dry with paper towels.
4. When ready to serve, place the spinach and bacon in a large mixing bowl. Add the Italian dressing. Toss until lightly coated.
5. Arrange in serving bowls or on salad plates. Top with the sliced hard-boiled eggs.

POTATO SALAD v

There's no single "right" way to make Potato Salad. It's likely that almost every family in America has its own recipe. Here's a basic recipe to get you started. You can substitute 2 to 3 small red russet potatoes (about 1 handful total) for each baking potato.

What You Need:

4 medium baking potatoes

2 eggs

¼ medium white onion

1 stalk celery

¾ cup mayonnaise or mayonnaise-like salad dressing

1 teaspoon prepared mustard

½ teaspoon celery seed

½ teaspoon salt

½ teaspoon pepper

1 teaspoon granulated sugar (optional)

What You Do:

1. Rinse potatoes under cold, running water and place in a Dutch oven. Cover with water. Boil for 30 to 35 minutes, until tender when pierced with a fork. Drain and let cool. Peel and cut into ¾" cubes. Place in a large mixing bowl.
2. While the potatoes are cooking, hard-boil the eggs (see Boiled Egg recipe in Chapter 1). Peel and chop the eggs. Add to the potatoes. Chop the onion and celery. Add to the potatoes.
3. In a separate, small mixing bowl, stir together the mayonnaise, mustard, celery seed, salt, and pepper until well blended. (Taste the mixture. Add 1 teaspoon sugar if you like.) Pour over the potato mixture. Gently stir until the potatoes are well coated. Refrigerate for at least 1 hour before serving.

This potato salad is traditionally served warm. If the dressing is too tangy for your taste, use 1 additional teaspoon of sugar.

HOT GERMAN POTATO SALAD

What You Need:

4 medium potatoes

6 slices bacon

½ small white onion

2 tablespoons all-purpose flour

4 teaspoons granulated sugar

1½ teaspoons salt

½ teaspoon celery seed

⅛ teaspoon pepper

⅔ cup water

6 tablespoons vinegar

What You Do:

1. Rinse potatoes and place them in a 2-quart saucepan. Cover with water. Bring to a boil over high heat. Boil for 8 to 10 minutes, until the potatoes are soft when pierced with a fork. Drain and let cool. Peel and slice crosswise into ¼"-thick pieces.
2. Fry the bacon in a large frying pan (see Makin' Bacon recipe in Chapter 1). Leave the fat in the pan. Drain the bacon on paper towels. When the bacon is cool, break it into crumbles. Set aside.
3. Chop the onion. Heat the bacon fat over medium-high heat. Cook the onion in the bacon fat until tender. Reduce heat to low. Stir in the flour, sugar, salt, celery seed, and pepper until well blended and the mixture bubbles. Remove the frying pan from the heat.
4. Stir in the water and vinegar. Return the frying pan to the stovetop over medium-high heat. Stir constantly until the mixture boils. Continue boiling for 1 minute. Remove from heat.
5. Gently stir in the potatoes and bacon until well coated. Cover to keep warm until ready to serve.

CHAPTER 5

Main Dishes for Carnivores—Beef and Pork

ROAST BEEF

This recipe makes 2 servings per pound.

When people talk about "meat and potatoes," they're talking about beef. Because roast beef is simple and unadorned, it can be served with a wide variety of interesting salads and side dishes with or without sauces. Serve with Garlic Mashed Potatoes (see recipe in Chapter 9), Green Bean Casserole (see recipe in Chapter 9), or Broccoli-Cauliflower Salad (see recipe in Chapter 4).

What You Need:

1 (any size) rump or round roast

Garlic salt, to taste

Salt and pepper, to taste

What You Do:

1. Preheat oven to 325°F. Place the meat fat-side up in a roasting pan or ovenproof baking pan. Insert a meat thermometer into the thickest part of the meat (optional). Sprinkle with garlic salt, salt, and pepper.
2. For rare meat, roast for 22 to 26 minutes per pound, or until the meat thermometer reads 140°F. For medium, roast for 26 to 30 minutes per pound, or until the meat thermometer reads 160°F. For well done, roast for 33 to 35 minutes per pound, or until the meat thermometer reads 170°F.
3. Remove from oven. Let roast sit for about 5 minutes before slicing. Note: As the roast sits outside the oven, it will continue to cook. So if you like rare or medium-rare meat, cook it for the smaller amount of time listed.

What Are the Cooking Times for Bone-In Roasts?

If you had two beef roasts that weighed the same, but one had a bone and the other didn't, you'd have to cook the one without the bone a bit longer. Leaving the bone in the meat helps it cook faster, because the bone conducts heat and helps cook the meat.

CHEESEBURGERS

You can grill burgers outdoors, or cook them inside on the stovetop or under the broiler. Top with your favorite cheese, and serve with your choice of lettuce, sliced onion, sliced tomatoes, pickles, mustard, ketchup, and mayonnaise. Serve with Old-Fashioned Coleslaw (see recipe in Chapter 4) and Baked Beans (see recipe in Chapter 9).

What You Need:

1½ pounds ground beef

Garlic salt, to taste

Pepper, to taste

4 slices Cheddar, Swiss, or other cheese (optional)

4 hamburger buns

What You Do:

1. Preheat the broiler, if using. Place the ground beef in a large mixing bowl. Gently squish it with your hands. Use ¼ of the beef for each burger. Shape into tight, round patties. Sprinkle with garlic salt and pepper.
2. Place patties on a broiling pan, and cook under the broiler for 3 to 5 minutes. Or, place the patties on an outdoor grill, or in a large frying pan over medium-high heat. Cook for 3 to 5 minutes until blood oozes out the top. Use a spatula to turn once. Cook for another 3 to 5 minutes.
3. During the last minute on the grill or in the frying pan, top each with one slice of cheese, if using. Cook until the cheese melts. (If broiling, remove from the broiler and top with the cheese.) Remove from the heat. Serve on the hamburger buns.

Here's an easy favorite you're probably used to buying at fast-food drive-up windows. Instead, make your own. Serve with sour cream and Fresh Tomato Salsa (see recipe in Chapter 10).

TACOS

What You Need:

1 pound ground beef
2 tablespoons chili powder or 1 (1.25-ounce) packet dry taco seasoning mix
1 tablespoon dried minced onion (optional)
¼ head iceberg lettuce
1 large tomato
6–8 prepared taco shells or 6" flour tortillas (for soft tacos)
1 cup shredded Cheddar cheese
½ cup salsa or picante sauce
2 tablespoons sour cream

What You Do:

1. In a frying pan, brown the ground beef (see the "How Do I Brown Ground Beef?" sidebar with the Chili Blue recipe in Chapter 3) along with chili powder (or taco seasoning mix) and the onion (if using). Drain off the fat. Cover to keep warm.

2. While the meat is browning, shred the lettuce using the large holes on a grater. (Or slice into narrow strips with a knife.) Place in a serving bowl. Chop the tomato and place in a small serving bowl.

3. Heat the taco shells according to package directions. (If you're using flour tortillas for soft tacos, omit this step. Instead, wrap the tortillas together in aluminum foil. Set the oven to the lowest temperature, about 200°F, and place the tortillas in the oven before you begin browning the meat. Remove the tortillas from the oven when you are ready to serve. Or, you can wrap the tortillas individually in damp paper towels and heat them for 40 seconds on high in the microwave. Heated flour tortillas taste better, and they are easier to roll up.)

4. To serve, spoon about ¼ cup of the beef mixture into each taco shell. Top each with some lettuce, tomato, cheese, salsa, and sour cream.

LEVEL **E**

SERVINGS **8**

This mild but hearty casserole makes a fine, Italian-style main course for a crowd, without the need for last-minute preparation. You won't have to rattle around in the kitchen boiling noodles after your guests arrive. Prepare ahead and store in the refrigerator until ready to bake. Serve with grated Parmesan cheese, a mixed greens salad, and French bread (see the "How Do I Prepare French Bread?" sidebar with this recipe). Cover and store leftovers in the refrigerator for up to 4 days.

BAKED SPAGHETTI

What You Need:

1 (10-ounce) package thin spaghetti

1 pound ground beef

¼ cup milk

1 egg

1 (28-ounce) jar spaghetti sauce (any kind)

2 cups shredded mozzarella cheese

What You Do:

1. Break the uncooked spaghetti into thirds and cook according to package directions (boil for about 8 minutes, until the noodles are tender but still firm).
2. While the noodles are cooking, brown the ground beef (see the "How Do I Brown Ground Beef?" sidebar with the Chili Blue recipe in Chapter 3) in a large frying pan. Drain off the fat.
3. Preheat the oven to 350°F. Spray a 9" × 13" ovenproof baking pan with nonstick cooking spray. When the noodles are done, drain. Pour the noodles into the baking pan.
4. In a small mixing bowl, quickly stir together the milk and egg with a fork until well blended. Pour the mixture onto the noodles and stir until the noodles are well coated.
5. Stir the beef into the noodles. Add the spaghetti sauce and gently stir until well blended. Cover the surface with shredded mozzarella. Bake uncovered for 30 minutes.

VARIATION:
VEGETARIAN BAKED SPAGHETTI v

For a vegetarian version of Baked Spaghetti, omit the beef. For more substance, add 1 (7-ounce) can of sliced mushrooms or mushroom stems and pieces (drained), and/or use a jar of spaghetti sauce with vegetable chunks. Or, substitute 1 diced eggplant for the meat.

How Do I Prepare French Bread?

Purchase an unsliced loaf of French bread. Preheat the oven to 400°F. Slice into 1"-thick pieces. Leave standing in a loaf shape. Take a heel piece and spread butter or margarine on the interior side. Replace the heel back on the end of the loaf. One by one take out a slice, spread butter on both sides. Replace it in the loaf. When finished, wrap entire loaf in aluminum foil. Bake for 10 minutes. Plan for 2 to 3 slices per person. If you don't need an entire loaf, cut the amount you need from the whole loaf. Tightly wrap the portion you won't use in aluminum foil and freeze for another meal or for Hot Cheese Toast (see recipe in Chapter 8).

LEVEL **E**

SERVINGS **4**

Round steak is the tastiest choice for this recipe. However, because this dish cooks slowly, you can use arm steak or chuck roast, which are less expensive cuts. Serve with a green vegetable and baked potatoes (see the "How Do I Bake a Potato?" sidebar with the Beef and Onion Roast recipe in this chapter).

SLOW-COOKED SWISS STEAK

What You Need:

1 pound round steak, about 1" thick

½ medium white or yellow onion

1 (28-ounce) can stewed tomatoes, with juice

¼ teaspoon garlic salt

Salt and pepper, to taste

What You Do:

1. Cut the meat into serving-sized pieces. Place into a slow cooker or a 9" × 13" ovenproof baking pan that has been sprayed with nonstick cooking spray.
2. Slice the onion and place on top of the meat. Pour the tomatoes and juice over the top. Sprinkle with garlic salt, salt, and pepper.
3. Cover the slow cooker or baking pan. In a slow cooker, cook on high for 1 hour. Reduce heat to low and cook for another 8 or 9 hours until the meat is tender. In the oven, bake at 350°F for 1½ to 2 hours, until the meat is tender. To serve, place the meat on a serving plate. Spoon onions, tomatoes, and drippings over the meat.

LEVEL **E**

SERVINGS **4**

VARIATION: CREAMY SWISS STEAK

Substitute 1 (10.5-ounce) can condensed mushroom soup for the tomatoes. When meat is done, use the drippings as gravy.

HAMBURGER-MUSHROOM PIZZA CASSEROLE

This dinner entrée tastes like pizza, but you don't have to spin dough over your head. Serve with grated Parmesan cheese and a Tossed Salad (see recipe in Chapter 4) with Vinaigrette or Honey-Mustard Dressing (see recipes in Chapter 4).

What You Need:

2 pounds ground beef

1 (7-ounce) can mushroom stems and pieces (optional)

1 (15-ounce) can pizza sauce

1 (7.5-ounce) can refrigerator biscuits

1 cup grated Parmesan cheese

What You Do:

1. Brown the ground beef in a frying pan (see the "How Do I Brown Ground Beef?" sidebar with the Chili Blue recipe in Chapter 3). Drain off the fat. Reduce heat to low. Drain the mushrooms (if using), and add to the beef along with the pizza sauce. Stir.
2. Lay the uncooked biscuits on top of the meat. Sprinkle with cheese. Cover and simmer for 20 to 25 minutes, until the biscuits are cooked.

TOMATO RICE WITH BEEF CASSEROLE

This casserole is a meaty variation of a Mexican side dish. You can substitute cooked pork from a leftover roast or pork chops for the beef. You also can substitute 2 servings of instant rice.

What You Need:

2 cups water

1 cup uncooked rice

1 teaspoon salt

1 pound ground beef

1 medium onion

1 (14.5-ounce) can stewed tomatoes, with juice

Salt and pepper, to taste

What You Do:

1. In a saucepan over high heat, bring the water, rice, and salt to a boil. Reduce heat to low and cover. Simmer for about 15 minutes, until all the water is absorbed.
2. While the rice is cooking, crumble the ground beef into the frying pan. Chop the onion and add it to the frying pan. Brown the beef and onion (see the "How Do I Brown Ground Beef?" sidebar with the Chili Blue recipe in Chapter 3). Drain off the fat.
3. Stir in the stewed tomatoes with juice until well blended. Sprinkle with salt and pepper. Stir in the rice. Cook uncovered for 5 to 10 minutes, until heated through.

BEEF AND ONION ROAST

This easy entrée cooks slowly, so you can use a less expensive cut of beef and it will still turn out tender and juicy. Serve with baked (see "How Do I Bake a Potato?" sidebar with this recipe) or Mashed Potatoes (see Mashed Potatoes recipe in Chapter 9) and sliced fresh tomatoes or steamed green beans.

What You Need:

2–3 pounds beef rump, round, or chuck roast

2 (1-ounce) packets dry onion soup mix

What You Do:

1. Place the meat on a large piece of aluminum foil. Sprinkle with the onion soup mix and pat it into the meat. Bring the two short ends of the foil together and fold down several times to seal the meat. Place in an ovenproof baking pan.

2. Cook at 300°F for 3 hours. Take it out of the oven and let it sit for 5 to 10 minutes. Be careful not to burn yourself with the hot steam when you unwrap the meat.

How Do I Bake a Potato?

One of America's favorite side dishes is a simple baked potato, served with a variety of toppings: butter, sour cream, chopped chives, or cottage cheese. Or, try sour cream mixed with ranch- or French onion–flavored dried soup or dip mix. To bake a potato, rinse the potato under cold, running water. Cut two slits in an "X" shape on the top of the potato to let heat escape during baking. Place directly on baking rack in oven. (Or, for a softer potato skin and mushy flesh, rub butter or margarine on the skin and wrap the potato in aluminum foil before placing in oven.) Bake at 350°F for 1 hour. Test for doneness by piercing with a fork or gently squeezing potato (while holding a potholder). When done, potato will feel soft.

Tired of spaghetti sauce that comes in a jar? Make your own and add tasty meatballs for an authentic Italian dinner. Serve over spaghetti cooked according to the directions on a 10-ounce package.

SPAGHETTI AND MEATBALLS

What You Need:

MEATBALLS

1 pound ground beef
2 eggs
⅛ teaspoon dried minced garlic
¼ cup grated Parmesan cheese
1 teaspoon salt
3 tablespoons vegetable oil

SAUCE

1½ cups water
2 (6-ounce) cans tomato paste
1 teaspoon dried basil
1 teaspoon salt
⅛ teaspoon pepper
½ teaspoon granulated sugar
1 (10-ounce) package thin spaghetti, cooked according to package instructions

What You Do:

1. **For the Meatballs:** To make the meatballs, crumble the ground beef into a large mixing bowl. In a separate, small mixing bowl or cup, beat the eggs with a fork until well blended. Add to the beef, along with the garlic, cheese, and salt. Use your hands to squish the ingredients together until well blended. Wet your hands with tap water, and form the beef mixture into about 16 meatballs. Pour the vegetable oil into a large frying pan over medium heat. Fry in the oil until well browned. Drain off the fat. Reduce the heat to low.

2. **For the Sauce:** Heat the water in a saucepan over high heat until small bubbles form. Pour into a heatproof bowl. Stir in the tomato paste, basil, salt, pepper, and sugar until well blended. Pour the sauce over the meatballs in the frying pan. Cover and cook over low heat for at least 1 hour, stirring occasionally.

3. **To Serve:** Pour over cooked spaghetti noodles.

THE EASIEST LASAGNA IN THE WORLD

This popular layered pasta dish is a favorite at potluck dinners. You can use cottage cheese in place of the ricotta for a lower-fat option.

What You Need:
1 pound ground beef
1 (32-ounce) jar spaghetti sauce
1 egg
12 ounces ricotta cheese
1 cup shredded mozzarella cheese
1 teaspoon dried basil
1 teaspoon dried oregano
Salt and pepper, to taste
⅛ teaspoon chili powder (optional)
9 uncooked lasagna noodles
¼ cup grated Parmesan cheese

What You Do:

1. Brown the ground beef (see the "How Do I Brown Ground Beef?" sidebar with the Chili Blue recipe in Chapter 3). Drain off the fat. Stir in the spaghetti sauce.
2. In a large mixing bowl, beat the egg with a fork until well blended. Stir in the ricotta and mozzarella, along with basil, oregano, salt, pepper, and chili powder.
3. Preheat oven to 350°F. Use just enough of the sauce mixture to cover the bottom of an ovenproof 7" × 11" × 3" baking dish. Place 3 of the uncooked noodles on top of the sauce in a row to form a layer. Spread about ⅓ of the cheese mixture on the noodles; then spread about ⅓ of the sauce mixture on top of the cheese. Repeat the process twice: 3 noodles, cheese mixture, sauce mixture; 3 noodles, cheese mixture, sauce mixture.
4. Sprinkle with Parmesan cheese. Cover with aluminum foil. Bake for 1 hour. Uncover and bake 15 minutes more or until the noodles are soft. Let stand 10 to 15 minutes before cutting.

BOILED CORNED BEEF AND CABBAGE

Nothing is more traditional for St. Patrick's Day than boiled corned beef and cabbage. Use leftover corned beef for a Grilled Reuben Sandwich (see recipe in Chapter 2).

What You Need:

3–4 pounds packaged corned beef brisket with spice packet

Water, as needed (about 1 quart)

2 small heads green cabbage

What You Do:

1. Place the meat in a Dutch oven or large stew pot. Cover with water. Stir in the contents of the spice packet. On the stovetop, cover and bring to a boil over medium-high heat. Reduce heat to low. Simmer for 2½ hours or until the meat is tender when pierced with a fork.

2. Remove and discard the outer leaves from the cabbages. Rinse the cabbages under cold, running water. Cut each head in half from top to bottom. Cut each half from top to bottom in half again to make wedges. Place the cabbage wedges in the pot surrounding the meat. Cover and cook another 30 minutes. (In a slow cooker, place the cabbage in the pot first. Place the meat on top of the cabbage. Cover with water. Cook on low for 8 to 10 hours.)

How Do I Choose and Store Cabbage?

Cabbage is high in vitamin C and very low in sodium. When purchasing, avoid heads with outer leaves that have separated from the stem. Do not rinse cabbage before storing. (Moisture favors decay.) If shredding, do it only when ready to use. Do not store shredded cabbage for future use. It quickly spoils once it's cut. Even tightly wrapped halves or quarters of head cabbage last only one or two days in the refrigerator.

COWBOY HASH

How easy is this? It makes you feel right at home on the range.

Serve with Hot Cheese Toast (see recipe in Chapter 8) and ketchup, barbecue sauce, or chunky salsa.

What You Need:

4 small white or red russet potatoes

1 small white or yellow onion

1 green bell pepper (optional)

¼ cup vegetable oil

1 pound ground beef

1 teaspoon chili powder

1 teaspoon salt

¼ teaspoon pepper

What You Do:

1. Peel and slice the potatoes. Set aside. Chop the onion and green bell pepper. Pour the vegetable oil into a large frying pan over medium-high heat. Add the onions and green bell pepper. Cook until tender but still firm, stirring frequently.

2. Crumble the ground beef into the pan and brown it (see the "How Do I Brown Ground Beef?" sidebar with the Chili Blue recipe in Chapter 3). Gently stir in the potatoes. Add the chili powder, salt, and pepper; mix well. Continue frying for about 30 minutes, stirring often. Cook until the potatoes are tender and golden brown. Drain off excess fat before serving.

This is best when prepared with rump or eye of round roast. But because this cooks slowly, you can cook it with a less expensive cut of beef, such as chuck roast or arm roast. Serve with Garlic Mashed Potatoes (see recipe in Chapter 9).

POT ROAST

What You Need:
POT ROAST

4 carrots

3 stalks celery

1 medium white or yellow onion

2 tablespoons vegetable oil

1 (2-pound) beef round, chuck, or arm roast

Salt and pepper, to taste

½ cup water

OPTIONAL GRAVY

3 tablespoons all-purpose flour

⅓ cup cold water

What You Do:

1. **For the Pot Roast:** Rinse the carrots and celery under cold, running water. Peel the carrots. Cut the carrots and celery diagonally into 1–1½"-long sections. Chop the onion. Place the carrots, celery, and onion in a slow cooker.

2. Heat the vegetable oil in a large frying pan over medium-high heat. Place the roast in the hot oil and brown on one side. Turn the roast. Generously sprinkle salt and pepper over the browned side. When the second side is browned, sprinkle with salt and pepper. Place in a slow cooker.

3. Pour ½ cup water over the beef. Cover. Cook on low for 8 to 10 hours (or on high for 4 to 5 hours).

4. **For the Optional Gravy:** At the end of the cooking time, pour the cooking liquid from the slow cooker into a large saucepan over medium-high heat.

(continued on next page)

POT ROAST — CONTINUED

5. (Leave the beef and vegetables in the cooker to keep warm.) In a small mixing bowl, stir together the flour and ⅓ cup cold water until well blended. Pour into the cooking liquid. Stir constantly until the mixture bubbles and thickens.
6. When ready to serve, place the meat on a serving dish. Use a slotted spoon to remove the vegetables. Spoon them around the beef to form a border along the edge of the serving dish. Serve the gravy on the side.

LEVEL **M**

SERVINGS **2**

If you like hot tamales, this one-dish meal is for you. You can omit the onion if you prefer.

HOT TAMALE CASSEROLE

What You Need:
1 (15-ounce) can beef chili (with or without beans)
¼ medium white or yellow onion (about 2½" in diameter)
1 (15-ounce) can tamales (with liquid)
1 (8-ounce) package shredded Cheddar cheese

What You Do:

1. Preheat oven to 350°F. Spray a 9" × 12" ovenproof baking pan with nonstick cooking spray. Pour chili into the pan.
2. Chop the onion. Stir into the chili. Stir in the liquid from the tamale can until well mixed.
3. Remove any paper from the tamales. Arrange tamales in a row on top of the chili. Top with Cheddar cheese. Bake uncovered for 30 minutes until cheese melts and tamales and chili are heated through. Or, cover and zap in the microwave for about 5 minutes on high until cheese melts and ingredients are heated through.

THEY'LL THINK YOU'RE A GENIUS BEEF BRISKET

*This recipe makes 2 servings per pound.

Prepare this recipe the day before you plan to serve it.

What You Need:

1 (3–6-pound) beef brisket

½ (3.5-ounce) bottle liquid smoke

1 cup lemon juice

1 tablespoon celery seed

½ teaspoon garlic salt

¼ teaspoon pepper

½ cup water

About ¾ cup bottled barbecue sauce

What You Do:

1. Place the brisket in a shallow roasting pan, fat-side up. Pour the liquid smoke and lemon juice over the top. Sprinkle with celery seed, garlic salt, and pepper. Bake uncovered at 275°F for 1½ hours.
2. Remove from oven. Pour water into the side of the roasting pan (not on top of the meat). Tightly cover with aluminum foil. Return to the oven. Cook for another 2½ hours.
3. Uncover. Pour the barbecue sauce over the top of the meat. Reseal the foil. Cook for another 30 minutes. Remove from oven. Remove the foil until the meat has cooled. Cover and refrigerate in the juices overnight. (Don't cut the meat before it's chilled!)
4. Preheat oven to 350°F. Remove brisket from the juices and place on cutting board. (Discard juices.) Thinly slice the cold brisket crosswise. Place in an ovenproof baking pan that has been sprayed with nonstick cooking spray. Cover and heat in the oven for 20 to 30 minutes, until warmed through.

Don a sombrero and invite some friends over for a fiesta!

ENCHILADAS

What You Need:

1¼ cups canned red enchilada sauce
1 (10.5-ounce) can condensed cream of mushroom soup
1 (10.75-ounce) can condensed tomato soup
1 small white or yellow onion
2 pounds ground beef
1½ cups shredded Cheddar cheese
10 (6") flour tortillas

What You Do:

1. Spray a 9" × 13" ovenproof baking pan with nonstick cooking spray. Set aside. In a large saucepan, stir together the enchilada sauce, undiluted mushroom soup, and undiluted tomato soup. Cook over medium heat for about 8 to 10 minutes until mixture is warm and the colors are well blended. Remove from heat.

2. Chop the onion. Place in a large frying pan. Crumble the ground beef into the pan. Brown the beef and onion together (see the "How Do I Brown Ground Beef?" sidebar with the Chili Blue recipe in Chapter 3). Drain off fat. Stir in ½ cup of the enchilada sauce mixture and ½ cup of the shredded cheese.

3. Preheat oven to 350°F. Scoop ⅓–½ cup of the beef mixture and spoon it in a 2"-wide line down the middle of a flour tortilla. Fold the bottom ¼ of the tortilla over the beef mixture. Wrap the right side of the tortilla halfway over the beef mixture (and the already folded bottom section). Wrap the left side of the tortilla over the right side. Carefully turn over the enchilada and place seam-side down in the baking pan. Repeat until all the enchiladas are prepared and placed in the baking pan.

4. Pour the remaining sauce mixture over the enchiladas. Top with the remaining cheese. Bake uncovered for 30 minutes.

STUFFED GREEN BELL PEPPERS

The green peppers in this recipe double as serving bowls. You can use instant rice to make ½ cup cooked rice if you like.

What You Need:

¼ cup uncooked rice

2 large green bell peppers

Water, as needed (about 2 quarts), divided for boiling and baking the peppers

½ small white or yellow onion

¾ pound lean ground beef

1 (8-ounce) can tomato sauce

Salt and pepper, to taste

2 slices American cheese

What You Do:

1. Cook the rice according to package directions. Set aside.
2. Rinse the green bell peppers under cold, running water. Cut off the tops of the green peppers. Remove the seeds and carefully cut out the ribs from the insides of the peppers. Fill a 2-quart saucepan about three-quarters full with water. Bring to a boil. Place the green peppers in the boiling water. Cover and cook for 5 minutes to soften. Drain.
3. While the peppers are cooking, chop the onion. Brown the ground beef along with the onion (see the "How Do I Brown Ground Beef?" sidebar with the Chili Blue recipe in Chapter 3). Drain off the fat. Stir in the tomato sauce, cooked rice, salt, and pepper.
4. Preheat oven to 325°F. Place the green peppers open-side up in a 1-quart ovenproof baking pan that has been sprayed with nonstick cooking spray. Spoon ½ of the beef mixture into each pepper. Top each filled pepper with 1 slice of cheese. Use a knife or your fingers to tear off any cheese that hangs over the edge of the pepper.
5. Add ¼ cup water to the bottom of the baking pan. Bake uncovered for 1 hour, or until the peppers are tender.

MEAT LOAF

Meat loaf makes an inexpensive entrée, and you can use leftovers for cold meat loaf sandwiches the next day. Serve with baked potatoes (see the "How Do I Bake a Potato?" sidebar with the Beef and Onion Roast recipe in this chapter).

What You Need:

¾ pound ground beef

3 slices white bread

2 tablespoons dried minced onion

½ teaspoon salt

⅛ teaspoon pepper

⅛ teaspoon dry mustard

⅛ teaspoon celery salt

⅛ teaspoon garlic salt

1½ teaspoons Worcestershire sauce

½ cup milk

1 egg

½ cup bottled barbecue sauce

What You Do:

1. Preheat oven to 350°F. Use your hands to crumble the ground beef into a large mixing bowl. Tear the bread, including the crusts, into small (½"–1") pieces. Add to the beef in the bowl. Sprinkle with minced onion, salt, pepper, dry mustard, celery salt, garlic salt, and Worcestershire sauce.
2. In a small mixing bowl, beat together the milk and egg until well blended. Pour over the beef mixture.
3. With your hands, squish together all ingredients until well blended. Form into a loaf shape. (Always wash your hands with soap and water after handling raw meat, especially raw ground meat.) Place in a shallow roasting pan that has been sprayed with non-stick cooking spray. Pour the barbecue sauce over the loaf. Bake for 1 hour. To serve, cut crosswise into slices about 1" thick.

MEXICAN MEAT LOAF

What You Need:

SAUCE

2 teaspoons canned chipotle peppers

1 cup ketchup

¼ cup apricot jam

MEAT LOAF

2 pounds ground beef

¾ cup bread crumbs

1 (1-ounce) packet fajita seasoning

1 (4-ounce) can diced green chilies

2 large eggs

What You Do:

1. **For the Sauce:** Drain the chipotle peppers and chop.
2. In a small mixing bowl stir together the ketchup, apricot jam, and chopped chipotle peppers until well blended.
3. **For the Meat Loaf:** Preheat oven to 350°F. Use your hands to crumble the ground beef into a large mixing bowl.
4. Add the bread crumbs and fajita seasoning.
5. Drain the green chilies, and add to mixture.
6. Crack the eggs into a small mixing bowl. Beat with a fork until smooth. Add to the meat mixture.
7. With your hands, squish together meat mixture until well blended. Form into a loaf shape. Place into a shallow roasting pan that has been sprayed with non-stick cooking spray.
8. Top with half the sauce and bake for 1½ hours. Let cool for 10 minutes. Top with remaining sauce and serve.

Although this recipe calls for beef, traditional shepherd's pie is made with lamb. You can substitute cooked chopped lamb if you prefer. Serve with a Cold Mixed Veggies Salad (see recipe in Chapter 4) or cold sliced peaches.

SHEPHERD'S PIE

What You Need:

2½ pounds baking potatoes

4 tablespoons butter, divided

1 cup milk

Salt and pepper, to taste

1 medium white or yellow onion

2 cloves garlic (or ¼ teaspoon dried minced garlic)

1 tablespoon vegetable oil

1½ pounds ground beef

1 tablespoon all-purpose flour

½ cup beef broth

1 teaspoon dried thyme

1 teaspoon dried rosemary

⅛ teaspoon nutmeg

What You Do:

1. Boil and mash potatoes (see Mashed Potatoes recipe in Chapter 9) with 2 tablespoons of the butter, the milk, and salt and pepper. Set aside.

2. Chop the onion and mince the garlic. Pour the vegetable oil into a large frying pan over medium heat. Stir in the onion and garlic and cook about 5 to 7 minutes until onions are tender. Crumble the ground beef into the pan. Brown the meat (see the "How Do I Brown Ground Beef?" sidebar with the Chili Blue recipe in Chapter 3). Drain off the fat.

3. Stir in the flour. Continue stirring for 2 to 3 minutes to thicken. Stir in the beef broth, thyme, rosemary, and nutmeg. Season with salt and pepper, to taste. Reduce heat to low. Cook, uncovered, for 15 minutes, stirring occasionally. Remove from heat.

(continued on next page)

SHEPHERD'S PIE — CONTINUED

4. Pour the mixture into a deep-dish pie pan or oven-proof baking dish that has been sprayed with non-stick cooking spray. Spread the mashed potatoes in an even layer over the mixture, covering it completely (as though you are frosting a cake). Cut the remaining 2 tablespoons butter into small pieces and place a few inches apart on top of the mashed potatoes. Bake for 35 minutes, until the mashed potatoes are lightly browned.

How Do I Choose Ground Beef?

Types of ground beef depend on the cut of meat ground. The more expensive the cut, the higher the price (unless it's on sale). For the best value, choose ground beef or ground chuck. Ground round and ground sirloin taste great but may not be worth the extra expense. Still, lower-fat ground beef choices have greater value because less fat cooks out, leaving more meat. To kill bacteria that can cause illness, always cook ground meat until there is no tinge of pink inside. And wash your hands with soap and warm water after handling raw, ground beef.

LEVEL **H**

SERVINGS **4**

BEEF STROGANOFF

Sour cream makes this creamy dish fit for a king—or a Russian baron. Serve over fluffy cooked rice or egg noodles cooked according to package instructions. You can substitute ground beef for the round steak if you like.

What You Need:

1 pound round steak or cubed stew beef

¼ medium white or yellow onion

¼ cup butter

⅛ teaspoon dried minced garlic

2 tablespoons all-purpose flour

¼–½ teaspoon salt, to taste

¼ teaspoon pepper

1 pound fresh sliced mushrooms

1 (10.5-ounce) can condensed cream of chicken soup

1 cup sour cream

1 tablespoon dried parsley flakes

What You Do:

1. Cut the beef into 1"–2" cubes (if not already cubed). Set aside. Chop the onion. Melt the butter in a large frying pan over medium heat. Stir in the onion. Cook about 5 to 7 minutes until tender. Stir in the beef and garlic. Cook until the meat is browned, stirring often.
2. Stir in the flour, salt, and pepper until thickened. Reduce heat to low. Add the mushrooms and cream of chicken soup. Cook for 15 minutes, stirring often.
3. Stir in the sour cream. Remove from heat. Sprinkle with parsley flakes. Serve hot.

*This recipe makes 2 servings per pound

Applesauce is a traditional side dish with pork. Serve with your favorite potato dish and Waldorf Salad (see recipe in Chapter 4).

PORK ROAST

What You Need:

1 (any size) pork roast

Salt and pepper, to taste

Garlic salt, to taste (or seasoned salt)

What You Do:

1. Preheat oven to 350°F. Place the meat fat-side up in a roasting pan or ovenproof baking pan. (Always wash your hands with soap after handling raw meat.) Insert a meat thermometer into the thickest portion of the meat (optional). Sprinkle with salt, pepper, and garlic salt.
2. Roast according to the following times: loin or center cut roast, 35 to 40 minutes per pound; leg roast, 25 to 40 minutes per pound; shoulder roast, 35 to 40 minutes per pound; butt roast, 45 to 50 minutes per pound.
3. Check for doneness. The meat thermometer should read 185°F. If you don't use a meat thermometer, cut into the center of the roast and check color. Pork is done when there is no tinge of pink.

Which Cut of Pork Should I Roast?

You can roast loin end, center cut, leg, butt, and shoulder cuts of pork. However, center cut roasts have a bone running through the middle, which makes serving difficult. Boneless pork roasts are more expensive, but you'll have no waste. Roast all cuts at 350°F until a meat thermometer reads 185°F. Time varies according to cut. To kill any harmful bacteria, all cuts should be cooked until well done.

EASY PORK TENDERLOIN

Sweet and tender, pork tenderloin makes a romantic entrée for your dinner date. Serve with peas and applesauce. Do not substitute white vinegar for the cider vinegar used in this recipe.

What You Need:

2 tablespoons cider vinegar

¼ cup honey

2 tablespoons firmly packed brown sugar

1 tablespoon prepared spicy, whole-grain mustard

1 (1-pound) pork tenderloin

What You Do:

1. Preheat oven to 425°F. In a large mixing bowl, stir together the vinegar, honey, brown sugar, and mustard until well blended.
2. Place the pork in a roasting pan. (Always wash your hands with soap after handling raw meat.) Pour the honey mixture over the pork. Roast for 25 minutes or until the juices run clear and the pork has no tinge of pink. If using a meat thermometer, it should read 185°F.

Be sure to buy "fully cooked" ham for this recipe. Serve with Old-Fashioned Coleslaw (see recipe in Chapter 4) and Baked Beans (see recipe in Chapter 9). Use leftovers for Cold Ham and Lima Beans (see recipe in this chapter).

BAKED HAM

What You Need:

½ (7–10-pound) fully cooked ham

1 cup firmly packed brown sugar

2 tablespoons honey

3 tablespoons Dijon mustard

¼ teaspoon salt

2 tablespoons water

What You Do:

1. Place the ham fat-side up in a shallow roasting pan. Bake at 325°F for 2 hours.
2. Make the glaze: Stir together the brown sugar, honey, Dijon mustard, salt, and water.
3. Remove the ham from the oven. Use a large knife to remove the brown outer skin, and discard. Make ¼"-deep cuts across the fat on top of the ham in parallel lines about 1" apart. Cut again crosswise to create a checkerboard pattern. Brush the glaze all over the outside of the ham. Return to the oven. Bake for 1 more hour.
4. During the last hour of cooking, open the oven and brush the ham with the drippings in the bottom of the pan two or three times.
5. At the end of the cooking time, insert a meat thermometer into the thickest part of the meat, without touching the bone. It should read 140°F. Remove from the oven. Let the ham sit (or "rest") for 20 minutes before slicing.

SLOW-COOKED PORK CHOPS IN CHERRY SAUCE

A slow cooker makes this dish extremely easy to prepare. To serve, pour the remaining sauce into a serving bowl. Spoon the sauce over the meat.

What You Need:

1 tablespoon vegetable oil

4 pork chops

Salt and pepper, to taste

⅔ cup canned cherry pie filling

1¼ teaspoons lemon juice

¼ teaspoon instant chicken bouillon granules

$\frac{1}{16}$ teaspoon ground mace

1 teaspoon dried parsley flakes

What You Do:

1. Place the vegetable oil in a large frying pan over medium-high heat. Brown the pork chops on both sides, but don't cook through. Remove from heat. Sprinkle with salt and pepper.
2. Place the cherry pie filling in a slow cooker. Stir in the lemon juice, bouillon granules, and mace until well mixed. Place the browned pork chops on top of the sauce. Cover and cook on low for 4 to 5 hours. To serve, place the pork chops on a serving plate. Spoon the sauce over top. Sprinkle with parsley.

LEVEL **E**

SERVINGS **2**

Here's a dinner entrée version of a football concession stand favorite. Start cooking early and turn on the game! Serve with cold, raw veggies.

SLOW-COOKED POLISH SAUSAGE AND KRAUT

What You Need:

1 pound Polish sausage

1 (14-ounce) can sauerkraut, with liquid

¼ teaspoon caraway seed

1½ tablespoons granulated sugar

1 tablespoon dried minced onion (or ¼ cup chopped fresh onion)

2 cups water

What You Do:

1. Slice each sausage into 4 pieces of equal length. Place in a slow cooker or a large saucepan.
2. In a medium mixing bowl, stir together the sauerkraut, caraway seed, sugar, and onion. Place on top of the sausage. Add the water and cover.
3. In a slow cooker, cook on low for 3 to 4 hours. On the stovetop, cook over low heat for 1 hour.

HAM FETTUCCINE CASSEROLE

Romano cheese and garlic add Italian flavor to this plentiful pasta dish. You can use cooked ham steak, turkey ham, deli-style ham, or leftover ham in this recipe.

What You Need:

1 (12-ounce) package uncooked fettuccine

½ pound cooked ham

3 tablespoons butter or margarine

2 tablespoons olive oil

¼ teaspoon dried minced garlic

1½ cups frozen broccoli florets

1 (14-ounce) can diced tomatoes, with juice

Salt, to taste

¼ teaspoon black pepper

¼ cup grated Romano cheese

What You Do:

1. Cook the fettuccine according to package instructions.
2. While the noodles are cooking, slice the ham into 2"–3"-long flat strips about the width of cooked fettuccine noodles.
3. Place the butter (or margarine) and olive oil in a large frying pan and heat over medium-high heat until the butter melts. Add the ham, garlic, and broccoli; sauté, stirring constantly, for about 5 minutes. Stir in the tomatoes and juice. Season with salt and pepper. Cook until the broccoli is tender but still firm.
4. Drain noodles when done. Add to the frying pan. Gently stir until all the ingredients are well mixed and heated through. Sprinkle with cheese.

HAM AND ASPARAGUS ROLL-UPS

This makes a nice light supper. Serve with bread and a fruit salad.

What You Need:

2 (15-ounce) cans whole asparagus spears

8 slices packaged deli-style ham

1 (10.75-ounce) can condensed Cheddar cheese soup

4 tablespoons milk

2 teaspoons prepared mustard

¼ teaspoon paprika

What You Do:

1. Preheat oven to 350°F. Drain the asparagus. Divide the asparagus spears evenly among the ham slices. Place 3 or 4 spears near one edge on top of each slice of ham. Roll the ham over the asparagus. Place ham rolls seam-side down in an ovenproof baking pan that has been sprayed with nonstick cooking spray.
2. In a medium mixing bowl, stir together the soup, milk, and mustard. Pour the mixture over the ham. Sprinkle with paprika. Bake uncovered for 30 minutes, until heated through.

What Can You Tell Me about Asparagus?

First known in the Mediterranean area more than 2,000 years ago, asparagus was enjoyed by ancient Greeks, who gathered wild asparagus, and Romans, who cultivated it. In the 1600s in France, royal gardeners grew it in greenhouses so King Louis XIV could eat it year-round. About the same time, asparagus made its way to the New World from England and Northern Europe.

HAM SLICE WITH PINEAPPLE

If you have leftover cooked ham, you can use it in this recipe by reducing the cooking time to 30 minutes. You can also substitute 2 peeled and sliced tart apples (McIntosh, Granny Smith, or Jonathan varieties) and ¼ cup water or apple juice for the pineapple and juice in this recipe.

What You Need:

1 (1-pound) uncooked ham slice

4 whole cloves

½ cup canned crushed pineapple, with juice

3 tablespoons firmly packed brown sugar

What You Do:

1. Place the ham in an ovenproof baking dish that has been sprayed with nonstick cooking spray. Stick the cloves into the ham several inches apart.
2. Spoon the pineapple and juice over the ham. Sprinkle with brown sugar.
3. Cover with aluminum foil (or a baking dish lid). Bake at 325°F for 1 hour and 15 minutes. Uncover and bake for 15 minutes more.

PORK CHOPS WITH RICE

To serve, carefully remove the chops from the pan, maintaining the layered ingredients for a nice visual effect. Top each pork chop with a sprig of parsley.

What You Need:

4 pork chops

Salt and pepper, to taste

1 tablespoon vegetable oil

4 thin (about ⅛"-thick) slices white or yellow onion

4 thin (about ⅛"-thick) slices green bell pepper

¼ cup uncooked rice

1 (28-ounce) can whole peeled tomatoes

What You Do:

1. Sprinkle the pork chops with salt and pepper. In a large frying pan, brown the pork chops on both sides in the vegetable oil over medium-high heat. Spray a 9" × 13" ovenproof baking pan or a roasting pan (large enough for all the pork chops to lie flat) with nonstick cooking spray. Place the pork chops in the bottom of the pan.
2. Place 1 slice of onion and 1 slice of green pepper on top of each pork chop. Spoon 1 tablespoon uncooked rice inside of each pepper ring, and place 1 whole tomato on top of the rice. Pour the juice from the tomatoes, along with any leftover tomatoes, around the sides of the pork chops.
3. Cover with baking pan lid or aluminum foil. Bake at 350°F for 1½ hours, until the meat is tender and has no tinge of pink.

SLOW-COOKED PORK IN MUSHROOM SAUCE

Cook this dish in a slow cooker. Serve with rice or Mashed Potatoes (see recipe in Chapter 9) and a steamed green vegetable (see Appendix C). To serve, remove the pork chops from the cooker. Stir the remaining liquid and use as gravy.

What You Need:

4 pork chops or 2 pounds pork shoulder

1 medium white or yellow onion

½ cup canned sliced mushrooms (or stems and pieces), drained

1 can cream of mushroom soup

½ cup milk

Salt and pepper, to taste

What You Do:

1. Place the pork chops in a slow cooker. Slice the onion. Separate the rings. Add to the pot.
2. In a small mixing bowl, stir together the mushrooms, soup, and milk. Pour over the onions. Season with salt and pepper. Cover and cook for 4 to 5 hours on high or for 1 hour on high plus 6 to 8 hours on low.

ROASTED ITALIAN SAUSAGE

This one-pot dinner in a dish is easy and tasty. Serve with spicy mustard and breadsticks. For best results choose a crisp red apple that's good for cooking, such as Braeburn, Cortland, Empire, Fuji, Gala, Rome, or Winesap varieties. Or, substitute fresh Bartlett pears for the apples.

What You Need:

2 small apples

2 leeks

½ pound yellow potatoes

9 sprigs fresh thyme

2 tablespoons olive oil

¼ teaspoon salt

¼ teaspoon pepper

1½ pounds your choice of mild, medium, or hot Italian sausage links

What You Do:

1. Preheat the oven to 475°F. Wash the apples. Leaving on the peel, cut into quarters or slice using an apple corer (see "How Do I Use an Apple Corer?" sidebar with the Apple Oatmeal recipe in Chapter 1). Remove the seeds and core. Place in a large roasting pan that has been sprayed with nonstick cooking spray.
2. Cut away the dark green parts of the leeks. Rinse under cold water. Cut the white and light green parts in half both lengthwise and horizontally. Add to the roasting pan.
3. Rinse the potatoes. Leave on the skin, and cut into wedges about ½" thick. Add to the roasting pan.
4. Add the whole thyme leaves, oil, salt, and pepper. Toss until the apples, potatoes, and leeks are well mixed and lightly coated. Roast uncovered for 15 minutes. Remove the thyme leaves after cooking.
5. Remove the pan from the oven and stir. Cut the sausages into 8 equal lengths. Arrange among the vegetables in the pan. Place in the oven for 15 to 20 more minutes until the potatoes and apples are tender and the sausage juices run clear.

OVEN-BAKED PORK RIBS

The meat from this recipe is so tender it falls off the bone. So you'll need forks for serving. If you choose spareribs, ask for St. Louis style. Or, ask the butcher to remove the membrane and flap of tough meat on top of the rack. You can omit step 3 if you prefer ribs without a smoky flavor. Wash hands with soap after handling the raw meat.

What You Need:

1 rack baby back ribs or spareribs
1 teaspoon garlic salt
1 teaspoon ground cumin
½ teaspoon freshly ground black pepper
1 teaspoon paprika
1 teaspoon chili powder
1 teaspoon dried oregano
¼ cup firmly packed brown sugar
1 teaspoon liquid smoke
1 tablespoon water
1–2 cups bottled barbecue sauce, as needed for cooking and serving

What You Do:

1. Set out the ribs to warm to room temperature. Line an ovenproof baking pan with aluminum foil. If needed, remove the membrane and flap of tough meat from the top of the spareribs.
2. Place the garlic salt, cumin, pepper, paprika, chili powder, oregano, and brown sugar in a small mixing bowl. Stir until well blended.
3. When the chill is gone from the meat, mix the liquid smoke and water in a separate small dish. Use a barbecue brush to coat both sides of the meat.
4. Place the ribs in the baking pan, bottom-side up. With your fingers, rub half of the spice mixture into the meat. Turn over the meat and rub in the remaining mixture on top. Cook uncovered for 2 hours in a 250°F oven. Remove from the oven.
5. Brush barbecue sauce on top of the ribs to coat evenly. Seal the baking pan with more aluminum foil. Bake covered for 2 hours more until the meat starts to separate from the bone. Serve with remaining bottled barbecue sauce.

LEVEL **M**

SERVINGS **4**

Curry powder wakes up the lima beans in this tasty, cold casserole you can make with leftovers. Add tomato slices on the side.

COLD HAM AND LIMA BEANS

What You Need:

4 hard-boiled eggs (see Boiled Egg recipe in Chapter 1)

2 cups cubed cooked ham (½" cubes)

1 cup chopped celery

2 cups cooked lima beans (drained)

1 tablespoon minced onion

½ cup mayonnaise

½ teaspoon curry powder

Salt and pepper, to taste

What You Do:

1. Peel and chop the hard-boiled eggs and place in a medium mixing bowl.
2. Add the ham and celery to the bowl.
3. Stir in the lima beans, onion, mayonnaise, curry powder, salt, and pepper until well mixed.
4. Refrigerate at least 1 hour before serving.

Here's an entrée with a touch of the exotic. You can substitute chicken or beef for the pork. For fun, purchase prebaked fortune cookies. Use clean tweezers to remove fortunes and insert ones you write yourself.

ASIAN FRIED RICE

What You Need:

1½ cups uncooked rice

½ pound raw pork loin

1 large white or yellow onion

¼ cup vegetable oil

⅜ teaspoon dried minced garlic

1 tablespoon soy sauce

1 teaspoon salt

½ teaspoon pepper

1 teaspoon granulated sugar

1 cup frozen or leftover vegetables (your choice)

2 eggs

What You Do:

1. Cook rice according to package directions. Set aside.
2. Cut the pork into 1" cubes. Chop the onion.
3. Heat the oil in a large frying pan over medium heat. Add the meat, onion, minced garlic, soy sauce, salt, pepper, and sugar. Cook, stirring frequently, until the meat is done.
4. Reduce heat to low. Stir in the rice and vegetables. Heat until warm. Just before serving, beat eggs in a small mixing bowl. Stir into the mixture until the eggs are cooked.

This unusual dinner-in-a-dish with blended flavors goes well with simple sides like a tossed green salad or steamed green beans. You can use either dark brown or light brown sugar in this recipe.

HAWAIIAN PORK CHOPS WITH SWEET POTATOES

What You Need:

1 pound sweet potatoes

½ teaspoon salt

6 slices bacon

12 slices canned pineapple, divided

6 pork chops

6 tablespoons loosely packed brown sugar, divided

What You Do:

1. Rinse sweet potatoes under cold, running water. Place whole in a Dutch oven. Add the salt. Cover with water. Boil over high heat for 10 minutes.
2. Cut the bacon slices in half horizontally. Set aside.
3. Arrange 6 slices of pineapple in the bottom of a 9" × 13" × 2" ovenproof baking pan that has been sprayed with nonstick cooking spray. Place 1 pork chop on top of each pineapple slice. Top each pork chop with another pineapple slice.
4. Drain the sweet potatoes. Cool until comfortable to touch. Slice potatoes crosswise into circles about ¼" thick. Place one slice on top of each pineapple-pork chop-pineapple stack.
5. Sprinkle each stack with 1 tablespoon brown sugar.
6. Make an "X" on top of each stack with 2 bacon strip halves.
7. Bake at 375°F for 1 hour or until pork shows no sign of pink and juices run clear.

APPLE-GLAZED PORK CHOPS

Turn plain pork chops into a special meal with the traditional accompanying flavor of apple. The recommended apple varieties are especially good for baking, but you can substitute others.

What You Need:

1 tablespoon vegetable oil
2 tablespoons butter, divided
6 pork chops (about 6 ounces each)
Salt and pepper, to taste
2 Rome, Gala, or Granny Smith apples
1½ teaspoons minced garlic
¼ cup apple cider vinegar
1 teaspoon Dijon mustard
1 teaspoon minced fresh rosemary
⅛ teaspoon red pepper flakes

What You Do:

1. Place the vegetable oil and 1 tablespoon of the butter in a large frying pan over medium-high heat. Season the pork chops with salt and pepper. Add the pork chops to the pan and brown on both sides for 5 to 7 minutes per side (the meat should still have a touch of pink in the middle). Remove from the heat. Place pork chops onto a plate and set aside. Leave the juices in the pan.

2. Peel, core, and slice the apples. Place the pan back on medium-high heat. Add the apple slices. Cook 4 to 5 minutes, occasionally gently stirring, until just tender but not soft. Remove the apple slices, leaving the juices in the pan. Set aside.

3. Stir in the garlic and vinegar. Scrape up any browned bits from the bottom of the pan. Stir in the apple cider vinegar and Dijon mustard. Bring to a boil, stirring often, for 3 to 4 minutes until the sauce thickens. Stir in the rosemary and red pepper flakes. Sprinkle with salt and pepper to taste.

4. Return the pork chops to the pan for 1 minute. Use a spatula to flip to the other side. Top with the apple slices. Spoon the sauce over all. Cook for one more minute or until warmed through.

CHAPTER 6

Main Dishes for Carnivores—Poultry

Whole fryer chickens often cost less than packaged chicken parts. Cut leftovers into bite-sized pieces and refrigerate or freeze for later use in salads or casseroles.

ROAST CHICKEN

What You Need:

Salt, as needed (about ½ teaspoon)

1 whole fryer chicken

Vegetable oil or solid vegetable shortening, as needed (about 1 teaspoon)

What You Do:

1. Use your fingers to rub salt on the inside of the neck and body cavities. Place in roasting pan or ovenproof baking pan, breast-side up. Fold the wings back and under the chicken for support.

2. With your fingers, a paper towel, or a cooking brush, spread vegetable oil over the entire chicken. Insert a meat thermometer, if desired. (To prevent illness, always wash hands with soap and water after handling raw chicken. Also wash any utensils and surfaces that came in contact with raw chicken.) Roast the chicken in the oven at 375°F. For a 4-pound chicken, roast for about 1½ hours. Reduce or increase cooking time according to weight.

3. Test for doneness. When done, the juices should run clear and the drumstick should easily move in the joint. Protect your fingers with a paper towel or cloth and gently squeeze the large end of the drumstick. The meat should feel very soft. If using a meat thermometer, it should read 190°F.

LEVEL **E**

SERVINGS **4-6**

This fried chicken is cooked in only a small amount of oil for a healthier meal. Coat the chicken with the flour mixture just before frying so the coating doesn't gum up.

PAN-FRIED CHICKEN

What You Need:

½ cup all-purpose flour

1 teaspoon salt

½ teaspoon pepper

6–8 pieces cut-up chicken with skin attached

3 tablespoons vegetable oil

What You Do:

1. In a small mixing bowl, stir together the flour, salt, and pepper. Coat each piece of the chicken with the flour mixture, one piece at a time. Shake off any extra, and place pieces on a large plate.
2. Heat a large frying pan over medium-high heat. When hot, add the vegetable oil. Tilt the pan to lightly coat the bottom. Place the chicken in the frying pan in a single layer. Cook for 4 to 5 minutes on one side until golden brown. Turn and cook until the other side is golden brown. Reduce heat to medium.
3. Cook uncovered for another 10 minutes. Turn the chicken again, and cook for 10 minutes more until the juices run clear.

CRANBERRY CHICKEN

Here's your chance to use that potato masher in your kitchen drawer. If you don't have a potato masher, use a fork.

What You Need:

1 prepackaged cut-up fryer chicken

1 (8-ounce) can whole-berry cranberry sauce

1 (1.25-ounce) packet dry onion soup mix

What You Do:

1. Place the chicken in a roasting pan or a 9" × 13" oven-proof baking pan that has been sprayed with non-stick cooking spray. (Always wash hands with soap after handling raw chicken.)
2. In a small mixing bowl, mash the cranberry sauce. Stir in the onion soup mix until well blended. Spoon over the chicken pieces. Cover with aluminum foil and bake at 350°F for 2 hours.

When Do I Need to Preheat the Oven?

For cooking times less than 1 hour, preheat the oven to ensure even heating. Turn the oven dial to "preheat," and turn the temperature selector to the desired temperature. Electric ovens use both the top coil (the one used for broiling) and the bottom coil when set to preheat. Be sure to change the dial to "bake" before placing food in the oven. If you forget, the top of the food will heat too much. Some foods will be crusty, dry, or burned on top.

*This recipe makes 2
servings per pound*

Don't worry about
stuffing the turkey
before roasting.
Instead, use stuffing
mix, cooked on a
stovetop according
to package
directions. Serve
with Mashed
Potatoes (see recipe
in Chapter 9), jarred
gravy, and canned
cranberry sauce.
Use leftover turkey
as a substitute for
cooked chicken in
casserole recipes.

ROAST TURKEY

What You Need:

1 turkey (any size)

1 tablespoon vegetable oil

1 teaspoon salt

What You Do:

1. If you buy a frozen turkey, thaw it in the refrigerator
   for 24 to 48 hours before cooking. (Thawing at room
   temperature encourages growth of harmful bacteria.)
   Remove the neck and package of turkey innards from
   both cavities. (You can discard these pieces or place
   them in a saucepan and simmer until tender and
   cooked through. Some people like to chop them and
   add them to stuffing mix or gravy. Others feed them
   to their cat or dog.)
2. Place breast-side up in a large roasting pan (you can
   buy a disposable foil pan if you don't have a pan big
   enough). If you have a meat thermometer, insert it into
   the center of a thigh or breast. Be sure it doesn't touch
   bone, or it will register an inaccurate temperature.
3. Use your hands to spread vegetable oil all over the
   outside of the turkey. Sprinkle salt on your hand and
   rub it inside the neck and body cavities. Bend the
   wings up and under the turkey for support.
4. Roast the turkey at 325°F, checking it after 2 hours
   or so and every 30 minutes after that. Approximate
   turkey roasting times vary according to weight. Here
   are roasting times at 325°F.

Weight	Roasting Time
8–12 pounds	4–4½ hours
12–16 pounds	4½–5½ hours
16–20 pounds	5½–7 hours
20–24 pounds	7–8½ hours

(continued on next page)

ROAST TURKEY — CONTINUED

5. When the turkey is as brown as you like, make a tent with aluminum foil and place it loosely on top of the turkey so it won't brown further. The turkey is done when the meat thermometer reads 190°F, or when the drumstick easily twists out of the joint. If you buy a turkey with a built-in timer, roast until the timer pops up. Let the cooked turkey sit about 20 minutes before carving.

LEVEL **E**

SERVINGS **2**

¡Olé! Here's an easy, spicy chicken dish. Parmesan cheese adds extra zing, even though it's usually used in Italian-style dishes.

SALSA CHICKEN

What You Need:

2 boneless, skinless chicken breasts

1 cup salsa

¼ cup grated Parmesan cheese

What You Do:

1. Preheat oven to 350°F. Spray a 2-quart ovenproof baking pan with nonstick cooking spray. Cut the chicken breasts in half lengthwise. Place side by side in the baking pan.
2. Pour the salsa over the chicken. Top with Parmesan cheese.
3. Cover and bake for 30 minutes. Uncover and bake for another 10 minutes.

BAKED LEMON CHICKEN

In this easy and delicious dish, citrus brings out the flavor of the chicken. Serve with warm rice, if you like.

What You Need:

4 boneless, skinless chicken breast halves

½ cup butter or margarine

¼ cup plus 2 tablespoons lemon juice

1 teaspoon garlic powder

1 teaspoon poultry seasoning

½ teaspoon salt

½ teaspoon pepper

What You Do:

1. Place chicken in an ovenproof baking pan that has been lightly greased with solid shortening or sprayed with nonstick cooking spray.
2. Preheat oven to 350°F. Melt the butter (or margarine) in a small saucepan or frying pan. Pour into a medium, heatproof mixing bowl. Stir in the lemon juice, garlic powder, poultry seasoning, salt, and pepper until well blended. Pour over the chicken. Cover the pan with aluminum foil or a baking pan lid. Bake for 1 hour. While the chicken is cooking, frequently spoon sauce from the bottom of the pan over the chicken.

How Do I Prevent Salmonella Poisoning?

To avoid salmonella poisoning, always wash your hands with soap and warm water after handling raw chicken and turkey. Also wash all dishes, utensils, and surfaces that touched the raw poultry. Take along sanitary hand wipes to picnics or tailgate parties. Use before and after touching the chicken.

CHICKEN BREASTS AND BROCCOLI

This makes an elegant entrée when prepared with whole chicken breasts and whole broccoli spears. You can also make it as a casserole with frozen chopped broccoli and cooked chicken or turkey cut into bite-sized pieces. Serve with chilled canned whole spiced peaches placed on a piece of leaf lettuce.

What You Need:

1 (16-ounce) package frozen broccoli spears

4 boneless, skinless chicken breasts

2 (10.5-ounce) cans condensed cream of chicken soup

½ teaspoon curry powder

¼ teaspoon paprika

What You Do:

1. Spray a 10" × 13" ovenproof baking pan with nonstick cooking spray. Boil the broccoli for 5 minutes only. Drain.
2. Line the bottom of the prepared pan with the broccoli spears, alternating floret-side up and stem-side up, so the broccoli fits closely together. Arrange the chicken breasts on top of the broccoli.
3. Preheat oven to 350°F. In a small mixing bowl, stir together undiluted soup and curry powder. Pour over the chicken and broccoli. Lightly sprinkle with paprika. Bake uncovered for 40 to 45 minutes. Or, microwave on high for about 6 to 8 minutes until the chicken is tender and the juices run clear.

How Should I Thaw Frozen Meat and Poultry?

Thaw frozen meat and poultry in the refrigerator to avoid bacteria growth. You can also thaw meat in the microwave on the "defrost" setting. Underestimate defrosting time so the meat doesn't start to cook. You can always zap it again if not completely thawed. Once you have defrosted meat, never refreeze it.

CHICKEN AND STUFFING CASSEROLE

This meal-in-a-dish provides meat, bread, and dairy products. All you need is a vegetable or chilled canned fruit to complete the meal.

What You Need:

4 boneless, skinless chicken breast halves

4 slices Swiss cheese

1⅓ cups herb-seasoned stuffing mix

1 (10.5-ounce) can cream of chicken soup

10.5 ounces water (use the soup can to measure)

What You Do:

1. Preheat oven to 350°F. Place chicken in an ovenproof baking pan that has been sprayed with nonstick cooking spray. (Always wash your hands with soap after handling raw chicken.)
2. Place a slice of cheese on each piece of chicken. Sprinkle the dry stuffing mix on top of the cheese.
3. In a small mixing bowl, stir together the soup and water until well blended. Pour over the stuffing mix. Bake uncovered for 45 to 50 minutes.

How Can I Save Money When I Buy Chicken?

Purchase packaged chicken according to your preferred pieces. Or, purchase a whole fryer and cut it yourself at a lower price per pound. Use kitchen scissors and cut pieces apart at the joints. Cut into 2 wings, 2 breasts, 2 thighs, and 2 drumsticks, or leave wings attached to breasts and legs attached to thighs, depending on your preferences and cooking method. Wash hands, surfaces, and scissors with soap and warm water after handling raw chicken.

CHICKEN AND RICE CASSEROLE

Serve with chilled canned spiced peaches and frozen peas cooked according to package directions. If you have leftover mushrooms from another recipe, toss them in before heating.

What You Need:

2 cups uncooked rice

1 stalk celery

2 cups cooked chicken (see the "How Should I Save Cooked Chicken for Other Recipes?" sidebar with this recipe)

1 (10.5-ounce) can cream of mushroom soup

½ soup can milk

What You Do:

1. Cook the rice according to package directions. While the rice is cooking, chop the celery and cut the cooked chicken into bite-sized pieces.
2. Preheat oven to 350°F. Place the rice, chicken, and celery in a 2-quart ovenproof or microwave-safe baking pan. Stir in the mushroom soup and milk. Cover and bake for 30 minutes, or cover and microwave on high for 5 minutes, or until heated through.

How Should I Save Cooked Chicken for Other Recipes?

To cook chicken to use later in casseroles or salads, place in an ovenproof baking pan that has been sprayed with nonstick cooking spray. Sprinkle with salt and pepper. Put a pat of butter or margarine on each piece of chicken. (Always wash your hands with soap after handling raw chicken.) Cover with baking pan lid or aluminum foil. Bake at 350°F for 1 hour or until the chicken is tender and the juices run clear. Remove from the oven and let cool. Remove skin. Cut away the meat from the bones into bite-sized pieces. Separate into 1- or 2-cup servings. Cover and refrigerate or freeze until needed. About 3 pounds of chicken breasts or thighs yields 4 to 5 cups.

MARINATED GRILLED CHICKEN

You can marinate the raw chicken while you're waiting for the charcoal fire. Or, you can marinate as long as overnight before cooking. You can use the leftover marinade during cooking, but to kill bacteria associated with raw chicken, first boil the marinade when you remove the chicken.

What You Need:

¼ cup bottled Italian salad dressing

¼ cup olive oil

2 teaspoons lemon juice

4 boneless, skinless chicken breasts

What You Do:

1. In a small mixing bowl, stir together the salad dressing, olive oil, and lemon juice. Pour into a shallow baking pan large enough to hold the chicken.
2. Place chicken in the marinade. Cover and refrigerate for at least 30 minutes (turn once after about 15 minutes). Remove chicken from marinade and place on a plate until ready to grill.
3. Bring the remaining marinade to a boil in a small saucepan over medium-high heat to kill bacteria from the raw chicken. Wash hands with soap and water.
4. Cook the chicken on a gas or charcoal grill over a medium-high fire (375–450°F) for about 2 to 3 minutes per side, brushing with the boiled marinade as it cooks until the chicken juices run clear.

What Is Meat Marinade?

Marinating is soaking meat, fish, poultry, or vegetables in a marinade, a mixture of vinegar or lemon juice, oil, herbs, and other ingredients. A marinade adds flavor before cooking, but contrary to widely held belief, it does nothing to tenderize meat. Be sure to marinate foods in the refrigerator to keep bacteria from forming. Also, if you marinate raw chicken or fish, bring the marinade to a boil before you reuse or serve it. You can marinate either by letting food sit in the marinade mixture for ½ the allotted time, then turning to the other side, or by pouring the marinade over the food to coat it, then letting it sit. Marinate foods—except for all kinds of fish—for anywhere from 30 minutes to all day, or even overnight. Limit marinating fish, including shellfish, to 1 hour, because acid (such as that in lemon juice) begins to "cook" the fish after that time.

GORGONZOLA AND SAGE-STUFFED CHICKEN BREASTS

Gorgonzola is a type of blue cheese. If you don't like the taste of blue cheese, you can substitute provolone cheese for the Gorgonzola. Be sure to wash your hands, the knife, and the dinner plate with soap and warm water after contact with raw chicken.

What You Need:

4 boneless, skinless chicken breasts

4 ounces Gorgonzola cheese

⅓ cup sun-dried tomatoes packed in oil, drained (reserve 2 tablespoons of tomato oil)

12 fresh sage leaves

What You Do:

1. Cut a slit about ¾ of the way through each chicken breast to form a pocket similar to a taco shell. Place on a dinner plate.
2. Slice the cheese into 4 equal slices.
3. Place ¼ of the tomatoes, 1 slice of the cheese, and 3 sage leaves into each slit in the chicken.
4. Heat the tomato oil in a large frying pan over medium heat. When the oil is hot, add the chicken to the pan and cook for about 10 minutes. Use a spatula to flip the chicken to the other side, and cook another 10 minutes until the chicken juices run clear.

Traditional Cajun spices perk up ordinary chicken and transport you to the French Quarter in New Orleans. Serve for Mardi Gras, or anytime.

BAYOU CHICKEN

What You Need:

2 teaspoons paprika

2 teaspoons cayenne pepper or chili powder

1 teaspoon onion powder

¾ teaspoon garlic powder

¼ teaspoon ground cumin

Salt and pepper, to taste

½ cup milk

3 tablespoons butter

3 boneless, skinless chicken breasts

What You Do:

1. In a medium mixing bowl, stir together the paprika, cayenne pepper (or chili powder), onion powder, garlic powder, cumin, salt, and pepper.
2. Pour the milk into a small mixing bowl.
3. Melt the butter in a large frying pan over medium heat. Dip the chicken into the milk to coat. Place in the melted butter. Sprinkle the chicken with ½ of the spice mixture.
4. Cover and cook for 10 minutes. Uncover and sprinkle with the remaining spice mixture. Cook uncovered for 20 to 25 minutes more, until the juices run clear.

SIX-LAYER CASSEROLE

This tasty casserole is just as good made with ground beef if you prefer. If using beef, cook until the meat is browned but still has a touch of pink on the inside of the pieces. Serve with something green: steamed broccoli, asparagus, or a spinach salad.

What You Need:

1½ pounds ground turkey

2 medium potatoes

Salt and pepper, to taste

2 medium onions

½ cups uncooked rice

2 stalks celery

3 medium carrots

2 cups chicken broth

What You Do:

1. Brown the ground turkey in a large frying pan until turkey is cooked through. Drain excess fat. Set aside.
2. Preheat the oven to 350°F. Rinse the potatoes. Peel and slice them and arrange them in the bottom of an ovenproof baking pan that has been sprayed with nonstick cooking oil. Lightly sprinkle with salt and pepper.
3. Peel and slice the onions. Layer the onions on top of the potatoes. Lightly sprinkle with salt and pepper.
4. Spoon the turkey on top of the onions. Sprinkle the uncooked rice over the turkey. Lightly sprinkle with salt and pepper.
5. Rinse the celery and carrots under cold, running water. Peel and slice crosswise. Spread on top of the rice. Lightly sprinkle with salt and pepper.
6. Pour the broth over the entire casserole. Cover and bake for 40 to 45 minutes or until rice is cooked and the potatoes and onions are tender. Remove from oven, and let stand 10 minutes before serving.

SLOW-COOKED SPINACH CHICKEN LASAGNA

Easy, creamy, and yummy, this makes a good potluck dish or an entrée for company.

What You Need:

1 (10-ounce) package frozen chopped spinach

2 (10.75-ounce) cans cream of chicken soup

1 (9-ounce) package diced cooked chicken (or 3 breasts, cut up)

1 cup 1% or skim milk

1 (8-ounce) carton sour cream

½ cup grated Parmesan cheese

⅓ cup chopped onion

½ teaspoon salt

¼ teaspoon pepper

⅛ teaspoon nutmeg

9 uncooked lasagna noodles

1 cup shredded mozzarella cheese

What You Do:

1. Line a colander with a paper towel. Place the frozen spinach on the paper towel to thaw. When thawed, place another paper towel on top and press excess liquid out of the spinach. Place the spinach in a large mixing bowl.
2. Add the cream of chicken soup, cooked chicken, milk, sour cream, Parmesan, onion, salt, pepper, and nutmeg. Stir to combine.
3. Spray slow cooker with nonstick cooking spray. Place 3 lasagna noodles in the bottom of the cooker. Spoon ⅓ of the chicken mixture on top. Sprinkle with ⅓ of the mozzarella. Repeat layers until everything is used up.
4. Cook on high for 1 hour. Reduce heat to low for 5 hours more.

CHICKEN AND HAM CASSEROLE

This is a great use of leftover chicken and ham. You can use ham steak, deli-style ham slices, or turkey ham, which is less expensive than "real" ham. Serve with chilled canned pineapple slices and Easy Dinner Rolls (see recipe in Chapter 1).

What You Need:

1 cup cooked chicken, cut into bite-sized pieces

1 cup cooked ham, cut into bite-sized pieces

1 (10.5-ounce) can condensed cream of chicken soup

½ cup milk

4 slices Swiss cheese

2 teaspoons dried parsley flakes

What You Do:

1. Preheat oven to 350°F. Spray a 2-quart ovenproof baking pan with nonstick cooking spray. Place the chicken and ham in the baking pan.
2. In a small mixing bowl, stir together soup and milk until well blended. Pour over chicken and ham. Top with Swiss cheese. Sprinkle parsley flakes over the cheese.
3. Bake for 30 minutes or until cheese melts. Or, microwave for 3 to 5 minutes on high until cheese melts.

SLOW-COOKED GARLIC CHICKEN

This dish has lots of garlic, but don't worry. As the garlic cooks, it gives the chicken a nice aroma and slightly sweet taste. Keep side dishes simple to avoid competing flavors. Wash hands and utensils with warm, soapy water after handling raw chicken.

What You Need:

3 pounds chicken pieces

1 large onion

1 teaspoon salt

1 teaspoon paprika

½ teaspoon pepper

1 teaspoon olive oil

1 medium whole bulb garlic

What You Do:

1. Peel and slice the onion and place in a slow cooker lightly coated with cooking spray.
2. Place chicken on top of the onion.
3. In a small mixing bowl, blend the salt, paprika, pepper, and olive oil. The mixture will be thick. Spread onto the chicken pieces.
4. Separate the garlic into cloves. Leave on the peel. Add to the cooker under and on top of the chicken. Cover and cook 7 hours on low or 3½ hours on high until juices run clear.

CHICKEN AND BOW-TIE PASTA

All dressed up in formalwear, this casserole is good enough for company. For an everyday dinner, you can substitute shells or macaroni for the bow-tie pasta.

What You Need:

1 pound boneless, skinless chicken

1 tablespoon vegetable oil

1 onion

1½ cups fresh sliced mushrooms

1 (19-ounce) can stewed tomatoes, with liquid

1 cup water

1 teaspoon dried basil

2 cups uncooked bow-tie pasta

Salt and pepper, to taste

What You Do:

1. Cut the chicken into ½" cubes. Heat the oil in a large frying pan over medium-high heat. Add the chicken and cook, stirring constantly until juices run clear (about 5 to 7 minutes). Use a slotted spoon to transfer the chicken to a plate or bowl. Set aside.
2. Chop the onion. Add to the hot oil in the pan. Stir in the mushrooms. Reduce the heat to medium. Cook the vegetables, gently stirring, for about 4 to 5 minutes until tender.
3. Add the tomatoes, water, basil, and bow-tie pasta, and mix well. Cover. Reduce heat to low. Cook 8 to 10 minutes, stirring occasionally, until pasta is done.
4. Add the chicken. Sprinkle with salt and pepper. Stir ingredients to mix well. Cook uncovered another 5 minutes or until ingredients are heated through. While the chicken is cooking, wash hands and any utensils that touched raw chicken with warm, soapy water.

This classic Italian dish is quick, easy, and nutritious. Serve over buttered linguine or white rice cooked according to package instructions.

CHICKEN CACCIATORE

What You Need:

1 tablespoon olive oil

8 pieces boneless, skinless chicken (total 4–5 pounds)

1 large red onion

½ red bell pepper

½ yellow bell pepper

½ orange bell pepper

1 cup tomato sauce

1 (28-ounce) can diced or crushed tomatoes (with juice)

1 chicken bouillon cube

Salt and pepper, to taste

1 cup sliced white mushrooms

1 teaspoon dried oregano

¼ cup chopped fresh basil

What You Do:

1. On the stovetop, place a Dutch oven over high heat. When hot, pour in the olive oil. Add the chicken and cook for 5 minutes until golden brown. Use a spatula to flip over. Cook another 5 minutes until golden brown on the other side. Remove from heat. Take the chicken out of the pot, but leave the juices. Set aside.

2. Preheat oven to 375°F. Peel and slice the onion into pieces about ½" thick. Remove the stems and seeds from the red, yellow, and orange peppers. Slice into ½"-wide strips. Add the onion and peppers to the pot over high heat, stirring constantly for 5 minutes.

3. Stir in the tomato sauce, tomatoes with juice, and chicken bouillon cube. Sprinkle with salt and pepper. Reduce heat to low. Continue stirring. Add the mushrooms and oregano.

4. Use tongs to place the cooked chicken into the Dutch oven. Spoon the sauce over the chicken until well coated. Place the Dutch oven in the oven. Cook uncovered for 1¾ hours. Remove from the oven. Stir in the basil.

BAKED CHICKEN-POTATO CASSEROLE

This recipe is a new one-dish version of meat and potatoes using chicken instead of beef. Wash your hands and all utensils after contact with raw chicken.

What You Need:

2 pounds boneless, skinless chicken thighs
2 pounds red potatoes
1 yellow onion
1 red bell pepper
2 tablespoons olive oil
2 teaspoons minced garlic
2 teaspoons paprika
1 teaspoon salt
1 teaspoon pepper
1 whole lemon
½ cup fresh parsley leaves

What You Do:

1. Preheat the oven to 450°F. Generously coat a 9" × 13" ovenproof baking pan with nonstick cooking spray. Use kitchen scissors or a knife to cut the raw chicken into 1" cubes.
2. Rinse the red potatoes and cut into fourths (leave on the skin).
3. Peel the onion and cut into 8 wedges.
4. Remove the core and seeds from the red pepper, and slice into long slices.
5. Place the chicken, potatoes, onion, and red pepper in a large mixing bowl. Sprinkle with the olive oil, garlic, paprika, salt, and pepper. Use your hands to mix well. Place the mixture into the baking pan.
6. Rinse the lemon and cut into six wedges. Squeeze the juice from each wedge over the casserole, making sure to keep any seeds from falling into the pan. Scatter the juiced lemon wedges in the pan. Bake for 20 minutes. Remove from oven, and stir the mixture. Return to the oven and bake another 20 minutes.
7. Chop the parsley leaves. Discard the stems. When the casserole is done, remove from oven and sprinkle with the chopped parsley.

CHAPTER 7

Main Dishes for Carnivores—Seafood

TUNA NOODLE CASSEROLE

Quick, cheap, easy—and good. What more can you ask for? Serve with cooked frozen peas and Fruit and Coconut Salad (see recipe in Chapter 4).

What You Need:

2 eggs

1 stalk celery

2 cups uncooked egg noodles

1 (6-ounce) can tuna

1 (10.5-ounce) can condensed cream of mushroom soup

½ soup can milk

4 slices American or Cheddar cheese

What You Do:

1. Hard-boil the eggs (see Boiled Egg recipe in Chapter 1). Let cool. Peel and chop. Rinse the celery under cold, running water. Chop. Set aside.
2. Cook the noodles according to package directions. Drain. Place in a 2-quart ovenproof or microwave-safe baking pan that has been sprayed with nonstick cooking spray. Preheat oven to 350°F. Drain the tuna. Flake with a fork and add to the noodles. Gently stir in the mushroom soup and milk until well blended. Stir in the celery and eggs. Top with the cheese. Cover and bake for 30 minutes. Or, cover and microwave on high for 5 minutes.

BREADED OVEN-BAKED FISH

Fish is easier to cook than people think. You can use your favorite fish in this recipe, but sole, catfish, and halibut work well.

What You Need:

2 cups milk

1 tablespoon plus 1 teaspoon salt, divided

1½ pounds fish fillets

1 cup bread crumbs or cornmeal

½ cup butter

1 tablespoon lemon juice

What You Do:

1. In a large mixing bowl, stir together the milk and 1 tablespoon salt. Soak the fish in the salted milk for 10 minutes.
2. Preheat oven to 350°F. Place the bread crumbs (or cornmeal) in a medium mixing bowl. Drag both sides of the milk-soaked fillets through the bread crumbs so they stick to the fillets. Place the fish in a greased 9" × 13" baking pan.
3. Melt the butter and use a spoon to drizzle a few drops at a time over the fish. Sprinkle with lemon juice and about 1 teaspoon salt. Bake uncovered for 20 minutes or until the fish flakes easily with a fork.

ORANGE ROUGHY PICANTE

LEVEL **E**

SERVINGS **2**

This tasty fish with a southwestern flair makes an attractive, easy-to-prepare main course. You can substitute any other white fish fillet. You can also substitute bottled salsa for the picante sauce.

What You Need:

2 orange roughy fillets (about ½ pound each)

½ cup bottled picante sauce

1 cup shredded Cheddar cheese

What You Do:

Preheat oven to 350°F. Spray an ovenproof baking pan with nonstick cooking spray. Place the fillets in the bottom of the pan. Cover each fillet with ½ of the picante sauce. Top with shredded cheese, then bake uncovered for 20 minutes or microwave on high for 3 to 4 minutes until the cheese melts and the fish flakes easily.

LEVEL **E**

SERVINGS **4**

BAKED FILLET OF SOLE

Quick to prepare, this dish is so easy it almost cooks itself. You can substitute cod, flounder, or haddock for the sole.

What You Need:

4 sole fillets

1 (10.5-ounce) can cream of celery soup

What You Do:

1. Preheat the oven to 400°F. Spray a shallow baking dish with nonstick cooking spray. Arrange the sole fillets in the dish. Bake for 20 minutes.
2. After 12 to 15 minutes, place the undiluted soup in a small saucepan, and heat over low heat until warm.
3. Remove the fish from the oven. Turn down the oven heat to 300°F. Pour the soup over the fish. Return the fish to the oven for another 15 minutes.

HOT BOILED SHRIMP

Shrimp is expensive, but it's quick and easy to prepare. Serve with baked potatoes (see the "How Do I Bake a Potato?" sidebar with the Beef and Onion Roast recipe in Chapter 5), a salad, French bread (see the "How Do I Prepare French Bread?" sidebar with the Baked Spaghetti recipe in Chapter 5), and bottled cocktail sauce (or homemade—see the "How Can I Make My Own Easy Cocktail Sauce?" with this recipe). Cut a whole fresh lemon into wedges and place on serving plates.

What You Need:

1 quart water

½ (3-ounce) package shrimp and crab boil spices (1 bag)

1 tablespoon salt

¼ cup lemon juice

2 pounds uncooked shrimp in the shell

What You Do:

1. Pour the water into a Dutch oven. Add the boil spices, salt, and lemon juice. Bring to a boil over high heat.
2. Place the shrimp into the Dutch oven. Bring back to a boil. Cook for 3 to 5 minutes. Test 1 shrimp for tenderness after the first 3 minutes. Shrimp should be firm, not chewy (undercooked) or rubbery (overcooked). Continue to test 1 shrimp every minute until all are pink and tender. Drain. Serve hot in the shell, or let cool and chill in the refrigerator for about 1 hour to serve cold.

How Can I Make My Own Easy Cocktail Sauce?

If bottled cocktail sauce is too spicy or too mild, make your own. Pour contents of 1 (12-ounce) bottle chili sauce into a small mixing bowl. Stir in 1 teaspoon lemon juice. Stir in horseradish (from a jar) ½ teaspoon at a time, to taste. Look for horseradish in a refrigerated section of the store. Chill at least 1 hour to let flavors blend. This sauce goes well with crab, shrimp, and fish. Store leftover sauce in the chili sauce bottle in the refrigerator. When using horseradish keep in mind that it has a pungent flavor that can rival hot chili peppers in its ability to make your eyes water! So use only a small amount at a time. Horseradish is often used as a condiment with ham, roast beef, and steak, as well as in cocktail sauce.

BROILED SALMON

Fresh herbs give salmon a delicate flavor. For a different taste, substitute fresh thyme for the dill weed. Choose salmon steaks or ½ of a whole salmon fillet. Garnish with sliced fresh lemon. If you use olive oil, you don't have to heat it first. Serve with Cheesy Asparagus (see recipe in Chapter 9) and a baked potato (see the "How Do I Bake a Potato?" sidebar with the Beef and Onion Roast recipe in Chapter 5).

What You Need:

¼ cup butter

2 pounds salmon fillets

1 tablespoon lemon juice

Salt and pepper, to taste

½ (0.75-ounce) package fresh prewashed dill weed (or dried dill weed, as needed)

What You Do:

1. Melt the butter in a small saucepan over low heat.
2. Preheat the broiler. Place the salmon skin-side down on the rack of a shallow broiling pan that has been sprayed with nonstick cooking spray. Drizzle the butter over the salmon. Sprinkle with lemon juice, salt, and pepper.
3. Lay sprigs of fresh dill weed diagonal to the length of the fish, evenly spaced about 1½" apart. (Or, lightly sprinkle with dried dill.)
4. Broil for 6 to 10 minutes. Test for doneness. The salmon should be opaque and flake easily with a fork.

Why Do People Serve Lemon with Fish?

Many people like to squeeze fresh lemon juice from a lemon wedge (about ¼ of a lemon, cut lengthwise) to add flavor according to their own taste as they dine. So, if you're serving seafood, make lemon wedges available. However, flavor is only one reason to use lemon juice with fish. It also helps remove the fishy smell from your hands after preparing or eating "hands-on" dishes like shrimp and crab legs.

BAKED COD

Here's a quick-fix recipe you can serve in minutes. If you can't find cod, you can substitute any white fish in this recipe.

What You Need:

4 cod fillets

1 large white or yellow onion

2 tablespoons butter or margarine

2 tomatoes

What You Do:

1. Preheat oven to 400°F. Place the fillets in an oven-proof baking pan that has been sprayed with non-stick cooking spray.
2. Slice the onion. Layer the slices over the fish. Melt the butter (or margarine) in a small saucepan or frying pan over low heat. Pour over the fish and onion. Bake uncovered for 20 minutes.
3. While the fish is cooking, rinse the tomatoes under cold, running water. Slice the tomatoes. When the fish is done, remove from oven. Layer the tomato slices on top.
4. Return to the oven and bake for 10 minutes more.

LEVEL **E**

SERVINGS **4**

Transform frozen fish sticks into a tasty entrée that adults—as well as kids!—will love. Serve with a green salad and sliced fresh fruit.

FANTASTIC FISH STICKS

What You Need:

16 frozen fish sticks

1 (10.5-ounce) can cream of celery soup

½ cup milk

1½ tablespoons chopped fresh chives

1 tablespoon lemon juice

¼ cup shredded Cheddar cheese

1–2 teaspoons paprika

What You Do:

1. Set out the fish sticks to thaw. Preheat the oven to 425°F. Spray a shallow ovenproof baking pan with nonstick cooking spray. Arrange the fish sticks in the pan.
2. In a small mixing bowl stir together the cream of celery soup and milk until smooth. Measure out just 1 cup of the mixture. (Discard the rest or save for lunch.) Return the 1 cup of the soup mixture to the bowl. Stir in the chives, lemon juice, and cheese.
3. Pour over the fish sticks. Sprinkle with paprika. Bake for 20 minutes.

SHRIMP PESTO PASTA

Even though shrimp can be expensive, this recipe calls for a small enough amount to be affordable and still contribute its seafood flavor. Look for basil pesto sauce in the dairy section of the grocery store, or make your own Pesto (see recipe in Chapter 9).

What You Need:

½ pound raw tiger shrimp

8 ounces uncooked bow-tie pasta

2 tablespoons olive oil

½ (7-ounce) package basil pesto sauce or ¼ cup homemade Pesto (see recipe in Chapter 9)

Grated Parmesan cheese, as needed

What You Do:

1. Peel off the shrimp shells by holding the "feet" and peeling off the outer shell. Use your thumbnail to remove the veins from the shrimp backs. Rinse the cleaned shrimp under cold, running water.
2. Cook the pasta according to package directions (boil for about 11 minutes).
3. While the pasta is cooking, cook the shrimp in the olive oil in a large frying pan over medium-high heat, stirring constantly to keep them from sticking. Cook for 5 to 8 minutes, until the shrimp just turn pink. (Be careful not to overcook the shrimp, or they will become rubbery.)
4. Drain the pasta and return it to the pot. Stir in the pesto sauce. Spoon the pasta onto serving plates. Top with shrimp. Sprinkle with grated Parmesan cheese.

BAKED TUNA LOAF

Take a break from tuna salad with a tuna dish served warm. Serve with Chilled Pea Salad (see recipe in Chapter 4) or sliced fresh tomatoes and a steamed green vegetable (see Appendix C).

What You Need:

Shortening or vegetable oil, as needed

1 (12-ounce) can tuna

1 stalk celery

3 cups unseasoned bread crumbs

1 egg

1 tablespoon dried minced onion

1 teaspoon salt

¼ teaspoon pepper

½ (7-ounce) can mushroom stems and pieces

1 (10.5-ounce) can condensed cream of chicken soup

What You Do:

1. Preheat oven to 375°F. Use a paper towel and solid shortening (or vegetable oil) to grease a shallow, ovenproof 9" × 13" baking pan. Set aside.
2. Drain the tuna. Use a fork to flake the tuna into a large mixing bowl.
3. Chop the celery. Add to the tuna along with the bread crumbs, egg, minced onion, salt, and pepper.
4. Use your hands to squish together all the ingredients, until well blended. Form into a loaf shape. Place in the prepared baking pan.
5. Drain the mushrooms and place in a small mixing bowl. Stir in the soup (do not dilute). Pour over the tuna loaf. Bake uncovered for 30 minutes.

CRABMEAT CASSEROLE

Here's an economical casserole that provides the flavor of crabmeat without the expense and without the effort of removing the shell. Serve with Cucumber Salad (see recipe in Chapter 4), Cold Mixed Veggies Salad (see recipe in Chapter 4), or a steamed green vegetable (see Appendix C).

What You Need:

½ cup milk

¾ cup bread crumbs, plus extra for sprinkling over the top

2 (4.5-ounce) cans cooked crabmeat (or 8 ounces imitation crab)

3 hard-boiled eggs (see Boiled Egg recipe in Chapter 1)

¾ teaspoon salt

⅛ teaspoon dry mustard

⅛ teaspoon cayenne pepper

3 tablespoons butter

Shortening, vegetable oil, or nonstick cooking spray, as needed

What You Do:

1. In a large mixing bowl, stir together the milk and bread crumbs. Drain the crabmeat (if using canned) or chop the imitation crab. Add to the bowl.
2. Peel the hard-boiled eggs. Cut the eggs in half lengthwise and separate the whites and yolks. Chop whites into small pieces. Add to bowl.
3. Preheat oven to 450°F. Place the egg yolks on a saucer or in a separate small bowl. Mash with a fork. Add to the crab mixture along with salt, dry mustard, and cayenne pepper.
4. Melt the butter and drizzle it over the ingredients in the bowl. Gently stir the ingredients together until well mixed.
5. Pour mixture into a greased baking dish. Top with bread crumbs. Bake uncovered for 15 minutes or until heated through.

GARLICKY PASTA WITH VEGGIES AND SHRIMP

This simple and yummy pasta has tons of variations. Use your imagination (or whatever leftovers you have in your fridge) to make this quick pasta dish. You can use fresh or frozen cooked or raw shrimp in this recipe. If precooked, thaw first. If raw, thaw and cook in 1 tablespoon of olive oil over medium-high heat just until almost tender. (They will cook more when combined with the other ingredients.) Cremini or button mushrooms are both good choices to use in this recipe.

What You Need:

16 large precooked shrimp (thaw if frozen)
2 fresh plum or Roma tomatoes
1 red bell pepper
½ cup fresh spinach or frozen chopped spinach (thawed)
½ medium white or yellow onion
2 cloves garlic (or ¼ teaspoon dried minced garlic)
2 tablespoons olive oil
½ (8-ounce) package sliced fresh mushrooms
8 ounces uncooked penne rigate pasta
1 tablespoon lemon juice
Salt and pepper, to taste
1–2 tablespoons grated Parmesan or Romano cheese

What You Do:

1. Remove the shells, tails, and veins from the shrimp, if necessary. Rinse the tomatoes and pepper under cold water. Remove the seeds and inner ribs from the pepper. Chop the tomatoes, bell pepper, and spinach. Set aside. Chop the onion and mince the garlic by chopping the cloves into very small pieces.

2. Pour the olive oil into a large frying pan over medium-high heat. Stir in the onion and fresh garlic and cook for 1 minute, stirring constantly. (If you're using dried minced garlic, add it later with the rest of the vegetables instead.) Reduce heat to medium. Add the tomatoes, bell pepper, and mushrooms. Cook the vegetables, stirring constantly, until they are tender but still firm.

3. Cook the pasta according to package directions until tender but still firm. Drain and rinse immediately with cold water. Stir into the vegetable mixture along with the shrimp and spinach. Use 2 forks to toss until well mixed.

4. Add the lemon juice, salt, and pepper. Stir until heated through. Sprinkle with cheese.

The smoked flavor of this dish makes it a favorite example of Scottish cuisine. Serve with sliced tomatoes and a steamed green vegetable (see Appendix C).

BAKED AND FLAKED HADDOCK WITH RICE CASSEROLE

What You Need:

½ pound smoked haddock fillets

1 cup uncooked rice

1 hard-boiled egg (see Boiled Egg recipe Chapter 1)

2 tablespoons butter or margarine

2 tablespoons lemon juice

2 teaspoons dried parsley flakes

Salt and pepper, to taste

What You Do:

1. Preheat oven to 400°F. Place the fillets in an oven-proof baking pan that has been sprayed with non-stick cooking spray. Bake uncovered for 25 minutes. Remove from oven.
2. While the fish is cooking, cook the rice according to package directions.
3. When the fish is done, flake it with a fork. (Remove the skin if present.) Peel and crumble the hard-boiled egg. In a large frying pan, melt the butter (or margarine) over low heat. Add the fish. Cook for 3 minutes, stirring to reheat the fish evenly. Stir in the cooked rice, egg, lemon juice, parsley flakes, salt, and pepper. Serve immediately.

CRAB TETRAZZINI

There's nothing like the sweet taste of crabmeat to turn everyone into a seafood lover. Serve with steamed green beans (see Appendix C). Add ½ cup water or milk to the leftover tomato soup and serve for lunch the next day.

What You Need:

½ (10-ounce) package uncooked spaghetti

Shortening, vegetable oil, or nonstick cooking spray, as needed

½ small white or yellow onion

1 tablespoon butter or margarine

¼ pound sliced fresh mushrooms

½ (10.75-ounce) can condensed tomato soup

¾ cup crabmeat or imitation crab

1 cup tomato juice

Salt and pepper, to taste

1 cup shredded sharp Cheddar cheese

What You Do:

1. Break the spaghetti into thirds and cook according to package directions. Drain. Preheat oven to 350°F. Grease an ovenproof baking pan with shortening or vegetable oil, or spray with nonstick cooking spray.
2. While the noodles are cooking, chop the onion. Melt the butter (or margarine) over medium heat in a small saucepan. Stir in the onion and mushrooms; cook until tender. Transfer the mixture to the prepared baking pan.
3. Stir in the soup, crabmeat, tomato juice, salt, pepper, and ½ of the cheese. When the noodles are done, drain. Gently stir into the crab mixture. Top with the remaining cheese. Bake for 35 to 40 minutes.

TUNA CHOW MEIN

With crispy noodles and crunchy cashews, this dish presents tuna as you may never have tasted it before. Serve with sliced fresh tomatoes.

What You Need:

1 (6-ounce) can tuna

1 cup chopped celery

½ cup salted cashew pieces

¼ cup dried minced onion

¼ cup water

¼ teaspoon pepper

1 (10.5-ounce) can condensed cream of mushroom soup (undiluted)

1 (5-ounce) can chow mein noodles

What You Do:

1. Drain and flake tuna with a fork. Place in a 2-quart saucepan.
2. Add celery to the saucepan. Stir in the cashews, onion, water, pepper, and mushroom soup. Add ½ of the noodles. Heat over medium heat until heated through. (Or, zap in the microwave for 3 minutes or so.)
3. Top with the rest of the noodles and serve.

HOT AND SPICY SALSA SHRIMP

You can squeeze fresh lime juice or use juice made from concentrate in this recipe. Serve piping hot over rice cooked according to package directions.

What You Need:

1½ pounds medium raw shrimp

1 tablespoon olive oil

1½ teaspoons chili powder

1 teaspoon garlic salt

1 teaspoon ground cumin

2 tablespoons lime juice, divided

2 cups canned black beans

1½ cups whole kernel corn

¾ cup bottle salsa

1 tablespoon dried parsley flakes

What You Do:

1. Peel the shrimp and remove the vein running across the back.
2. Heat the olive oil in a large frying pan over medium-high heat. In a small mixing bowl, stir together the chili powder, garlic salt, and cumin. Place the shrimp in the frying pan. Sprinkle with the spices and 1 tablespoon of the lime juice. Cook 3 to 5 minutes, stirring constantly until shrimp is tender. Transfer the shrimp to a large mixing bowl. Set aside.
3. Drain the black beans in a colander. Rinse with cool, running water. Set aside.
4. Drain the corn. Add the corn to the frying pan, stirring constantly until corn is lightly coated with oil. Stir in the salsa, parsley, and black beans. Cook 30 seconds. Add the remaining 1 tablespoon lime juice. Cook until warmed through. Pour the sauce over the shrimp. Serve over rice.

LINGUINE AND CLAM SAUCE

For seafood lovers only, this creamy, filling dish is a good choice for a cold winter evening. Serve with steamed broccoli (see Appendix C).

What You Need:

½ cup canned minced clams, with liquid

4 cups water

1 (16-ounce) package uncooked linguine

1 cup heavy cream

8 tablespoons butter, divided

1 tablespoon minced fresh garlic, or 1 teaspoon dried

4 tablespoons chopped fresh parsley

1 tablespoon chopped fresh basil

1 teaspoon thyme

½ cup grated Parmesan cheese

Salt and pepper, to taste

What You Do:

1. Drain the clams over a large cooking pot. Set clams aside. Add the water to the clam liquid in the pot. Bring to a boil over high heat. Cook linguine in the liquid according to package instructions.
2. While noodles are cooking, pour the cream into a small saucepan. Heat over medium heat just to boiling then reduce heat to low. In a separate, medium saucepan, melt ½ of the butter over low heat. Add the clams, garlic, parsley, basil, thyme, and pepper. Stir in the cream.
3. Drain the linguine. Return to the cooking pot, away from the heat. Pour the clam sauce over the noodles and toss together. Add remaining butter and toss again. Sprinkle with the Parmesan cheese. Sprinkle with salt and pepper to taste.

LEVEL **H**

SERVINGS **2**

BROILED ORANGE ROUGHY

You'll find orange roughy fillets in the frozen foods section of your supermarket. Thaw before cooking.

What You Need:

1 pound orange roughy fillets

½ cup mayonnaise

½ cup grated Parmesan cheese

1 tablespoon lemon juice

Garlic salt, to taste

⅛ teaspoon paprika

1 medium white or yellow onion

¼ cup dried parsley flakes

What You Do:

1. Spray a broiler pan with nonstick cooking spray. Place the fillets on the pan.
2. In a small mixing bowl, stir together the mayonnaise, cheese, lemon juice, garlic salt, and paprika. Spread the mixture onto the fillets.
3. Preheat the broiler. Thinly slice the onion. Arrange the slices on top of the fillets. Sprinkle with parsley. Cover the pan with aluminum foil. Broil for 7 minutes. Remove from oven. Uncover and broil for 5 to 6 minutes more, until golden brown. (No need to turn the fillets.)

These tasty patties are a fish alternative to hamburgers. Serve with fresh lemon wedges and bottled tartar sauce or seafood cocktail sauce.

CRAB CAKES

What You Need:

1 (16-ounce) can crabmeat

⅓ cup butter cracker crumbs (like Ritz)

3 scallions (also called green onions)

½ cup chopped green pepper

1 egg

¼ cup mayonnaise

1 teaspoon Worcestershire sauce

1 teaspoon dry mustard

1 tablespoon lemon juice

¼ teaspoon garlic powder

1 teaspoon salt

⅛ teaspoon cayenne pepper

Vegetable oil, as needed for frying

1–2 cups all-purpose flour, as needed for dusting

What You Do:

1. Drain the crabmeat. Use a fork to flake the crabmeat into a large mixing bowl.
2. Add the cracker crumbs to the bowl.
3. Rinse the scallions in cold, running water and remove outer skin and "tassels." Slice the scallions, including the dark green tops. Add to the bowl. Stir in the green pepper with the fork.
4. In a small mixing bowl, use the fork to beat the egg enough to break the yolk and slightly mix it with the white. Add to the crabmeat mixture.
5. Add the mayonnaise, Worcestershire sauce, dry mustard, lemon juice, garlic powder, salt, and cayenne pepper.

(continued on next page)

CRAB CAKES – CONTINUED

6. Use your hands to form the mixture into 10 cakes, as you would make hamburger patties.
7. Pour the vegetable oil to about ¼" deep in a large frying pan over medium heat. Place about ½ cup of the flour on a saucer, and dip both sides of each patty into the flour. Replace with more flour as needed. When the oil is hot, place the cakes in the frying pan. Cook for 4 minutes or until the bottom is crisp and golden brown. Use a spatula to flip to the other side. Cook for another 4 minutes or until golden brown. Serve warm.

JAMBALAYA

You can use any type of poultry, sausage, fish, or seafood in this Cajun favorite. For the best results, use a combination of 2 or 3 of these ingredients. For traditional flavor, choose from Andouille sausage, chicken, shrimp, oysters, crayfish, or alligator, but any fish or sausage will work, particularly the spicy and flavorful chorizo sausage popular in Mexico. Common combinations include chicken/sausage and shrimp/oysters.

What You Need:

3 cups cooked poultry, sausage, fish, and/or seafood

1 medium white or yellow onion

1 green bell pepper

2 stalks celery

2 tablespoons vegetable oil

¼ teaspoon dried minced garlic

1 teaspoon cayenne pepper

Salt and pepper, to taste

1 (14.5-ounce) can chicken or vegetable broth

¼ cup water

1 cup uncooked rice

What You Do:

1. Cut the meat and/or fish into bite-sized pieces. Set aside. Chop the onion, green bell pepper, and celery. Keep chopped ingredients separate.
2. Pour the vegetable oil into a large frying pan. Cook the meat/fish, onion, and garlic in the oil over medium-high heat for 5 minutes, stirring often. Stir in the green bell pepper and celery; cook 3 minutes more. Sprinkle with cayenne pepper, salt, and pepper.
3. Stir in the broth and water. Bring to a boil. Add the rice. Cover and cook for about 20 minutes, stirring occasionally, until the rice is tender.

SALMON-POTATO PATTIES WITH LEMON-BASIL SAUCE

Serve with a fruit salad or green vegetable. You can use 2 cups of leftover mashed potatoes in place of the instant ones. If you make this change, just omit the water. It's already cooked into them.

What You Need:
LEMON-BASIL SAUCE

½ cup mayonnaise

¾ teaspoon dried minced garlic

½ teaspoon dried basil

½ teaspoon lemon juice

½ teaspoon Dijon mustard

¼ teaspoon lemon pepper

SALMON-POTATO PATTIES

2¼ cups water

2 cups instant mashed potato flakes

1 (14.5-ounce) can red salmon

½ cup grated Parmesan cheese

¼ cup vegetable oil

What You Do:

1. **For Lemon-Basil Sauce:** Combine the mayonnaise, garlic, basil, lemon juice, Dijon mustard, and lemon pepper in a small mixing bowl. Stir until well blended. Refrigerate until ready to serve.

2. **For the Salmon-Potato Patties:** Boil the water in a large saucepan over high heat. Remove from heat. Measure out 2 cups. Discard any remainder. Pour the 2 cups back into the saucepan. Use a fork to stir in the potato flakes.

3. Drain the salmon. Use a fork to flake it into the potatoes in the saucepan.

4. Stir in the Parmesan cheese. Let cool enough that you can use your hands to work with the mixture.

(continued on next page)

SALMON-POTATO PATTIES WITH LEMON-BASIL SAUCE — CONTINUED

5. With your hands, form the mixture into 8 patties. Place them on a cookie sheet. Refrigerate for 10 minutes.

6. Preheat the oven to 250°F. Heat the vegetable oil in a large frying pan over medium heat. When the oil is hot, fry four of the patties on one side for about 4 minutes or until lightly browned. Use a spatula to flip over the patties. Cook for another 4 minutes or until the second side is lightly browned and the patty is heated all the way through.

7. Cover the first batch with aluminum foil and place in the oven to keep warm while you fry the rest of the patties. Serve warm with the sauce on the side.

CHAPTER 8

Vegetarian Entrées

RAMEN NOODLES EXTREME v

Turn Ramen noodles from a side dish into a vegetarian meal. This dish is inexpensive, tasty, and full of vitamin C and other nutrients.

What You Need:

4 (3-ounce) packages Ramen noodles, any flavor

1 cup frozen peas

1 (14.5-ounce) can diced tomatoes

1 tablespoon butter or margarine

Grated Parmesan cheese, to taste

What You Do:

1. Cook the noodles in a medium saucepan according to package directions. While cooking, stir in the frozen peas. Drain the noodles and peas and return to the saucepan.

2. Reduce heat to low. Drain the tomatoes. Add the tomatoes and butter (or margarine) to the noodles and peas. Heat until butter has melted and the peas are tender. Spoon into serving bowls and sprinkle with Parmesan cheese.

How Can I Use Frozen Veggies as First Aid?

You can use bags of frozen vegetables as first aid for headaches, bumps, and sprains. Just grab the bag from the freezer and use it as an ice pack. Don't place the frozen vegetable bag (or any ice pack) directly on the skin. Instead, place a kitchen towel between the injury and the ice. This tip is especially useful if you're babysitting someone's son or daughter. When you tell the parents about the big bump on their child's forehead, smile and say, "Don't worry, I put broccoli on it."

MAC 'N' CHEESE v

LEVEL E

SERVINGS 4

Packaged macaroni and cheese is so easy, you might prefer to make that. However, if you prefer homemade flavor, here's an easy recipe. Serve this vegetarian dish with sliced fresh tomatoes and steamed asparagus (see Appendix C).

What You Need:

3 quarts water

2 cups uncooked macaroni (about 8 ounces)

3 tablespoons butter or margarine

½ cup shredded Cheddar cheese

1 cup milk

Paprika, to taste

What You Do:

1. Bring the water to a boil in a large saucepan over high heat. Add the macaroni. Cook according to package directions for about 8 minutes until the noodles are tender but still firm. Drain. Return the noodles to the pan and reduce heat to low.
2. Stir in the butter (or margarine) and cheese until melted. Stir in the milk. Cook until heated through, stirring often. Sprinkle with paprika and serve.

LEVEL E

SERVINGS 4

VARIATION: NUTTY MAC v

Pecans add a sweet flavor, and sour cream adds body for a main course or side dish. You'll never want plain macaroni and cheese again. Follow the recipe for Mac 'n' Cheese, but in place of butter (or margarine) add ½ cup sour cream and ½ cup chopped pecans.

PARMESAN NOODLES v

These cheesy noodles can serve as a tasty lunch, dinner entrée, or side dish. Although fresh ingredients taste better, you can use dried parsley flakes and pre-grated Parmesan cheese.

What You Need:

8 ounces medium egg noodles

¼ cup butter or margarine

¼ teaspoon garlic powder

2 tablespoons chopped fresh parsley

2 tablespoons grated Parmesan cheese

What You Do:

1. In a large saucepan, cook the noodles according to package directions. Drain and return to the pan.
2. While the noodles are cooking, melt the butter (or margarine) in a separate small saucepan. Add the garlic powder. When the noodles are ready, pour the butter over them. Stir until the noodles are well coated.
3. Sprinkle the parsley and Parmesan cheese over the noodles. Serve warm.

What Is the Easiest Way to Measure Butter?

The easiest way to measure butter or margarine in stick form is to look at the markings on the wrapper. Lines indicate 1 tablespoon increments. Here are commonly called-for amounts:

4 tablespoons = ½ stick = ¼ cup

5⅓ tablespoons = ⅓ cup

8 tablespoons = 1 stick = ½ cup

For non-vegetarians, you can add chunks of cooked chicken. Top with Easy Guacamole or Fresh Tomato Salsa (see recipes in Chapter 10) and sour cream.

CHEESE QUESADILLAS v

What You Need:

1 tablespoon butter or margarine

2 (10") flour tortillas

1 cup shredded Cheddar cheese

What You Do:

1. Melt the butter (or margarine) in a small or medium frying pan over low to medium heat. Place 1 tortilla in the pan. Top with the cheese. Place the second tortilla on top. Heat until the bottom tortilla is golden brown.
2. Flip, as you would a pancake, to the other side. Heat until golden brown. Remove from the pan and place on a serving plate. Cut into six wedges.

EGGPLANT SURPRISE v

No need for fancy dishes with this entrée. The eggplant shell placed on a dinner plate becomes your serving bowl. For a vegan variation, omit the cheese.

What You Need:

1 whole eggplant

1 Roma tomato (also called plum tomato)

1 scallion (also called green onion)

¼ cup sliced fresh mushrooms

¼ teaspoon minced dried garlic

⅛ teaspoon freshly ground black pepper

½ teaspoon dried basil

2 tablespoons olive oil

½ cup shredded mozzarella cheese

Grated Parmesan cheese, to taste

What You Do:

1. Cut the eggplant in half lengthwise. Remove the seeds, and scoop out the flesh. Leave ¼"–½" of flesh attached to the interior of the shell for support. Set aside the shells.
2. Cut the eggplant flesh and tomato into 1" cubes.
3. Rinse the scallions in cold, running water and remove outer skin and "tassels." Slice about 4" of the scallion, including about half of the dark green part.
4. In a large frying pan over medium-high heat, cook the eggplant, tomato, onion, mushrooms, garlic, pepper, and basil in the olive oil, stirring constantly until the eggplant is tender but still firm. Remove from heat. Add the mozzarella cheese. Set aside until the cheese melts.
5. With a slotted spoon to drain off the oil, spoon half of the mixture into each eggplant shell half. Sprinkle with grated Parmesan cheese. Serve warm.

BROILED PORTABELLA MUSHROOM CAPS v

This colorful, easy entrée looks and tastes like gourmet cooking, especially if you use fresh herbs. You can make this recipe as an attractive side dish by using baby portabellas about 3" to 4" in diameter. Use 1 baby mushroom cap per serving.

What You Need:

2 tablespoons butter or margarine

2 portabella mushroom caps (about 4"–5" in diameter)

2 small tomatoes

1 clove garlic (or ⅛ teaspoon dried minced garlic)

2 tablespoons chopped fresh basil (or ¼–½ teaspoon dried basil)

2 tablespoons olive oil

Freshly grated Parmesan cheese, as needed

What You Do:

1. Melt the butter (or margarine) in a small frying pan over medium-high heat. Place the mushroom caps, rounded-side up, in the frying pan. Move the mushroom caps around during the cooking, until the mushrooms are tender. Remove from frying pan. Place caps rounded-side down in an ungreased pie tin (don't use glass).

2. Preheat oven broiler. Chop the tomatoes and garlic and stir together in a small mixing bowl with the basil. Spoon the tomato mixture into the mushroom caps. Drizzle olive oil over the tomato mixture. Generously sprinkle with Parmesan cheese. Broil for 5 minutes, until the cheese bubbles. Serve warm.

STIR-FRY VEGGIE COMBO v

Chickpeas, also known as garbanzo beans, are high in protein, enabling this dish to be served over rice as a vegetarian main course. Or, you can serve this combo as a side dish for Pot Roast (see recipe in Chapter 5) or Roast Chicken (see recipe in Chapter 6).

What You Need:

1 green bell pepper

1 stalk celery

¼ medium white or yellow onion

3 small zucchini (about 6" long)

1 medium tomato

2 tablespoons olive oil

½ cup chickpeas

What You Do:

1. Cut the green pepper in half and remove the stem, seeds, and inner ribs. Chop the green pepper, celery, and onion. Place in a small mixing bowl. Set aside. Cut the zucchini in half lengthwise and then slice crosswise into ½"-thick pieces. Keep separate from the celery mixture. Cut the tomato into ½" cubes. Set aside.
2. Pour the olive oil into a large frying pan over medium-high heat. Stirring constantly, cook the green pepper, celery, onion, and chickpeas in the olive oil for 6 minutes. Reduce heat to medium. Stir in the zucchini and cook for 5 more minutes. Stir in the tomatoes and continue cooking just until the tomato is tender.

What could be more delicious than garlicky pesto flavor in a cheesy tomato pasta dish? Serve with a simple mixed greens salad and French bread (see the "How Do I Prepare French Bread?" sidebar with the Baked Spaghetti recipe in Chapter 5). You can substitute linguine for the rigatoni. Just change the name to Pesto Linguine.

PESTO RIGATONI v

What You Need:

3 pints cherry or grape tomatoes

1 whole head fresh garlic

½ cup fresh basil (or 2 tablespoons dried basil)

½ cup pine nuts

2 tablespoons olive oil

1 teaspoon salt

1 (16-ounce) package rigatoni

½ cup grated Parmesan cheese

What You Do:

1. Rinse the tomatoes under cold, running water. Slice lengthwise into halves. Mince the garlic by cutting it into small pieces. Roughly chop the basil. Place the pine nuts in a small, dry frying pan over medium heat. Stir until they turn brown. Remove from heat.

2. In a large saucepan, heat the olive oil on low. Add the tomatoes and salt. Cook for 3 minutes. Add the garlic and cook for 1 minute. Stir in the roasted pine nuts and the basil. Stir occasionally until the tomato mixture cooks down into a sauce.

3. Cook the pasta in a Dutch oven according to package directions. Drain. Return the pasta to the Dutch oven. Pour the sauce over the pasta. Stir until well mixed. Cook over low heat for about 2 minutes until heated through. Add the Parmesan and toss to mix.

BRIE LINGUINE WITH TOMATOES AND BASIL v

This dish is best made in summer from homegrown, vine-ripened tomatoes and fresh basil. Serve as a side dish or entrée immediately upon mixing the pasta and dressing. You'll also enjoy leftovers served warm or cold the next day.

What You Need:

4 tomatoes

1 pound Brie cheese

1 cup fresh basil

3 cloves garlic

¾ cup extra-virgin olive oil

½ teaspoon salt

½ teaspoon seasoned salt

½ teaspoon pepper

1½ pounds uncooked linguine

1 cup grated Parmesan cheese

What You Do:

1. Dice the tomatoes and place in a large glass serving bowl.
2. Remove the rind from the Brie and tear the cheese into irregular pieces. Chop the basil. Chop the garlic into very small pieces. Add the Brie, basil, and garlic to the tomatoes.
3. Stir in the olive oil, salt, seasoned salt, and pepper until well blended. Cover with a kitchen towel. Let sit at room temperature for 2 to 4 hours.
4. When ready to serve, fill a large pot with water. Cook the linguine according to package directions, but for only 10 minutes, so the noodles are tender but still firm.
5. Drain the pasta and add to the tomato dressing. Toss until noodles are well coated. Sprinkle with the Parmesan cheese.

SPINACH AND FETA QUESADILLAS v

Two delicious flavors combine for a festive entrée or appetizer. Top with bottled salsa or Fresh Tomato Salsa (see recipe in Chapter 10). Be sure to wash your hands with soap and water after handling the chilies and before touching your mouth or eyes! You can omit the cilantro if you prefer.

What You Need:

4 serrano or jalapeño chilies
½ cup cooked spinach
2 tablespoons chopped fresh cilantro
4 ounces feta cheese
¼ cup ricotta cheese
5 (8") flour tortillas
Water, as needed
Vegetable oil, as needed

What You Do:

1. Remove stems and seeds from the chilies. Chop. Place in a large mixing bowl.
2. Drain and chop the spinach. Add to the bowl.
3. Add the cilantro to the bowl. Stir in the feta and ricotta cheeses until well blended.
4. Place a piece of damp paper towel on a microwave-safe plate and place 1 tortilla on top. Cover with another damp paper towel and another tortilla until all the tortillas are in the stack with a damp paper towel on top. Microwave on high for 45 seconds to 1 minute until soft. Cover with a paper or cloth towel to keep warm.
5. Place ⅕ of the filling on one half of each tortilla. Moisten the tortilla edges with water and fold in half. Press together, then brush both sides of the tortillas with the vegetable oil. Brown one side of the quesadilla on a hot frying pan. Flip and brown on the other side. Cut each tortilla into three triangles.

What If My Red Hot Chili Peppers Are Too Hot?

If a chili pepper is too spicy for your liking, combine with cheese, sour cream, or another dairy product. During preparation, you can reduce the "heat" by removing some or all of the ribs, inner membranes, and seeds, or by soaking for 30 minutes or less in cold water with about ⅛ teaspoon of salt or a little vinegar.

LEVEL **M**

SERVINGS **4**

COUSCOUS WITH TOMATO SAUCE v

This main dish looks a bit like spaghetti, with couscous replacing the spaghetti noodles. Chickpeas, which are also known as garbanzo beans, provide a protein source. Serve with a Tossed Salad (see recipe in Chapter 4).

What You Need:

2 cups water

1⅓ cups uncooked couscous

1 (28-ounce) jar chunky vegetable spaghetti sauce

1 (15-ounce) can chickpeas

¼ teaspoon red pepper flakes

2 tablespoons chopped fresh parsley

4 tablespoons grated Parmesan cheese

What You Do:

1. Boil the water in a medium saucepan over high heat. Add the couscous and stir. Cover and remove from the heat. Let it steam for 5 minutes or until all the water is absorbed.

2. While the couscous is cooking, place the spaghetti sauce, chickpeas, and red pepper flakes in a separate large saucepan. Stir well. Cook uncovered over medium heat until ingredients are heated through (about 5 to 7 minutes).

3. Use a fork to loosen the couscous. Spoon onto serving plates.

4. Spoon the sauce over each serving. Sprinkle 1 tablespoon of chopped parsley and 1 tablespoon of Parmesan cheese on each serving.

Full of flavor and fiber, this stew will warm a cold winter night. The fennel seed adds a hint of licorice. If you're not a vegetarian, you can substitute a can of pork and beans for the vegetarian baked beans. Serve with your favorite bread or Easy Dinner Rolls (see recipe in Chapter 1).

FOUR-BEAN STEW v

What You Need:

1 (15.5-ounce) can butter beans

1 (15.5-ounce) can red kidney beans

1 (16-ounce) can vegetarian baked beans

1 (9-ounce) package frozen baby lima beans

3 carrots

1 small onion

1 (14.5-ounce) can stewed tomatoes with Italian seasoning, with liquid

½ teaspoon garlic salt

⅛ teaspoon cayenne pepper

⅛ teaspoon fennel seed

What You Do:

1. Drain and rinse the butter beans and kidney beans. Place in a 4-quart slow cooker, along with the baked beans and lima beans.
2. Thinly slice the carrots. Chop the onion. Add to the pot.
3. Stir in the tomatoes. Use the side of a cooking spoon to break the tomatoes into small pieces, if necessary. Sprinkle mixture with garlic salt and cayenne pepper. Crush the fennel seed and add to the pot. Cover. Cook on low for 8 hours or on high for 4 hours.

BLACK BEANS AND RICE v

You don't have to be a vegetarian to love this tasty, aromatic dish. It's even better when stored in the refrigerator for a day or two to give the flavors a chance to blend. (Wait to cook the rice until ready to serve.) Serve with warm Corn Bread (see recipe in Chapter 1) and fresh lime wedges.

What You Need:

1 large carrot
½ small red bell pepper
1 large onion
1 tablespoon olive oil
½ teaspoon minced dried garlic
1 teaspoon dried oregano
½ teaspoon ground cumin
1 teaspoon chili powder
2 (15.5-ounce) cans black beans
1 (15-ounce) can crushed tomatoes (with juice)
¾ cup vegetable broth or water
1 bay leaf
Salt and pepper, to taste
4 cups cooked white or brown rice

What You Do:

1. Peel and chop the carrot, and place in a medium mixing bowl. Remove the stem and seeds from the red pepper and chop. Add to the bowl. Set aside.
2. Peel and chop the onion. Heat the olive oil in a Dutch oven over medium heat. When hot, cook the onion for about 5 to 7 minutes until tender and translucent. Add the carrot, red pepper, and garlic. Cook for about 2 more minutes until the vegetables are just tender, but still firm.
3. Stir in the oregano, cumin, and chili powder. Cook for 1 minute.
4. Drain and rinse the beans in a colander. Add to the Dutch oven. Stir in the tomatoes with juice, broth or water, and bay leaf. Reduce heat to low. Cook uncovered for 20 minutes. Sprinkle with the salt and pepper.
5. While the beans are cooking, cook the rice according to package instructions. Place the rice on serving plates. Remove the bay leaf, and spoon the beans onto the rice.

HOT CHEESE TOAST v

What You Need:

½ scallion (also called green onion)

¼ cup shredded sharp Cheddar cheese

¼ cup shredded Monterey jack cheese

¼ cup mayonnaise

Garlic powder, to taste (less than ⅛ teaspoon)

Cayenne pepper, to taste

¾ teaspoon dried parsley flakes

4 slices French bread, about 1½" thick

1 tablespoon grated Parmesan cheese

What You Do:

1. Rinse the scallions in cold, running water and remove outer skin and "tassels." Slice the scallion, including part of the dark green top. Place in a medium mixing bowl. Stir in Cheddar cheese, Monterey jack cheese, mayonnaise, garlic powder, cayenne pepper, and parsley until well blended.
2. Spread the cheese mixture on one side of each slice of bread. Sprinkle the Parmesan cheese on top. Place face up on an ungreased baking sheet or on the rack of a toaster oven. Broil until the cheeses melt and bubble. Serve hot.

QUICK VEGAN ENCHILADAS v

If you don't eat meat, you can still enjoy the fiesta flavor of these enchiladas made with tofu instead of beef. Top with tofu sour cream (see the "How Do I Make Tofu Sour Cream?" sidebar with this recipe). Serve with shredded lettuce, black olives, or Easy Guacamole (see recipe in Chapter 10).

What You Need:

2 baking potatoes

1 (28-ounce) can red enchilada sauce

28 ounces water (use the enchilada sauce can to measure)

9 ounces firm tofu

1 medium white or yellow onion

1 (15.5-ounce) can chili beans

3 tablespoons chili powder

1 tablespoon ground cumin

2 tablespoons garlic powder

Salt and pepper, to taste

12 (8") flour tortillas

What You Do:

1. Rinse the potatoes under cold, running water. Peel and cut into quarters. Boil for about 20 minutes, until tender. (Check by piercing with a fork.) Drain and let cool. Cut the potatoes into ½" cubes. Place in a large mixing bowl. Set aside.
2. Pour the enchilada sauce and water into a 1-quart saucepan over low heat. Stir often while preparing the rest of the tortilla filling.
3. Crumble the tofu or cut into ½" cubes. Chop the onion. Add tofu and onion to the potatoes in mixing bowl. Drain the beans. Add to the potatoes. Stir in the chili powder, cumin, garlic powder, salt, and pepper.
4. Preheat oven to 350°F. Spray a 9" × 13" ovenproof baking pan with nonstick cooking spray. Spoon in just enough enchilada sauce to cover the bottom of the pan.

(continued on next page)

QUICK VEGAN ENCHILADAS
— CONTINUED

5. Dip a tortilla into the remaining enchilada sauce in the saucepan and place in the baking pan. Spoon about ⅓ cup of the filling mixture across the tortilla. Fold the bottom ¼ of the tortilla over the filling mixture. Wrap the right side of the tortilla halfway over the filling (and the already folded bottom section). Wrap the left side of the tortilla over the right side. Carefully turn over the enchilada and place seam-side down in the baking pan. Repeat with the remaining tortillas. Pour the remaining enchilada sauce over the enchiladas. Bake for 20 to 25 minutes.

How Do I Make Tofu Sour Cream?
Use tofu sour cream to top your favorite dishes from Mexico and the American Southwest. In a small mixing bowl, use a wooden spoon or electric mixer to blend together 1 (12-ounce) package silken soft tofu, 2 tablespoons vegetable oil, 1 tablespoon lemon juice, 1½ teaspoons sugar (or honey), and ½ teaspoon salt. Makes about 1½ cups.

BAKED SPINACH AND EGGPLANT CASSEROLE v

Eggplant takes on the flavors of surrounding ingredients and makes this casserole tasty and filling. A great potluck dish.

What You Need:

3 fresh tomatoes

2 cups fresh spinach

1 tablespoon dried parsley flakes

1 cup uncooked macaroni

1¼ cups canned stewed tomatoes, with juice

1 eggplant

⅜ teaspoon dried minced garlic

⅓ cup olive oil

¾ teaspoon salt

¾ teaspoon pepper

What You Do:

1. Rinse the tomatoes under cold, running water. Slice them and place in a layer in the bottom of a greased ovenproof baking dish.
2. Rinse the spinach under cold, running water. Drain and chop. Sprinkle the tomatoes with the spinach and parsley.
3. Place the macaroni on a cutting board. Cover with waxed paper. Use a rolling pin to crush the macaroni. Sprinkle the crushed macaroni in a layer over the sliced tomatoes. Pour the canned tomatoes and juice over the crushed macaroni.
4. Preheat oven to 350°F. Rinse the eggplant under cold, running water. Slice in half lengthwise. Remove the seeds. Slice the eggplant crosswise. Place in a layer on top of the stewed tomatoes.
5. Mince the garlic by chopping it into very small pieces. Place in a small mixing bowl. Stir in the olive oil, salt, and pepper. Drizzle the mixture over the eggplant. Bake uncovered for 30 minutes.

Cilantro, also called Chinese or Mexican parsley, is an herb with a distinctive flavor similar to sage with citrus. Not everyone likes cilantro. If you've never tasted it, give it a try in a small quantity before adding to the entire recipe. If it's not for you, substitute chopped regular parsley or dried parsley flakes

BLACK BEAN BURRITOS v

What You Need:

1 cup uncooked rice

½ medium white or yellow onion

1 tablespoon vegetable oil

2 medium tomatoes

1 ripe avocado

4 (8") flour tortillas

1 (15-ounce) can black beans, with liquid

⅛ teaspoon ground cumin

⅛ teaspoon dried minced garlic

1 cup shredded Cheddar or Monterey jack cheese

¼ cup bottled salsa

¼ cup sour cream

½ cup fresh cilantro or 2 tablespoons dried parsley flakes (optional)

What You Do:

1. Cook the rice according to package directions. While the rice is cooking, chop the onion. Pour the vegetable oil into a large frying pan over medium-high heat. Add the onion and cook, stirring constantly, until lightly brown and tender. Remove from heat. Cover to keep warm. Set aside.
2. Preheat oven to 350°F. Chop the tomatoes. Set aside. Peel and slice the avocado. Set aside.

(continued on next page)

3. Place the tortillas on an ungreased baking sheet. Warm in oven for 10 minutes or until softened. (Or place between damp paper towels in the microwave on high for 40 seconds.) While the tortillas are warming, place the black beans and the liquid from the can into a medium saucepan over medium heat. Stir in the cumin and garlic until the mixture is heated through.

4. Remove the tortillas from the oven and place on serving plates. Spoon the onions in a line across the middle of each tortilla. Sprinkle with cheese and top with rice, the black bean mixture, the salsa, avocado, sour cream, and cilantro or parsley (if using).

5. Fold up the bottom ⅓ of each tortilla to cover the fillings. Fold side flaps in, over each other. Fold down the top ⅓ of the tortilla. Place on the serving plate seam-side down. Serve warm.

How Do I Know If an Avocado Is Ripe?

Fresh avocados should be stored at room temperature until they are ripe. Test for ripeness by gently squeezing the fruit. It should "give" to slight pressure. Most avocados remain green when ripe, although the lighter the color, the less ripe the fruit. The Hass variety turns black when ripe. The avocado's rough skin and pear shape have earned it the nickname "alligator pear." Both ancient Mayan and Aztec written records refer to the tropical fruit. In fact, the Aztecs considered avocados an aphrodisiac and protected all unmarried women during avocado season. The Spanish explorer Hernán Cortés ate avocados with Montezuma II in Mexico City in 1519.

MUSHROOM TOFU STIR-FRY v

Hoisin is an Asian sauce. Look for it and sesame oil in the international foods section close to such Chinese foods as canned water chestnuts. Serve this dish with white or brown rice cooked according to package instructions.

What You Need:

½ pound fresh shiitake mushrooms

4 cups hot water

1 medium white or yellow onion

1 bunch scallions (also called green onions)

1 clove garlic (or ⅛ teaspoon dried minced garlic)

2 tablespoons vegetable oil

1 tablespoon chopped fresh ginger root

3 tablespoons hoisin sauce

½ teaspoon sesame oil

½ teaspoon salt

½ teaspoon vinegar

1 (20-ounce) package silken tofu

1½ teaspoons cornstarch

1 tablespoon water

What You Do:

1. Soak the mushrooms in the 4 cups of hot water for at least 20 minutes. While the mushrooms are soaking, cut the onion in half lengthwise. Slice lengthwise. Set aside. Drain the mushrooms over a small mixing bowl to save the liquid. Remove the mushroom stems and cut the mushrooms into slices about ¼" thick. Set aside.

2. Rinse the scallions in cold, running water and remove outer skin and "tassels." Slice the scallions. Finely chop the garlic. Heat the vegetable oil in a large frying pan on medium-high. Add the scallions, garlic, mushrooms, and ginger root. Stir constantly for about 5 minutes or until the scallions are just tender and the onions are translucent. Reduce heat to low.

(continued on next page)

MUSHROOM TOFU STIR-FRY
— CONTINUED

3. In a small mixing bowl, stir together the hoisin sauce and sesame oil. Stir into the vegetables along with the salt, vinegar, and 1 cup of the soaking liquid from the mushrooms. Cook for 5 minutes, stirring occasionally.
4. Cut the tofu into 1" cubes. Set aside. Dissolve the cornstarch in 1 tablespoon water. Stir into the vegetables until well mixed and slightly thickened. Place the tofu cubes on top of the vegetables. Cover and cook for about 5 minutes, until the tofu is heated through.

How Should I Cook Mushrooms?

Grilling is only one of several ways you can cook mushrooms. Some recipes you may come across will specify a particular variety of mushroom for a particular cooking style, but in general, you can sauté, broil, bake, and microwave most types. To sauté, place about 1 tablespoon olive oil in a frying pan over medium-high heat, stirring constantly for about 3 minutes until tender. Before broiling, baking, or microwaving, brush mushrooms with olive oil, butter, or margarine. Broil for about 5 minutes, turning mushrooms after the first 2 minutes. Bake in a single layer in a shallow baking pan at 375°F for 12 to 15 minutes until brown. Microwave uncovered on high for 4 to 6 minutes.

Serve this delicious dish with tomato sauce on the side.

EGGPLANT PARMIGIANA v

What You Need:

1 medium eggplant (about 1 pound)
Vegetable oil, for frying
3 eggs
½ cup milk
1 cup all-purpose flour
3 cups bread crumbs
1 (28-ounce) can tomato sauce
4 cups shredded mozzarella cheese
Chopped fresh Italian parsley or whole fresh basil
  leaves, as needed for garnish

What You Do:

1. Rinse the eggplant under cold, running water. Remove the stem. Cut in half lengthwise and remove the seeds. Thinly slice crosswise. Pour the vegetable oil to about ½" deep in a large frying pan. Heat on medium-high. Test for correct temperature by placing a piece of the eggplant in the oil. It will sizzle if the oil is ready.

2. In a small mixing bowl, beat together the eggs and milk. Place the flour on a dinner plate. Place the bread crumbs on another plate. Dip both sides of each eggplant slice first in the flour, then in the egg mixture. Place on the bread crumbs and press so the bread crumbs stick. Fry each piece of eggplant in the oil for about 3 minutes, until golden brown. Drain on paper towels.

3. Preheat oven to 350°F. Layer the eggplant slices in the bottom of an ovenproof baking dish that has been sprayed with nonstick cooking spray. Top each slice with 1 teaspoon of tomato sauce and a rounded teaspoon of the cheese. Bake for 15 minutes, until the cheese melts and the dish is brown and bubbling. Sprinkle with fresh chopped parsley or fresh whole basil.

Here's a chance to use the broiler in your oven for hot open-face sandwiches you can serve for lunch or a dinner entrée. Or, cut the bread slices in half and serve as an appetizer.

OPEN-FACE VEGGIE MELT v

What You Need:
½ eggplant (about 8 ounces)

1 medium zucchini, cut in half horizontally, then cut in half lengthwise

1 medium tomato, cut horizontally into 8 slices

3 slices mozzarella cheese, sliced into 4 strips

⅓ cup bottled Italian salad dressing

3 tablespoons mayonnaise

½ teaspoon dried basil

4 (¾"-thick) slices Italian bread

What You Do:
1. Rinse the eggplant and zucchini under cold, running water. Slice the eggplant into 8 (¼"-wide) slices.
2. Place the eggplant and zucchini on a cookie sheet that has been sprayed with nonstick cooking spray. Brush half of the salad dressing on the top sides of the slices. Adjust the top oven rack so it's 4" to 6" from the broiler. Cook 5 minutes.
3. While the veggies are cooking, place the mayonnaise and basil in a small mixing bowl. Stir until well blended. Set aside.
4. Remove the cookie sheet from the oven. Turn the vegetables so the cooked side is down. Brush the uncooked side with the remaining salad dressing. Broil another 4 to 7 minutes until tender and slightly browned. Remove from oven and set aside.
5. Place the bread slices on a clean cookie sheet. Broil 1 to 2 minutes until lightly browned.
6. Remove from the oven, leaving the bread on the cookie sheet. Spread ¼ of the mayonnaise mixture on each bread slice. Top with 2 slices each of eggplant, zucchini, and tomato. Top each sandwich with 3 pieces of mozzarella.
7. Return to the oven. Broil 1 to 2 minutes until tomatoes are hot and cheese melts.

CHAPTER 9

Side Dishes

MASHED POTATOES v

Serve with your favorite toppings: butter, sour cream, chopped chives, bacon bits, and/or shredded Cheddar cheese. Or try sour cream mixed with dry ranch or French onion salad dressing mix.

What You Need:

4–6 medium red potatoes or 2 large baking potatoes
¼ cup milk
2 tablespoons butter or margarine
¼ teaspoon salt
⅛ teaspoon pepper

What You Do:

1. Rinse the potatoes under cold, running water. Peel with a potato peeler or paring knife. Cut each potato into fourths and place in a 2-quart saucepan. Cover with water. Bring to a boil over high heat. Boil for 8 to 10 minutes, until the potatoes are soft when pierced with a fork. Drain in a colander. Reduce heat to low, and return the potatoes to the saucepan.

2. Add the milk, butter (or margarine), salt, and pepper. Using an electric mixer (or by hand using a masher), whip the ingredients together until not quite smooth. (Add more milk if needed.) Serve warm.

Is Gravy Easy to Make?

Our grandmothers learned to make gravy from their mothers. With years of practice, they made pretty good gravy. But, believe me, gravy is really difficult to make. It turns out too runny or too lumpy. It's easy to burn. And, it's not worth the trouble. So, take my advice. Buy jars of prepared gravy. Place in a saucepan over medium heat until warm. Hide the empty jars.

LEVEL **E**

SERVINGS **2**

VARIATION: **GARLIC MASHED POTATOES** v

Place mashed potatoes in an ovenproof baking pan that has been sprayed with nonstick cooking spray. Sprinkle ¼ teaspoon garlic powder over the top. Stir in ¼ cup mayonnaise. Top with ½ cup shredded Cheddar cheese. Cover with aluminum foil. Bake at 350°F for 30 minutes or until warmed through.

GREEN BEAN CASSEROLE v

In a hurry? Here's a quick, easy, and attractive side dish. French-style cut green beans look prettiest in this casserole, but you can use any style of cut beans. You can also substitute canned cut green beans for frozen.

What You Need:

1 (10-ounce) package frozen French-style cut green beans

½ (7-ounce) can sliced mushrooms or mushroom stems and pieces

½ (10.75-ounce) can condensed cream of mushroom soup

⅓ cup milk

⅛ teaspoon pepper

⅔ cup canned French-fried onions (plain or Cheddar flavor)

What You Do:

1. Set out the green beans to thaw slightly so you can separate them with a fork. Preheat oven to 350°F. Spray a 2-quart ovenproof baking pan with nonstick cooking spray. Drain the mushrooms.
2. Place the green beans and mushrooms in the prepared baking pan. Stir in the condensed mushroom soup, milk, pepper, and ½ of the French-fried onions; mix well. Top with the remaining onions. Bake uncovered for 30 minutes. Or, microwave on high for 3 to 4 minutes, until heated through.

Serve this casserole as a vegetarian side dish or as a main course. Use spaghetti sauce from a jar or make your own.

ITALIAN ZUCCHINI v

What You Need:

4 small zucchini (about 6"–8" long)

½ medium white or yellow onion

2 tablespoons butter or margarine

2 cups spaghetti sauce

¼ teaspoon garlic salt

2 tablespoons grated Parmesan cheese

What You Do:

1. Rinse the zucchini under cold, running water. Cut crosswise into ½"-thick slices. Chop the onion. Heat the butter (or margarine) in a large frying pan over medium heat. Add the zucchini and onion. Cook, stirring constantly, for 1 to 2 minutes.
2. Reduce heat to medium-low. Stir in the spaghetti sauce, garlic salt, and Parmesan cheese. Cover and simmer for 6 to 8 minutes, until the zucchini is tender but still firm.

What Kinds of Zucchini Are There?

Zucchini, which looks a little like a cucumber, is a type of squash known as "summer squash." Despite its name, summer squash is available year-round. Summer squash, which has a soft shell and edible seeds, is distinguished from winter squash, which has a hard shell. Zucchini has a mild flavor. You can cook zucchini or eat it raw by itself or with dip or in salad. When purchasing, look for firm texture and shiny skin that is free from pits or other injury. Also avoid zucchini with yellowish areas on the skin. Smaller zucchini are more tender than large ones.

CHEESY ASPARAGUS v

A creamy Cheddar topping adds color and flavor to the asparagus for an attractive accent to entrées without sauces. Do not substitute canned asparagus—it will be too mushy and too salty.

What You Need:

1 pound fresh asparagus

Seasoned salt, to taste

2 eggs

¼ cup evaporated milk

½ cup shredded Cheddar cheese

¼ teaspoon salt

⅛ teaspoon pepper

½ cup shredded mozzarella cheese

What You Do:

1. Steam the asparagus (see Appendix C) and sprinkle with seasoned salt. Spray a shallow 9" × 12" ovenproof baking pan with nonstick cooking spray. Preheat oven to 350°F.
2. Place the asparagus in the prepared pan. Use a fork to stir together the eggs (break the yolks), milk, Cheddar cheese, salt, and pepper. Pour the mixture over the asparagus. Top with mozzarella cheese. Bake uncovered for 15 to 20 minutes, until the cheese melts.

What Is Evaporated Milk?

Evaporated milk, also called condensed milk, is whole milk cooked until only 40 percent of its water content remains. You can buy evaporated milk or evaporated skim milk in 5-ounce or 12-ounce cans, usually found in the baking aisle of the grocery store. Do not confuse evaporated milk with sweetened condensed milk, which has added sugar, and never substitute evaporated or condensed milk for the sweetened variety.

ORANGE-GLAZED CARROTS v

If you use whole carrots, clean, peel, and slice them before cooking. You can substitute canned or frozen carrots for fresh without precooking them.

What You Need:

1 cup fresh baby carrots

⅛ teaspoon salt

2 tablespoons butter or margarine

1½ teaspoons granulated sugar

¼ cup orange juice

1 tablespoon dried parsley flakes

What You Do:

1. Place the carrots in a small saucepan. Add the salt and about ½" of water in the bottom of the pan. Bring to a boil over high heat. Cover and cook for 10 to 15 minutes, until tender. Drain.
2. While the carrots are cooking, melt the butter (or margarine) over low heat in a small frying pan. Add the sugar and orange juice. Stir until the sugar dissolves.
3. When the carrots are done (and drained), stir in the orange juice mixture. Cover and heat over low heat until warm. Sprinkle with parsley.

You might think you don't like these vegetables that look like little cabbages, but before you give up on them, try them this way.

BRUSSELS SPROUTS TO DIE FOR v

What You Need:

16 fresh Brussels sprouts

Olive oil, as needed

Coarse sea salt or kosher salt, as needed

What You Do:

1. Preheat the oven to 375°F. Rinse Brussels sprouts under cold, running water. Remove stems and outer leaves. Place the sprouts in an ovenproof baking pan.
2. Generously sprinkle with olive oil.
3. Generously sprinkle with coarse sea salt or kosher salt.
4. Bake uncovered 45 minutes to 1 hour until tender.

This recipe turns boring peas into a delightful side dish that goes well with seafood, pork, or poultry, and a baked potato (see the "How Do I Bake a Potato?" sidebar with the Beef and Onion Roast recipe in Chapter 5).

PEAS WITH MINT BUTTER v

What You Need:

3 tablespoons butter

2 cups frozen peas

Water, as needed to cook the peas

1 tablespoon chopped fresh mint leaves

2 tablespoons lemon juice

What You Do:

1. Place the butter in a small mixing bowl. Set aside to soften.
2. Boil the peas in water until just tender.
3. While the peas are boiling, add the mint to the butter. Stir in the lemon juice.
4. Drain the peas and place in a serving bowl. Top with the butter mixture. Gently stir until nicely coated.

Butternut squash is known as butternut pumpkin down under in Australia and New Zealand. It tastes sweet and nutty, like cooked pumpkin flesh.

ROASTED BUTTERNUT SQUASH   v

What You Need:

1 butternut squash (about 1 pound)

2 tablespoons butter

1 tablespoon light or dark brown sugar

¼ teaspoon salt, plus more to taste, if needed

What You Do:

1. Preheat the oven to 450°F. Spray a rimmed cookie sheet with nonstick cooking spray.
2. Cut off the top and bottom of the squash so it can stand upright on the cutting board. Peel the thick skin with a vegetable peeler down to the orange flesh (this might take two or three tries with the peeler). Cut in half lengthwise. Scoop out the seeds. Cut the remaining flesh into 1½" cubes. Place in a large mixing bowl.
3. Melt the butter in a small frying pan over low heat. Drizzle over the squash. Sprinkle with the brown sugar and salt. Use two large spoons to toss the squash until evenly coated. Spread on the cookie sheet. Bake 25 minutes. Remove from oven and stir around. Put back in the oven for another 10 to 20 minutes until tender and nicely browned. Sprinkle with salt to taste, if needed.

STEAMED ARTICHOKES v

Here's a side dish you can serve as a fun appetizer for a small gathering. Teach guests how to remove the petal and enjoy.

What You Need:

2 artichokes

½ cup (1 stick) butter

Lemon juice, to taste (about 1 teaspoon)

What You Do:

1. To begin (unless you are using a thornless variety), cut off the tips and needles of each petal. For both varieties, cut off the top 1" of the whole artichoke so steam can flow through the inside. Pull off the lowest row of petals, and cut off the bottom ½" of the stem so the remainder is about 1" long. Rinse under cold, running water.

2. Set the artichokes stem-side down in a saucepan or steamer. Steam (see Appendix C) for 20 to 45 minutes, until tender. (Test by sticking a fork into the bottom of the stem. The fork should easily penetrate the stem.)

3. Cool for 2 to 4 minutes. In the meantime, melt the butter in a small saucepan. Stir in lemon juice to taste. Place the butter mixture in a serving dish to share. Serve warm.

How Should I Eat Steamed Whole Artichokes?

To eat a steamed whole artichoke, start from the bottom. Use your fingers to tear off a petal. Hold the tip of the petal between your thumb and index finger. Dip into butter mixture, place on tongue and pull off the flesh with your teeth. (You eat the larger end of the petal—the one that was attached to the plant.)

PESTO v

Pesto is a green sauce with lots of garlic that tastes good on almost everything. Spoon 1 to 2 tablespoons of the sauce onto Scrambled Eggs (see recipe in Chapter 1), pasta, or steak. Store covered in the refrigerator for up to 2 weeks. For the best results, use a food processor to make this sauce.

What You Need:

2 cups fresh basil leaves

½ cup olive oil

½ cup grated Parmesan cheese

3 cloves garlic

Freshly ground black pepper, to taste

3 tablespoons pine nuts or walnuts

What You Do:

1. Rinse the basil under cold, running water. Drain. Pat dry with paper towels. Place in a food processor. (If you don't have a food processor, cut all the ingredients into very small pieces and blend in an electric blender.)
2. Add the olive oil, cheese, garlic, pepper, and pine nuts (or walnuts). Process until the sauce is well blended. Cover and refrigerate until ready to use.

SWEET POTATO–APPLE BAKE v

For the best results, choose McIntosh, Granny Smith, or Jonathan apple varieties for this recipe. For a different flavor, you can substitute unpeeled orange slices for the apples.

What You Need:

2 sweet potatoes

2 apples

4 teaspoons butter or margarine

½ cup firmly packed brown sugar

1 teaspoon salt

Shortening, vegetable oil, or nonstick cooking spray, as needed

What You Do:

1. Rinse the sweet potatoes under cold, running water. Peel them and place in a medium saucepan and cover with water. Bring to a boil over high heat. Boil for 30 to 35 minutes. Drain and let cool. Slice crosswise into circles.
2. While the sweet potatoes are cooling, peel the apples and use a knife to remove the cores or use an apple corer (see "How Do I Use an Apple Corer?" sidebar with the Apple Oatmeal recipe in Chapter 1). Wedge into 3 pieces. In a separate medium saucepan, melt the butter (or margarine) over low heat. Stir in the brown sugar and salt. Take off heat and set aside.
3. Preheat oven to 350°F. Grease an ovenproof baking pan with solid shortening or vegetable oil, or spray with nonstick cooking spray. Layer ½ of the sweet potato slices in the bottom of the prepared baking pan. Layer ½ of the apple slices on top. Drizzle ½ of the butter mixture over the apples. Repeat with another layer of sweet potato slices, apple slices, and the remaining butter mixture. Bake for 1 hour.

Using fresh potatoes (instead of canned yams) is important in this recipe with a secret. The secret is the white potato added to the mixture. (Don't tell!)

MASHED SWEET POTATOES

What You Need:

5 large sweet potatoes

2 large baking potatoes

2 tablespoons butter

¼ cup firmly packed brown sugar

⅛ teaspoon salt

¼ cup whole milk

2 cups miniature marshmallows (optional)

What You Do:

1. Peel and slice the sweet potatoes and baking potatoes. Place in a large saucepan and cover with water. Boil over high heat for about 20 minutes or until tender. Drain.

2. Preheat oven to 350°F. Add the butter, brown sugar, and salt to the potatoes. Use a potato masher or electric mixer to mash. Add milk 1 tablespoon at a time until the mixture has the consistency of mashed potatoes. (Add more milk if necessary.)

3. Place the mixture in a 9" × 12" ovenproof baking pan that has been sprayed with nonstick cooking spray. Top with miniature marshmallows (if using). Refrigerate to let flavors blend about an hour until almost ready to serve. Bake for 20 to 25 minutes, until the marshmallows are melted and slightly browned.

BAKED SLICED POTATOES & ONION v

This potato side dish is easier and more flavorful than regular baked potatoes— in half the time. Garnish with fresh parsley.

What You Need:

2 baking potatoes

½ medium white or yellow onion

2½ tablespoons butter or margarine

¼ teaspoon garlic salt

Salt and pepper, to taste

What You Do:

1. Preheat oven to 350°F. Rinse the potatoes under cold, running water. Peel and cut crosswise into slices. Place in a 9" × 12" ovenproof baking pan. Slice the onion. Separate into individual rings and mix in with the potato slices.

2. Cut the butter (or margarine) into pats and spread around the top of the potatoes and onions. Sprinkle with garlic salt, salt, and pepper. Cover tightly with aluminum foil. Bake for 30 minutes. Or, cover with baking pan lid or plastic wrap, and microwave on high for about 6 minutes until the potatoes are tender. (Do not use aluminum foil in a microwave.)

What Is the Difference Between Slicing and Dicing?

"Slice" means to cut pieces of food using parallel lines. You can slice foods lengthwise or crosswise. For roasted meat, you want to slice against the grain, or crosswise. If you cut meat with the grain, you'll see long lines in the meat. Cutting crosswise makes the meat easier to chew. "Dice" means to cut into cubes. The easiest way to dice is to slice lengthwise but keep the food in place as if it were still whole. Then slice crosswise.

This sauce adds zesty flavor to fresh asparagus. You can substitute 1 teaspoon cornstarch for the 2 teaspoons flour. A wooden spoon works well to stir the sauce to prevent sticking or burning.

ASPARAGUS WITH ALMOND SAUCE

What You Need:

¼ cup slivered almonds

1 tablespoon butter or margarine

⅓ cup water

2 teaspoons all-purpose flour

½ teaspoon chicken-flavored bouillon granules

2 teaspoons lemon juice

⅛ teaspoon pepper

1 pound fresh asparagus

What You Do:

1. Cook the almonds in the butter (or margarine) in a large frying pan over medium-high heat for 3 to 5 minutes, stirring constantly until golden brown. Reduce heat to low.
2. In a medium mixing bowl, stir together the water, flour, bouillon granules, lemon juice, and pepper until well blended. Add to the almonds in the frying pan. Cook over medium heat, stirring constantly, until the mixture comes to a boil. Boil for 1 minute. Remove from heat. Keep warm.
3. Steam the asparagus (see Appendix C). Arrange on a serving platter. Pour the sauce over the asparagus. Serve immediately.

STIR-FRY PARSNIP MEDLEY v

Consider color combinations when planning your menu. This bright orange and white dish offers a nice contrast with green vegetables or salads. You can bake the unused half of the sweet potato and serve with butter and brown sugar. Or, use it in Curried Vegetable Stew (see recipe in Chapter 3).

What You Need:

1 carrot

1 parsnip

½ sweet potato

2 tablespoons olive oil

¼ teaspoon minced dried garlic

What You Do:

1. Rinse the carrot, parsnip, and sweet potato under cold water and peel. Cut the vegetables into sticks about 3" long and about ¼" wide and ¼" thick.
2. Coat the bottom of a large frying pan with olive oil and heat on medium-high. Stir in the carrot, parsnip, sweet potato, and garlic. Stirring constantly, cook until tender but still firm.

What Is a Parsnip?

A parsnip is a specialty root vegetable that looks like a white carrot and tastes like a sweet potato. You may have to ask where they are in the produce section of your grocery store, as parsnips don't get the same shelf space allotment as other more popular vegetables.

BROCCOLI-CAULIFLOWER BROIL v

You can substitute 1 cup each of frozen cauliflower and broccoli. If you use frozen, you don't steam them. Thaw before chopping.

What You Need:

½ head cauliflower

½ head broccoli

⅓ cup sour cream

½ cup shredded Cheddar cheese

What You Do:

1. Rinse the cauliflower and broccoli under cold, running water. Steam them (see Appendix C). Chop and place in an ovenproof baking pan that has been sprayed with nonstick cooking spray. Move the top oven rack into a position closest to the broiler element. Preheat broiler.

2. In a medium mixing bowl, stir together the sour cream and cheese. Spoon the mixture over veggies. Broil for 10 to 15 minutes until lightly browned and heated through.

Hot and cheesy, this yummy side dish goes well with Roast Beef (see recipe in Chapter 5), Pork Roast (see recipe in Chapter 5), or Roast Chicken (see recipe in Chapter 6).

TWICE-BAKED POTATO CASSEROLE

What You Need:
6 red russet potatoes
1 cup water
2 chicken bouillon cubes
4 scallions (also called green onions)
1½ cups sour cream
¾ cup small-curd cottage cheese
2 cups shredded Cheddar cheese, divided

What You Do:

1. Bake the potatoes (see the "How Do I Bake a Potato?" sidebar with the Beef and Onion Roast recipe in Chapter 5). Let cool. Peel and cut into 1" cubes. Place in a 10" × 15" ovenproof baking pan that has been sprayed with nonstick cooking spray.
2. Preheat oven to 350°F. In a small saucepan, bring the water to a boil over high heat. Add the chicken bouillon cubes. Stir until dissolved. Pour over the potatoes.
3. Rinse the scallions in cold, running water and remove outer skin and "tassels." Slice the scallions, including the green tops. Add to the potatoes, along with the sour cream, cottage cheese, and 1 cup of the Cheddar cheese. Gently stir until well blended. Top with remaining Cheddar cheese. Bake uncovered for 30 to 35 minutes, until the cheese melts and bubbles.

LEVEL **M**
SERVINGS **6**

VARIATION: BAKED MASHED POTATO CASSEROLE v

Instead of baking the potatoes, boil them until tender and mash them. Omit the chicken bouillon cubes and water. Sprinkle with paprika.

You can serve this cheesy rice dish as a vegetarian main course or as a side dish for non-vegetarians with beef, chicken, or pork.

RICE CASSEROLE v

What You Need:

1 cup uncooked rice

1 medium white or yellow onion

½ cup butter

1 (8-ounce) can sliced, diced, or crushed tomatoes, with juice

2 cups shredded Cheddar cheese

1 cup water

Salt and pepper, to taste

What You Do:

1. Preheat oven to 350°F. Place the rice in an ungreased 2½-quart ovenproof baking pan.
2. Chop the onion and add to the baking pan. Slice the butter into chunks of about 2 tablespoons each. Add to the pan. Stir in the tomatoes, cheese, and water. Sprinkle with salt and pepper. Cover and bake for 1 hour.

HOT BEANS AND CORN v

Hot! Too hot! You have to love spicy to enjoy this dish. Serve with something cheesy to balance the meal. Keep a pitcher of ice water handy.

What You Need:

1 medium white or yellow onion

1 tablespoon vegetable oil

1 (16-ounce) can baked beans

1 (10-ounce) package frozen corn

2 teaspoons vinegar

½ teaspoon hot pepper sauce

What You Do:

1. Chop the onion. Pour the oil into a large saucepan over medium-high heat. Add the onion. Cook until the onion is tender, stirring constantly. Stir in the beans and corn, and bring the mixture to a boil.
2. Reduce heat to low. Cover and cook for about 5 minutes or until warmed through. Stir in the vinegar and hot pepper sauce. Serve warm.

This tangy side dish goes well with sausages, Hot German Potato Salad (see recipe in Chapter 4), or other German dishes.

WARM RED CABBAGE

What You Need:
1 head red cabbage
1 small white or yellow onion
2½ cups water, divided
2 teaspoons salt, divided
4 slices bacon
2 tablespoons firmly packed brown sugar
2 tablespoons all-purpose flour
⅓ cup white vinegar
⅛ teaspoon pepper

What You Do:

1. Shred the cabbage using the large holes on a grater. Set aside. Slice the onion. Set aside.
2. Place the cabbage in a large saucepan. Add 2 cups of the water and 1 teaspoon of the salt. Bring to a boil over high heat. Cover and reduce heat to low. Cook for 5 to 8 minutes, until cabbage is tender but still firm. Remove from heat. Drain and return the cabbage to the saucepan. Cover to keep warm and set aside.
3. Fry the bacon (see Makin' Bacon recipe in Chapter 1). Move bacon to paper towels to drain. Pour ½ of the bacon fat into an empty can, chill in refrigerator until solid, and discard or pour into a heat-proof container and save to flavor eggs or other foods. (Do not pour bacon fat down the sink; it will clog your pipes.) Leave ½ of the bacon fat in the pan. Reduce heat to low.
4. Add the brown sugar and flour to the bacon fat remaining in the frying pan. Stir until well blended. Stir in the onion, remaining ½ cup water and 1 teaspoon salt, the vinegar, and pepper. Cook for about 5 minutes or until the mixture thickens.
5. Pour the dressing over the cabbage in the saucepan. Crumble the bacon over the top. Cook over low heat, stirring until well coated and heated through. Serve warm.

BAKED POTATO LATKES v

You can make the latkes the night before, cover, and store in the refrigerator overnight. Reheat for about 10 minutes at 350°F. Serve with applesauce or sour cream and sugar. For party appetizers, make latkes 1" in diameter.

What You Need:

1 tablespoon vegetable oil

1 (20-ounce) package frozen hash brown potatoes

3 eggs

½ cup all-purpose flour

2 teaspoons salt

½ teaspoon pepper

6 scallions (also called green onions)

What You Do:

1. Use 1 teaspoon of the vegetable oil to grease each of 2 cookie sheets. Preheat oven to 450°F. Set out frozen potatoes to slightly thaw in a medium mixing bowl. In a separate, large mixing bowl, beat eggs. Stir in flour, the remaining 1 teaspoon of vegetable oil, salt, and pepper. Set aside.

2. Rinse the scallions in cold, running water and remove outer skin and "tassels." Cut scallions into very small pieces, including about 6" of the dark green tops (to make about 1 cup). Add to the egg mixture in the large mixing bowl. Add hash browns about 1 cup at a time. Use 2 forks to toss ingredients. Repeat until all ingredients are well mixed.

3. Pour about ⅓ cup of the potato mixture onto a cookie sheet for each latke. Use a spatula to spread and slightly flatten the mixture into a pancake shape.

4. Bake 10 minutes or until golden brown on the bottom. Remove from oven. Use a spatula to flip over latkes. Switch position of the cookie sheets, so that the one that was on the top oven rack is now on the bottom and vice versa. Bake about 5 more minutes until second side is golden brown.

This recipe turns ordinary green beans into a flavorful delight. The pecans add a sweet crunch, and the garlic just makes them taste good.

GARLIC GREEN BEANS WITH PECANS v

What You Need:

4 cloves garlic

2 tablespoons butter

⅛ teaspoon cayenne pepper

1 pound whole green beans

Salt, to taste

⅛ teaspoon granulated sugar

½ cup water

Black pepper, to taste

4 tablespoons chopped pecans

What You Do:

1. Remove the skin from the garlic cloves. Slice crosswise.
2. Melt the butter in a large, covered frying pan over medium heat. Add the garlic. Sprinkle with the cayenne pepper. Stir until the garlic is lightly toasted.
3. Add the green beans. Sprinkle with the salt and sugar. Cook for 2 minutes, stirring occasionally.
4. Add the water. Cover. Cook for 5 to 6 minutes, until beans are just tender. Leave on the heat and uncover. Continue cooking until the water evaporates.
5. Season with the pepper. Add the pecans and stir until evenly distributed.

RED BEANS AND RICE

You'll have to start preparing this traditional dish from the Big Easy the night before serving. Choose your favorite sausage. Serve with cooked rice, either on the side or mixed together with the beans. For faster preparation, you can substitute 2 (16-ounce) cans of red beans (drained), omit the overnight soaking, and reduce the cooking time until the onion and green bell pepper are just tender.

What You Need:

1 (16-ounce) package dried small red beans

Water, as needed

1 medium white or yellow onion

½ green bell pepper

2 cloves garlic

½ pound sausage

Cayenne pepper, to taste

Salt and pepper, to taste

What You Do:

1. Place the dried beans in a colander and rinse with cool, running water. Place the beans in a large mixing bowl or Dutch oven. Fill with enough cold water to cover the beans. Set aside for 8 hours or overnight (but not longer than 24 hours).
2. Drain the beans and rinse with cold water. Drain again. Place the beans in a Dutch oven or large pot.
3. Chop the onion, green bell pepper, and garlic. Add to the beans. Slice the sausage and add it to the beans. (If using ground sausage, crumble into the beans.) Cover the ingredients with water. Season with cayenne, salt, and pepper. Cover and cook over medium heat, stirring occasionally, until the beans are tender, about 1 to 1½ hours. During the cooking, add water as needed to keep all the ingredients simmering in thick gravy.

ROASTED PEPPERS v

This colorful side dish goes well with roasted or grilled meat or fish and rice.

What You Need:

2 red bell peppers

2 yellow bell peppers

1 clove garlic

1 tablespoon olive oil

8 large leaves fresh basil

2 tablespoons lemon juice

Salt and pepper, to taste

What You Do:

1. Preheat the broiler. Cut the peppers in half lengthwise. Remove the stems and seeds. Place on a broiling pan, cut-side down. Broil for about 5 minutes until the peeling skin is black. Remove from the oven and place in a covered bowl to cool.
2. Remove the skin from the garlic clove and slice crosswise. Place in a small frying pan with the olive oil over medium heat. Cook until lightly browned. Remove from heat. Set aside.
3. When the peppers have cooled, peel and cut into ½" × 1½" strips and place in a serving bowl.
4. Add the basil leaves to the small frying pan with the garlic and olive oil. Add the lemon juice, salt, and pepper. Sprinkle over the peppers. Toss until well mixed.

Even if you don't think you like cooked spinach, you may like this creamy, nutritious side dish. Just ask Popeye!

WARM SPINACH AND CREAM v

What You Need:

1 (10-ounce) box frozen chopped spinach

¼ cup chopped onion

Water, as needed

¼ cup butter

⅛ teaspoon salt

½ cup sour cream

1 teaspoon vinegar

What You Do:

1. Place the spinach and the onion in a large saucepan with about 1" of water. Cover. Boil over high heat until the spinach is just tender. Pour the mixture into a colander and top with paper towels. Press to squeeze out as much water as possible.
2. Melt the butter in the same saucepan over medium heat. Stir in the spinach and onion mixture. Add the salt and sour cream. Stir until well blended. Stir in the vinegar. Serve warm.

BAKED BEANS

This summer favorite goes well with anything grilled or smoked outdoors. Serve warm alongside hamburgers, hot dogs, chicken, or ribs. For indoor cooking, serve with Baked Ham (see recipe in Chapter 5) or Pan-Fried Chicken (see recipe in Chapter 6).

What You Need:

2 slices bacon

1 (19-ounce) can red kidney beans

1 (19-ounce) can great northern beans

1 medium onion

¾ cup ketchup

½ cup water

2 tablespoons cider vinegar

2 tablespoons molasses

2 tablespoons prepared yellow mustard

Salt and pepper, to taste

What You Do:

1. Preheat the oven to 350°F. Cook the bacon in a large frying pan over medium heat until crisp (see Makin' Bacon recipe in Chapter 1). Remove from heat. Leave the fat in the pan. Drain the bacon on paper towels. Crumble and set aside.
2. Drain both cans of beans and rinse together in a colander. Set aside.
3. Peel and chop the onion. Cook in the bacon fat over medium heat for about 5 minutes until the onion is tender and lightly golden brown. Stir in the ketchup, water, cider vinegar, molasses, mustard, beans, salt, and pepper. Reduce heat to low. Cook until the mixture forms small bubbles.
4. Spray an ovenproof baking pan with nonstick cooking spray. Transfer the mixture to the pan. Bake uncovered for 20 minutes. Stir well. Bake for another 20 minutes. Stir in the bacon. Bake 20 minutes more.

NATER'S TATERS v

Did you break up with the love of your life? Lose your job? Your cat? This mashed potato dish is the ultimate comfort food, but you'll have to work out for a month to make up for eating it! Lemon zest is the outer peel of a lemon. Serve alone or as a bed for serving grilled salmon or roast beef.

What You Need:

7 white potatoes

½ medium onion

2½ cups heavy cream

1 stick butter

1½ teaspoons salt or 1 tablespoon coarse sea salt or kosher salt

1 tablespoon freshly ground black pepper (or more, to taste)

1 whole bulb garlic

1 lemon

½ teaspoon liquid smoke

½ teaspoon Worcestershire sauce

½ teaspoon hot pepper sauce

2–3 cups grated Parmesan cheese, to taste

What You Do:

1. In a large pot, boil the whole potatoes with skin on 30 to 35 minutes over high heat until tender.
2. While the potatoes are cooking, cut the onion into two halves (¼ onion each) and place in a separate large saucepan over low heat. Add the heavy cream, butter, salt, and pepper.
3. Remove the skin of the garlic and separate and peel cloves. Mash garlic cloves and add to the cream mixture.
4. Rinse the lemon under cold, running water. Use a grater or a sharp knife to scrape off 1 teaspoon of the yellow peel (this is called "zest"). Add the lemon zest to the cream mixture. Juice the lemon and add the juice to the cream mixture. Stir in the liquid smoke, Worcestershire sauce, and hot pepper sauce until well blended. Stir occasionally.

(continued on next page)

NATER'S TATERS — CONTINUED

5. Drain the potatoes. Return the potatoes to the pot over high heat. Mash with a potato masher. Let sit uncovered on the hot burner for 3 minutes, until most of the moisture has evaporated.
6. Remove the cream mixture from the burner and turn off the heat. Reduce the heat under the potatoes to low. Use a slotted spoon to remove the onion and garlic from the cream mixture. Pour the mixture a little at a time into the mashed potatoes. Leaving the potatoes over the heat, use an electric mixer to blend to the preferred consistency. (The result will be thicker than traditional mashed potatoes.)
7. Sprinkle the Parmesan cheese over the potatoes. Continue cooking 2 to 3 minutes until heated through.

SPAGHETTI SQUASH AU GRATIN v

Spaghetti squash is an oblong winter squash with large seeds that look like pumpkin seeds. Its color varies from ivory to yellow to orange. You can substitute it for pasta in many recipes. If you'd like more spice, add more red pepper flakes than called for.

What You Need:

½ small yellow onion

1 medium spaghetti squash

Water, as needed

2 tablespoons butter

¼ teaspoon red pepper flakes, or more to taste

1 teaspoon fresh thyme

Salt and pepper, to taste

½ cup sour cream

½ cup shredded Cheddar cheese, divided

What You Do:

1. Peel and thinly slice the onion.
2. Cut the spaghetti squash in half lengthwise without cutting the stem. Use a spoon to scoop out the seeds. Place rind-side up in a microwave-safe dish. Add ¼ inch of water. Cover and microwave for 10 to 12 minutes until soft. Let cool for 10 minutes.
3. Preheat the oven to 375°F.
4. Use a fork to shred the squash flesh into strings that look like spaghetti. Place in a small mixing bowl.
5. Place the butter, onions, red pepper flakes, and thyme in a medium frying pan over medium heat. Stir as the mixture cooks. When the onions are slightly brown, sprinkle with salt and pepper. Remove from heat and add the mixture to the bowl of squash. Stir in the sour cream and half the cheese. Mix well.
6. Transfer the mixture from the bowl to an ovenproof baking dish that has been sprayed with nonstick cooking spray. Sprinkle with the rest of the cheese.
7. Bake for 15 to 20 minutes until golden brown.

RICE PILAF

Pilaf means rice cooked in a seasoned broth. If you find cooking rice on the stovetop challenging, you'll love this oven-baked recipe for a classic side dish.

What You Need:

½ onion

2 tablespoons butter

2 tablespoons olive oil

2 cups uncooked long-grain white rice

3 cups chicken stock

1½ teaspoons salt

¼ teaspoon cayenne pepper

What You Do:

1. Preheat oven to 350°F. Peel and chop the onion. Place the butter and olive oil in a large saucepan over medium heat. Add the onion. Stir about 7 to 8 minutes until the onion is light brown. Remove from heat.
2. Place the onions in a 9" × 13" ovenproof baking dish that has been sprayed with nonstick cooking spray. Stir in the rice. Set aside.
3. In a large saucepan over high heat, stir together the chicken stock, salt, and cayenne pepper. Cook until the mixture boils. Reduce heat to low. Cook uncovered for 5 minutes. Pour over the rice and onions in the baking pan. Stir well. Spread evenly. Tightly cover with heavy-duty aluminum foil. Place the baking dish on a cookie sheet. Put both in the oven for 35 minutes.
4. Take out of the oven. Leave covered for 10 minutes. Uncover and fluff with a fork.

Parmesan cheese adds a nice zing to ordinary broccoli. You can substitute panko crumbs for the bread crumbs.

PARMESAN BROCCOLI v

What You Need:

1 (16-ounce) package frozen broccoli florets, thawed

2 cloves garlic

1 tablespoon olive oil

Black pepper, to taste

½ cup plain bread crumbs, divided

½ cup grated Parmesan cheese, divided

What You Do:

1. Place an ovenproof baking pan on the bottom rack of the oven and preheat to 450°F.
2. Place the broccoli in a large mixing bowl.
3. Remove the skin from the garlic. Slice crosswise. Add to the broccoli along with the olive oil, pepper, ½ of the bread crumbs, and ½ of the Parmesan cheese. Toss to lightly coat.
4. Take the hot baking pan out of the oven. Place the broccoli mixture into it. Top with the rest of the bread crumbs and Parmesan cheese. Bake for 15 minutes or until just golden brown.

CHAPTER 10
Snacks and Appetizers

Easy

Medium

Hard

These picnic and potluck favorites also make a quick lunch or snack. Because they contain mayonnaise that can easily spoil, take care to keep them cold until ready to eat—especially on a hot day. If available, use a serving plate with depressions made especially for deviled eggs.

DEVILED EGGS v

What You Need:

6 eggs

¼ cup mayonnaise or mayonnaise-like salad dressing

½ teaspoon prepared mustard

Salt and pepper, to taste

Paprika, as needed

What You Do:

1. Hard-boil the eggs (see Boiled Egg recipe in Chapter 1). Peel off the shells. Cut the eggs in half lengthwise. Remove the yolks and place them in a medium mixing bowl. Place the egg whites, rounded-side down, on a serving plate.
2. Mash the yolks with a fork. Stir in the mayonnaise, mustard, salt, and pepper. (Adjust measurements to taste.) Use a spoon to heap the mixture back into the holes in the egg white halves. Sprinkle with paprika. Refrigerate until ready to eat.

This Popcorn is the perfect treat for movie night at home. When serving, add more melted butter or salt if you like. Enjoy the show.

POPCORN v

What You Need:

4 tablespoons butter (optional)

2 tablespoons vegetable oil

½ cup popping corn

Salt, to taste

What You Do:

1. Melt the butter (if using) in a small saucepan over low heat. Remove from the heat.
2. Place the oil in a large pot with a lid over medium-high heat. Throw in three or four pieces of the popping corn. Cover and wait until you hear the corn pop.
3. Add the rest of the popping corn to the pot. Cover and return to the heat. Use a potholder to hold the lid on and shake the pot a few times. When the popping increases in speed, keep shaking. When the pops slow down to about 3 seconds between each pop, remove from the heat.
4. Place popcorn in a large serving bowl. Drizzle with the melted butter (if using) and salt, to taste.

It takes just a minute to transform an ordinary apple into a tasty snack. This dip tastes best with tart apple varieties like Granny Smith and McIntosh. If you have time, make the dip ahead and let it chill before eating.

APPLE DIP v

What You Need:

1 (8-ounce) package cream cheese

1 cup loosely packed dark brown sugar

2 teaspoons vanilla extract (or imitation)

2 apples

Lemon juice, as needed (a few drops)

What You Do:

1. Let the cream cheese soften at room temperature for about 10 minutes. Place in a small mixing bowl. Add the brown sugar and vanilla extract. Stir until well blended. Cover and chill for at least 1 hour to give the flavors a chance to mingle.
2. Rinse apples under cold, running water. Pat dry with a paper towel. Cut apples in half. Remove cores. Slice apples. Or, use an apple corer (see "How Do I Use an Apple Corer?" sidebar with the Apple Oatmeal recipe in Chapter 1). Sprinkle a few drops of lemon juice on the apples to help prevent them from turning brown. Serve with the dip.

How Can I Keep Fruits from Turning Brown?

Fruits such as apples, bananas, and pears tend to turn brown after slicing. If you're using these fruits with dips or in salads, you can prevent this browning by sprinkling a few drops of lime or lemon juice on the fruit before serving. You can omit this step if the salad dressing includes lime or lemon juice as an ingredient.

S'MORES

What You Need:

2 graham cracker squares

½ flat-shaped chocolate bar (with or without nuts)

1 marshmallow

What You Do:

1. If outdoors, roast marshmallow on a stick over a wood fire and then assemble the s'more: graham cracker square, then chocolate square, then marshmallow, then graham cracker square. Otherwise, place chocolate square on top of 1 graham cracker square. Place marshmallow on top of chocolate.

2. Place on a microwave-safe plate. Microwave on high for 10 to 15 seconds until marshmallow softens. Remove from oven. Place second graham cracker square on top. Squish together.

Here's nutty granola for a quick snack or breakfast on the go. No need to refrigerate.

NUTTY HOMEMADE GRANOLA v

What You Need:

2 tablespoons butter or margarine

2 tablespoons honey

2 tablespoons firmly packed brown sugar

1 cup uncooked oatmeal (not instant)

¼ cup sunflower kernels

¼ cup sliced almonds

What You Do:

1. In a large frying pan, melt butter (or margarine) over low heat. Stir in honey and brown sugar until well blended. Stir in oatmeal, sunflower kernels, and almonds. Cook and stir for 4 to 5 minutes.
2. Spread (loose) on cookie sheet to cool. When cooled, store in an airtight container.

What would a party be without guacamole? Serve with corn or tortilla chips. Or, serve it as a garnish for Tacos (see recipe in Chapter 5), Quick Vegan Enchiladas (see recipe in Chapter 8), or other festive Mexican dishes.

EASY GUACAMOLE v

What You Need:

2 ripe avocados

2 tablespoons lemon juice

1–2 teaspoons cayenne pepper hot sauce, to taste

1 small tomato

1 small white onion

What You Do:

1. Cut the avocados in half lengthwise, cutting around the seed. Remove the seed. Hold ½ of the avocado by the peel and squeeze together to squeeze the avocado flesh into a small mixing bowl. Repeat with the other half. Mash with a fork. Stir in the lemon juice. Add the cayenne pepper hot sauce 1 teaspoon at a time, to taste.
2. Chop the tomato and onion. Stir into the mashed avocados. Chill for 1 hour before serving.

ARTICHOKE PARMESAN DIP v

The aroma of melting Parmesan cheese will fill the kitchen as you heat this tangy dip. Serve with wheat crackers. Do not substitute mayonnaise-like salad dressing for the mayonnaise in this recipe.

What You Need:

1 (14-ounce) can artichoke hearts

1 cup mayonnaise

⅓ cup grated Parmesan cheese

½ teaspoon garlic powder

What You Do:

1. Preheat oven to 350°F. Drain the artichoke hearts. Chop into very small pieces (about ¼" square or smaller). Place into an ungreased 9" × 12" ovenproof baking pan.
2. Stir in the mayonnaise, Parmesan cheese, and garlic powder until well mixed. Bake for 20 minutes or until bubbly.

What Else Can I Do with Artichokes?

If you're unfamiliar with artichokes, don't let their unusual appearance scare you away. Some varieties of fresh artichokes have prickly points, so use the stem as a handle during purchase and preparation. Before steaming, slice off the tip and the thorn from each petal. You can steam artichokes or microwave them together with about ⅜ cup water, 1 teaspoon vegetable oil, and 1 teaspoon lemon juice in a covered, microwave-safe bowl for 6 to 8 minutes. Prepare several at one time. Cover and refrigerate. Leftovers will store for several days for quick snacks.

For blue cheese lovers only! This dip has a strong flavor that goes well with sliced cucumbers; zucchini; red, yellow, and green peppers; and cool, crisp chunks of celery and baby carrots.

BLUE CHEESE VEGGIE DIP v

What You Need:

1 (8-ounce) package cream cheese

⅛ teaspoon garlic salt

⅛ teaspoon seasoned salt

Milk, as needed

4 ounces crumbled blue cheese

What You Do:

1. Unwrap the cream cheese and place in a mixing bowl. Set aside at room temperature for 10 to 15 minutes to soften.
2. Add the garlic salt and seasoned salt to the cream cheese, and stir in by hand or beat with an electric mixer. Add the milk 1 tablespoon at a time to thin the mixture. Beat until smooth. The mixture should be smooth and thick enough for a spoon to stand up in it.
3. Stir in the blue cheese. Refrigerate for at least 1 hour before serving.

Should I Use Block or Softened Cream Cheese?

When purchasing cream cheese for a recipe, choose the block of cream cheese that comes in a box unless otherwise specified. The whipped cream cheese that comes in a tub has added air. If you use that type, your measurement will be inaccurate, especially in recipes that call for heating the cream cheese.

TANGY MUSHROOMS v

These tangy mushrooms add variety to your party menu. They provide a nice contrast to appetizers with cheese or meat. Supply toothpicks for easy serving.

What You Need:

2 (7.3-ounce) jars or 2 (8-ounce) cans whole mushrooms
1½ teaspoons minced onion
1½ teaspoons dried parsley flakes
2 tablespoons bottled Italian salad dressing

What You Do:

1. Drain the mushrooms and place in small mixing bowl. Add the onion and parsley.
2. Sprinkle with salad dressing, and stir until heavily coated. (Excess dressing in the bottom of the bowl is okay.) Cover and refrigerate for at least 1 hour to let the flavors blend.

GOUDA GOODNESS v

The aroma of freshly baked dough and warm, creamy cheese will bring your guests into the kitchen before this delightful dish is out of the oven. You can substitute Edam, smoked Gouda, Cheddar, or any wheel-style cheese for the Gouda cheese. Provide a cheese or butter knife for cutting wedges.

What You Need:

1 (7-ounce) wheel Gouda cheese
1 (8-ounce) can refrigerated crescent roll dough

What You Do:

1. Preheat oven to 375°F. Unwrap the cheese and peel off and discard the wax covering.
2. Open the package of dough and unroll on a cutting board or other flat surface. Use your fingers to mold the dough around the cheese, so it completely covers the cheese.
3. Place the dough-covered cheese in the center of an ungreased baking sheet. Bake for 11 to 13 minutes until golden brown. Cheese should be warm and gooey, but not runny. Serve immediately.

Why just add bottled barbecue sauce to mini sausages like everyone else when this recipe is almost as easy and has a special zing? You can substitute peach preserves for the apricot. Serve with toothpicks.

TANGY SMOKED SAUSAGES

What You Need:

1 cup apricot preserves

½ cup Dijon mustard

2 scallions (also called green onions)

1 pound mini smoked sausages

What You Do:

1. Place the preserves and mustard in a small saucepan over low heat.
2. Rinse the scallions in cold, running water and remove outer skin and "tassels." Slice the scallions, including about ½ of the dark green tops. Add to the saucepan, along with the sausages. Cover and cook about 30 minutes, stirring occasionally, until heated through. Keep warm until ready to serve.

LEVEL **M**

SERVINGS **12**

WARM PECAN CHEESE DIP v

Based on appearance, your guests may expect this dip to taste spicy. Instead, it has a creamy, sweet flavor that tastes best with wheat crackers. Because the dip is served warm, prepare and serve it in a slow cooker, if possible. (During the party, stir every 30 minutes or so to keep the surface from hardening.)

What You Need:

1 (1-pound) block processed American cheese

1 cup heavy cream

1 (2-ounce) jar diced pimientos

1 (2.25-ounce) package chopped pecans

What You Do:

1. Cut the processed cheese into 1" to 2" cubes and put in a slow cooker. Add the heavy cream. Heat on high until the cheese melts. (If you don't have a slow cooker, you can complete this step in a 2-quart saucepan over low heat or in a microwave-safe mixing bowl in the microwave.)
2. When the cheese has melted, drain the pimientos, and add to the mixture. Stir in the pecans. Serve warm.

What Is Pimiento?

Pimiento is a red garden pepper often used to stuff green olives. You'll find pimiento in the canned vegetable aisle near pickles and olives. It comes in a small glass jar, so you'll have to look hard! If you can't find it, ask a grocery stocker or customer service representative.

Crustacean connoisseurs love this cracker spread. Look for bottled cocktail sauce in the ketchup aisle or near the seafood department.

CRAB CRACKER SPREAD

What You Need:

½ cup bottled cocktail sauce

1 (8-ounce) package cream cheese (do not used whipped)

1 (8-ounce) package imitation crab

1 sprig fresh parsley

What You Do:

1. Pre-chill the bottle of cocktail sauce. Unwrap the block of cream cheese and place it in the center of a serving plate. With your fingers or a fork, separate the crab into flakes. Place the flakes on top of the cream cheese, letting some pieces fall over the side. Chill in the refrigerator for at least 1 hour.
2. When ready to serve, pour the cocktail sauce over the crab. Top with parsley. Surround with crackers. Stick a cheese knife into the top for easy serving.

VARIATION: SHRIMP CRACKER SPREAD

For a shrimp variation, substitute 1 (6-ounce) can of shrimp (drained) for the imitation crab, and add ¼ teaspoon garlic powder. Both variations taste best with club crackers.

PIZZA ON RYE

Aromatic oregano adds Italian flavor to these easy and delicious party favorites. You may need several baking sheets. Or, heat in shifts. Remove warm appetizers from the oven. Place on serving tray. Cool and reuse the baking sheet for the next set of "pizzas."

What You Need:

1 pound mild or medium ground pork breakfast sausage

1 pound shredded Cheddar or mozzarella cheese

1 loaf party rye bread

Dried oregano, as needed

What You Do:

1. Brown the sausage in a frying pan as you would ground beef (see the "How Do I Brown Ground Beef?" sidebar with the Chili Blue recipe in Chapter 3). Drain off fat. Reduce heat to low.
2. Preheat oven to 350°F. Cut the cheese into 2" cubes. Add to the sausage. Stir together until the cheese melts.
3. Place the slices of party rye on ungreased baking sheets. Spoon about 1 tablespoon of the mixture onto each slice. Sprinkle with oregano. Bake for 5 to 10 minutes, until the mixture is bubbly. Serve warm.

What Can I Do with Party Rye Bread?

Look for party rye in the bread aisle. Loaves are small, and the slices are about ¼ the size of regular bread. For a quick snack, spread with softened cream cheese or spreadable Cheddar cheese. Or, make miniature bologna and cheese sandwiches to take to a potluck party.

Here's a tasty, high-protein appetizer everyone will love. Serve with warm pita bread or in a Hummus Pocket Sandwich (see recipe in Chapter 2). For the best results, use a food processor. If you don't have one, use an electric blender, an electric mixer, or a potato masher (this will take more elbow grease!) to make the dip smooth.

HUMMUS v

What You Need:

1 (15-ounce) can chickpeas (also called garbanzo beans)

¼ teaspoon garlic powder

3 tablespoons tahini

½ teaspoon salt

2–3 teaspoons ground cumin

2–3 tablespoons lemon juice, to taste

¼ cup olive oil

Water, as needed (up to ¼ cup)

Additional salt and pepper, to taste

Paprika (optional)

Chopped fresh parsley (optional)

What You Do:

1. Drain the chickpeas and rinse under cold water. Place in a food processor or electric blender. Add the garlic powder, tahini, ½ teaspoon salt, cumin, and 1 tablespoon of the lemon juice. Process until smooth, gradually adding the olive oil and water (up to ¼ cup) until the hummus reaches desired softness. Sprinkle with salt, pepper, and lemon juice, to taste.
2. Spread into a serving bowl. Drizzle a little olive oil and a few drops of lemon juice over the top. Sprinkle with paprika and parsley (if using).

SWEET WINGS

You can turn this Asian-flavored appetizer into a main dish by serving over cooked rice with a green vegetable or salad. Serve warm with lots of napkins.

What You Need:

2 pounds chicken wings

¼ cup soy sauce

½ cup honey

1 tablespoon butter or margarine

What You Do:

1. Rinse the chicken under cold, running water. Pat dry with a paper towel. Use a knife to separate each wing at the joint into 2 pieces. Set aside.
2. In a large mixing bowl, stir together the soy sauce and honey. Add the chicken wings to the bowl, making sure the wings are well coated with the mixture. Cover and refrigerate for at least 1 hour, or overnight.
3. Preheat oven to 400°F. Use the butter (or margarine) to grease a baking pan large enough to allow the wings to cook in a single layer. Remove the wings from the bowl and place in the pan. Spoon 2 to 3 tablespoons of the soy sauce mixture remaining in the bowl over the chicken.
4. Bake uncovered for 15 minutes. Repeat 3 times, using all of the sauce, for a total of 45 minutes of cooking time. (To prevent illness, wash hands, bowl, and any surfaces that touched the raw chicken with soap and warm water.)

Pizza flavor without the work. No long wait, and no need to tip for delivery. If you're a cheese lover, top with grated Parmesan cheese.

MINI PEPPERONI PIZZA

What You Need:

1 English muffin

¼ cup canned spaghetti sauce

Sliced pepperoni, as needed

1 scallion (also called green onion)

½ cup shredded mozzarella cheese

What You Do:

1. Preheat oven to 350°F. Slice the English muffin in half. Spread ½ of the spaghetti sauce on each half. Arrange the pepperoni slices on top of the sauce.
2. Rinse the scallion in cold, running water and remove the outer skin and "tassels." Slice the scallion, including the green top. Sprinkle ½ of the onion on each mini pizza. Top with cheese.
3. Place on a baking sheet. Bake for 10 to 12 minutes or until the cheese melts and bubbles.

BUFFALO WINGS

Some like 'em hot! You can adjust the "heat" by how much hot sauce you use. Start with a little at first to see what you like. Serve with a packet of dry ranch or blue cheese salad dressing mix made with sour cream according to package instructions.

What You Need:

HOT SAUCE
4 tablespoons butter
1–4 tablespoons bottled hot pepper sauce
2 tablespoons red or white wine vinegar
1 tablespoon minced garlic

WINGS
3 pounds chicken wings
2 tablespoons vegetable oil
Salt and pepper, to taste

What You Do:

1. **For the Hot Sauce:** Melt the butter in a small saucepan over low heat. Remove from heat. Stir in the hot sauce, wine vinegar, and garlic. Set aside until ready to use.
2. **For the Buffalo Wings:** Preheat the oven to 400°F. Use kitchen scissors or a knife to cut through the joints and separate the chicken wings into three parts. Discard the tips. Place the other two parts in a large roasting pan. Drizzle with the vegetable oil, and sprinkle with salt and pepper. Stir the wings until well coated. Spread into a single layer. Roast 25 to 35 minutes until the wings start to brown.
3. Remove the wings from the oven. Dip a barbecue brush into the chicken fat in the bottom of the pan and brush the wings. Tilt the pan and spoon out as much of the drippings as you can into a grease can and discard. See if the wings easily release from the bottom of the pan. If not, roast for another 5 to 10 minutes.
4. Turn the wings and brush with more of the drippings. Roast for another 15 to 20 minutes until the new side is browned and the wings easily come off the bottom of the pan.

(continued on next page)

BUFFALO WINGS — CONTINUED

5. Increase the oven heat to 450°F. Take the wings out of the oven, and spoon off any remaining fat from the bottom of the pan. Drizzle the sauce mixture over the wings, and stir them around until well coated. Spread out in a single layer. Return the wings to the oven and roast, stirring once or twice, for 5 to 10 minutes more until crisp.

FRESH TOMATO SALSA v

Serve this Fresh Tomato Salsa with corn chips, scrambled eggs, or hot dogs, as well as Mexican dishes. Cover and refrigerate to store up to 5 to 7 days, but serve at room temperature.

What You Need:

4 large tomatoes (about 1½ pounds)

1 medium white onion

1–2 jalapeño peppers

1 cup chopped fresh cilantro or parsley

3 tablespoons lime juice

2 teaspoons minced garlic

Salt and freshly ground black pepper, to taste

What You Do:

1. Rinse the tomatoes under cold, running water and cut into halves. Chop on a cutting board. Pour the tomatoes and the juice from the cutting board into a large mixing bowl.
2. Peel and chop the onion, and add to the bowl.
3. Cut off the stem side of the jalapeños crosswise and discard. Slice the pepper in half lengthwise. Remove the seeds and ribbing. Chop the pepper, and add to the bowl. Add the cilantro or parsley to the bowl, along with the lime juice, garlic, salt, and pepper. Mix well. Let stand at room temperature for 15 minutes.

SPINACH-STUFFED MUSHROOMS v

What You Need:

1 (12-ounce) package frozen spinach soufflé

2–3 pounds whole mushrooms

4–6 slices processed Swiss cheese

What You Do:

1. Preheat oven to 350°F. Remove the spinach soufflé from the freezer. Unwrap and place in a small mixing bowl. Thaw for about 15 to 20 minutes.
2. Wipe the mushrooms with a damp paper towel to clean. Remove the stems. Cover the stems and refrigerate for another use. Place the mushrooms cap-side down in a 9" × 13" ovenproof baking pan that has been sprayed with nonstick cooking spray.
3. Slice the cheese into 1" squares big enough to cover the top of the mushrooms without hanging over the edge.
4. Spoon about 1 to 2 teaspoons spinach soufflé into each mushroom cap. Top with a cheese square. Bake for 10 to 12 minutes, until the cheese melts.

Your party guests will want this recipe to pass along to all their friends. Don't tell them how easy it is! Serve warm with blue or yellow corn chips. (Do not use fresh Parmesan cheese in this recipe.)

SPINACH AND ARTICHOKE DIP v

What You Need:

1 (16-ounce) bag frozen chopped spinach, thawed

1 (14-ounce) can artichoke hearts

2 scallions (also called green onions)

1 cup mayonnaise

1 cup sour cream

1 cup powdered Parmesan cheese

1–2 teaspoons garlic salt, to taste

Pepper, to taste

What You Do:

1. Place spinach in a colander and rinse with cool, running water to thaw. Shake the spinach into a large, microwave-safe mixing bowl. Line the colander with paper towel. Return spinach to colander. With another paper towel on top, press the spinach to drain excess water. Rinse and dry the mixing bowl. Return spinach to the bowl.
2. Drain the artichokes. Cut into fourths. Add to the spinach.
3. Rinse the scallions and remove outer skin and "tassels." Slice crosswise. Add to the bowl.
4. Stir in the mayonnaise, sour cream, and powdered Parmesan cheese until well blended. Add garlic salt and pepper, to taste. Microwave on high for 5 minutes, and keep warm in a slow cooker. Or, instead of microwaving, heat in a slow cooker for 2 hours on low.

CHAPTER 11
Desserts

Eat as many of these Toll House Cookies as you can while they're still warm, then save the rest for later. Serve with a glass of cold milk for dipping. Or, make a chocolate chip ice cream sandwich by smearing about ¼ cup softened vanilla ice cream onto the flat side of one cookie and topping it with another, chips-side up.

TOLL HOUSE COOKIES v

What You Need:

1 cup butter

2¼ cups all-purpose flour

1 teaspoon baking soda

1 teaspoon salt

¾ cup white granulated sugar

¾ cup firmly packed brown sugar

1 teaspoon vanilla extract

2 large eggs

1 (12-ounce) package (about 2 cups) semi-sweet
 chocolate chips

1 cup chopped nuts (optional)

What You Do:

1. Set out the butter to soften. Preheat the oven to 375°F.
2. Place the flour, baking soda, and salt in a medium mixing bowl. Stir to mix well.
3. Place the softened butter, granulated sugar, brown sugar, and vanilla extract in a large mixing bowl. Use an electric mixer to beat until creamy. Add the eggs one at a time. Beat in each one until well blended.
4. Beat in the flour mixture about ¼ to ½ cup at a time. Stir in the chocolate chips and nuts, if using.
5. Scoop a rounded tablespoon of the batter onto an ungreased cookie sheet. Bake in batches of 1 dozen until you've used all the batter. (It helps to use more than one cookie sheet.) Bake 9 to 11 minutes until golden brown. Remove from the oven and let cool on the baking sheet for a couple of minutes. Then use a spatula to transfer the cookies to a wire rack to cool the rest of the way.

These cookies—the easiest ones you'll ever make—use no flour and bake like a dream. They make a great gift for coconut lovers.

COCONUT DROP COOKIES v

What You Need:

1 tablespoon solid vegetable shortening for greasing

1 (14-ounce) package flaked coconut

1 (14-ounce) can sweetened condensed milk

What You Do:

1. Preheat oven to 300°F. Use solid shortening and a paper towel or piece of waxed paper to grease a cookie sheet. In a medium mixing bowl stir together coconut and sweetened condensed milk until coconut is well coated.
2. Drop spoonsful of the mixture onto the cookie sheet. Make 3 rows of 4 drops. Bake 18 minutes or until golden brown. Use a spatula and gently move each batch to a wire cooling rack. Cool. Repeat until all of the coconut mixture has been used. Store cooled cookies in an airtight container.

These nutty cookies are fun to make. If you like, roll them in confectioners' sugar when they're still warm from the oven.

PECAN COOKIES v

What You Need:

¾ cup butter or margarine

½ cup firmly packed brown sugar

2 tablespoons vanilla extract (or imitation)

1 cup chopped pecans

What You Do:

1. Place the butter (or margarine) in a large mixing bowl to soften for 20 minutes before beginning.
2. Stir in the brown sugar until creamy. Stir in the vanilla.
3. Add the pecans to the bowl. Blend well.
4. Preheat the oven to 250°F. Break off about 1 tablespoon of the batter per cookie, and roll into a long, thin shape. Place on an ungreased cookie sheet. Repeat with the rest of the batter. Bake 10 minutes or until golden brown.

LEVEL **E**

SERVINGS **4**

Make this old-fashioned favorite in a modern slow cooker. Use leftover rice, or cook rice according to package directions.

SLOW-COOKED RICE PUDDING v

What You Need:

1½ tablespoons butter

1¼ cups cooked rice

¾ cup evaporated milk

⅓ cup granulated sugar

1 teaspoon vanilla extract (or imitation)

¼ teaspoon nutmeg

¼ cup raisins (optional)

2 eggs

What You Do:

1. Lightly coat a slow cooker with nonstick cooking spray. Place the butter in the cold slow cooker to soften for about 30 minutes.
2. Add the rice, evaporated milk, sugar, vanilla, nutmeg, and raisins (if using). Turn heat to low.
3. In a small mixing bowl, lightly beat the eggs. Add to the mixture in the slow cooker. Mix well. Cover and cook 1 hour. Remove cover and stir well. Cover and cook 1 more hour.

Use this recipe as a base for your favorite cheesecake. Top with 1 (21-ounce) can of cherry, blueberry, or strawberry pie filling or drizzle with chocolate syrup.

NO-BAKE CHEESECAKE v

What You Need:

1 (8-ounce) carton frozen whipped topping

13 ounces cream cheese

1 cup confectioners' sugar

1 (8" or 9") graham cracker crust

What You Do:

1. Set out the frozen whipped topping to thaw.
2. Unwrap the cream cheese and place in a large mixing bowl to soften for 15 to 20 minutes. When ready, add the sugar and beat with an electric mixer just until smooth. Add the thawed whipped topping, stirring from the bottom of the bowl to the top. Pour into the crust. Chill well before serving.

What's the Difference Between "Fold", "Beat", and "Whip"?

The term "fold" means to mix ingredients by sliding a spoon or spatula toward you along the bottom of the bowl, then up the side. In effect, you stir from the bottom to the top, blending ingredients by gently turning them over on top of each other. The terms "beat" and "whip" refer to rapid, circular stirring motions, using a wire whisk or electric mixer. Both methods add air to the ingredients. Beating makes ingredients smooth and fluffy. Whipping lightens the mixture and increases its volume.

This frosting traditionally tops Carrot Cake (see recipe in this chapter), but you can also use it on cookies, cinnamon rolls, or brownies. This recipe makes enough to frost a two-layer cake. You can add a little more milk or sugar to make this frosting the consistency you prefer.

CREAM CHEESE FROSTING v

What You Need:

¼ cup butter

1 (8-ounce) package cream cheese

4 cups confectioners' sugar

¼ cup milk

2 teaspoons vanilla extract

What You Do:

1. Unwrap the butter and cream cheese and place in a large mixing bowl. Set out to soften for about 20 minutes.
2. Use an electric mixer to beat the butter and cream cheese just until blended and creamy. (Do not overbeat.) While continuing to beat the mixture, slowly add the confectioners' sugar, milk, and vanilla just until well blended and creamy.

VARIATION: VANILLA BUTTER FROSTING v

Use the recipe for Cream Cheese Frosting, but omit the cream cheese and add an extra ¼ cup butter.

This creamy frosting will satisfy the chocolate lover in you. Use to frost a one-layer Yellow Cake, Homemade Brownies (see recipes in this chapter), or your favorite cake or cupcakes.

CHOCOLATE BUTTER FROSTING v

What You Need:

3 tablespoons butter or margarine

1 ounce unsweetened chocolate

2⅓ cups confectioners' sugar

¾ teaspoon vanilla extract (or imitation)

1–2 tablespoons milk

What You Do:

1. Before beginning, set out the butter (or margarine) for 10 to 15 minutes to soften at room temperature. In a saucepan over low heat, melt the chocolate. Remove from heat. Set aside.

2. Sift the confectioners' sugar into a mixing bowl or shake through a strainer 3 times. Set aside.

3. In a small mixing bowl, beat the butter with an electric mixer or by hand until fluffy. Stir in the melted chocolate, vanilla, 1 tablespoon milk, and ½ of the sugar. Beat until well blended. Slowly add remaining sugar. If the frosting becomes too thick, add more milk a little at a time until the frosting reaches the desired consistency.

HOMEMADE BROWNIES v

You can make brownies from a mix, but homemade are so much better. And they're not any harder to prepare. Be sure to cool completely before cutting. Serve plain, frost with Chocolate Butter Frosting (see recipe in this chapter), or dust on all sides with confectioners' sugar.

What You Need:

Shortening, as needed

4 (ounces) unsweetened baking chocolate

¾ cup butter or margarine

3 eggs

2 cups granulated sugar

1 teaspoon vanilla extract (or imitation)

1 cup all-purpose flour

1 cup chopped walnuts or pecans (optional)

What You Do:

1. Use the solid shortening to grease a 9" × 13" baking pan. Set aside. Preheat oven to 350°F. (If you're using a glass pan, preheat oven to 325°F.)
2. Place the baking chocolate and butter (or margarine) in a small saucepan and melt over low heat. Stir until well blended. Pour into a large mixing bowl.
3. Lightly beat the eggs and stir them into the mixing bowl, along with the sugar and vanilla, until well blended. Gently stir in the flour and nuts until all the ingredients are well mixed. Scrape into the prepared baking pan. Spread the mixture into an even layer.
4. Bake for 30 to 35 minutes. Test for doneness. Insert a toothpick into the center of the brownies and pull it out. The brownies are done if the toothpick has gooey crumbs sticking to it as opposed to wet batter. Cool completely in the pan before cutting.

BLONDIES v

What You Need:

¾ cup butter

1¾ cups tightly packed brown sugar

2 teaspoons vanilla extract

2 large eggs

1¾ cups all-purpose flour

¾ teaspoon baking soda

⅜ teaspoon salt

1 cup butterscotch chips or chopped walnuts, or ½ cup
of each

What You Do:

1. Preheat the oven to 350°F. Spray a 9" × 13" ovenproof
    baking pan with nonstick cooking spray.
2. Melt the butter in a medium saucepan over low heat.
    Remove from the heat. Stir in the brown sugar until
    well blended. Cool for 5 minutes. Stir in the vanilla.
    Crack the eggs one at a time, quickly stirring each
    into the batter.
3. Place the flour, baking soda, and salt in a small mix-
    ing bowl. Stir to mix well. Stir the flour mixture into
    the egg mixture in the saucepan until well mixed.
    Gently stir in the butterscotch chips and/or nuts.
4. Use a rubber spatula to scrape the batter into the bak-
    ing pan. Smooth the batter to distribute evenly. Bake
    24 to 28 minutes. The shorter time is for more chewy
    blondies. Test for doneness by inserting a wooden
    toothpick into the center of the blondies. It should
    come out clean. Remove from the oven and cool.
    When cool, cut into the desired number of blondies.

*Serves 9-12, depending on how you cut them.

This easy summer dessert is good any time of year. When cooled, sprinkle with confectioners' sugar, if you like. Use the leftover egg yolk in Scrambled Eggs (see recipe in Chapter 1).

LEMON BARS v

What You Need:
CAKE

¼ cup butter

¼ cup granulated sugar

1 cup all-purpose flour

¼ teaspoon salt

TOPPING

1 cup granulated sugar

2 tablespoons all-purpose flour

¼ teaspoon baking powder

⅛ teaspoon salt

1 large egg, plus 1 egg white

4 tablespoons lemon juice

What You Do:

1. **For the Cake:** Place the butter in a medium mixing bowl to soften for 10 to 15 minutes. Preheat the oven to 350°F. Spray an 8" square ovenproof baking pan with nonstick cooking spray. Use an electric mixer or a spoon with "elbow grease" to beat the butter and sugar together until the mixture is creamy. Stir in the flour and salt until well blended. Mixture will be crumbly. Spread the mixture evenly in the baking pan.
2. Bake for 8 to 10 minutes. Cake should be just golden brown on the edges. Remove from the oven and cool.
3. **For the Topping:** In a medium mixing bowl, stir together the sugar, flour, baking powder, and salt. Stir in the egg, egg white, and lemon juice until smooth. Pour over the cake. Bake 25 to 30 minutes until the topping is golden brown and bubbles form around the edges. Cool completely in the pan before cutting.

These treats are best served the same day you make them. But, you can freeze them in layers separated with waxed paper in an airtight container for up to 6 weeks. To thaw, set out at room temperature for 15 minutes.

CRISPY TREATS

What You Need:

3 tablespoons butter, plus 2 teaspoons to butter the spatula

1 (10-ounce) package regular marshmallows, or 4 cups miniature marshmallows

6 cups crispy rice cereal

What You Do:

1. Coat a 9" × 13" baking pan with nonstick cooking spray. Melt together the butter and marshmallows in a large saucepan over low heat, stirring until completely melted. Remove from heat.
2. Stir in the rice cereal 2 cups at a time. Coat well. Butter both sides of a rubber spatula. Scoop the mixture into the baking pan. Press mixture so it is evenly distributed. Cool well before cutting.

You don't need the sun to cast a shadow over these strawberries. Make your own shadow with melted chocolate. You can substitute chunks of banana for the strawberries—or use both.

SHADOW BERRIES v

What You Need:

1 pint fresh strawberries

1 tablespoon butter

1 (12-ounce) package semisweet chocolate chips

1 (11.5-ounce) bag milk chocolate chips

What You Do:

1. Rinse and clean the strawberries (see the "How Should I Clean Strawberries?" sidebar with the Fruit Pizza recipe in this chapter, except leave on the stems to use as little handles for dipping. Remove all moisture with paper towels.

2. In a saucepan over low heat, stir together the butter and both packages of chocolate chips until the chocolate melts. (Do not heat in a microwave unless you have a special dish for melting chocolate in a microwave. The heat is uneven and can affect the taste and texture.)

3. Place a cooling rack on top of several thicknesses of paper towel. Use a fork or fondue fork to "stab" each strawberry. Dip the strawberries in the melted chocolate. Place in the refrigerator for about 15 to 30 minutes only until the chocolate hardens. After that, store in a cool place, but not in the refrigerator.

FRUIT PIZZA v

This pizza really is a glorified cookie. But with fresh fruit, it tastes so good that you might forget it's good for you, too.

What You Need:

1 (18-ounce) tube refrigerated sugar cookie dough

2 (8-ounce) packages cream cheese

½ cup blueberries

½ cup green seedless grapes

½ cup strawberries

2 tablespoons confectioners' sugar

What You Do:

1. Using your hands, shape the cookie dough into a circle on an ungreased cookie sheet. Or, form the dough into a ball and use a rolling pin to roll into a circle. Bake according to package directions. Cool.
2. Let the cream cheese soften at room temperature for about 10 minutes. Spread the cream cheese in a thick layer over the cookie.
3. Rinse the blueberries and grapes under cold, running water. Drain. Pick the grapes off the stems. Slice grapes in half lengthwise. Clean the strawberries (see sidebar for more information), and slice in half lengthwise.
4. Spoon the fruit over the top of the pizza. With the back of the spoon or your fingers, gently press the fruit into the cream cheese to anchor it in place. Sprinkle with confectioners' sugar. To serve, cut into pie-shaped pieces.

How Should I Clean Strawberries?

Strawberries grow low to the ground, so rinse well to remove field dirt. Place strawberries in a large mixing bowl and soak several minutes in cold water. Pour into a colander. Repeat at least three times. With strawberries still in colander, rinse again under cold, running water. Drain. Remove the stem and green part (the large, green calyx called the hull) by cutting with a knife or using a huller, a small utensil that resembles tweezers with large flat prongs.

Here's an old-fashioned treat that's still a favorite with kids of all ages. You can omit the raisins and/or nuts if you prefer. The oats in this recipe are simply uncooked oatmeal.

OATMEAL COOKIES v

What You Need:

1 egg, lightly beaten

¼ cup butter

¼ cup firmly packed brown sugar

¼ cup white granulated sugar

¼ teaspoon vanilla extract (or imitation)

1 tablespoon milk

½ cup all-purpose flour

¼ teaspoon baking soda

¼ teaspoon salt

¾ cup oats

½ cup seedless raisins

½ cup chopped walnuts

What You Do:

1. In a large mixing bowl, stir together the egg, butter, brown sugar, white sugar, and vanilla. Stir in the milk.
2. In a separate, medium mixing bowl stir together the flour, baking soda, and salt. Slowly add the flour mixture to the large mixing bowl, stirring with a spoon or your hands until well mixed. Stir in the oats, raisins, and walnuts.
3. Preheat oven to 400°F. Scoop rounded teaspoons of dough onto an ungreased cookie sheet. Make 3 rows of 4 cookies each. Bake for 8 to 10 minutes. Use a spatula to remove the cookies from the cookie sheet. Let cool on a wire rack.

LEVEL **M**
SERVINGS **48**

Oatmeal cookies should be in every cook's repertoire, and this recipe has the added goodness of chocolate and cinnamon. You can use either regular or instant oatmeal in this recipe.

OATMEAL CHOCOLATE CHIP COOKIES v

What You Need:

1 cup (2 sticks) butter

1 cup firmly packed brown sugar

½ cup white granulated sugar

2 eggs

1 teaspoon vanilla extract (or imitation)

1½ cups all-purpose flour

1 teaspoon baking soda

2 teaspoons cinnamon

½ teaspoon salt

3 cups uncooked oatmeal

1 (12-ounce) package semisweet chocolate chips

What You Do:

1. Before you begin, place the butter in a large mixing bowl to soften for about 20 minutes. Use an electric mixer to beat together the butter, brown sugar, and white sugar until creamy. Preheat oven to 350°F.
2. In a small mixing bowl, lightly beat the eggs with a fork. Add to the bowl, along with the vanilla. Beat until smooth.
3. In a separate, medium mixing bowl, stir together the flour, baking soda, cinnamon, and salt until well mixed. Slowly add the flour mixture to the large mixing bowl, stirring with a spoon or your hands until well mixed. Stir in the oatmeal. Gently stir in the chocolate chips.
4. Scoop heaping tablespoons of the dough and drop onto an ungreased cookie sheet in 3 evenly spaced rows of 4 cookies each. Bake for 10 to 12 minutes, until golden brown. Remove from the oven and let cool for 1 minute. Use a spatula to move the cookies onto a wire rack.

(continued on next page)

VARIATION: OATMEAL CHOCOLATE CHIP BARS v

You can use the same recipe to make chocolate chip bars instead. When the dough is ready, pour into an ungreased 9" × 13" baking pan. Bake for 30 to 35 minutes. Cool in the pan. Cut into twelve 3" × 4" rectangles.

PEANUT BUTTER COOKIES v

There's nothing like warm peanut butter cookies straight from the oven. And they're quick and easy to make.

What You Need:

½ cup butter

½ cup solid shortening

1 cup peanut butter

1 cup white granulated sugar

1 cup firmly packed brown sugar

2 eggs

1 teaspoon vanilla extract (or imitation)

2¼ cups all-purpose flour

2 teaspoons baking soda

¼ teaspoon salt

What You Do:

1. Before beginning, set out the butter for 10 to 15 minutes to soften at room temperature. In a large mixing bowl, stir together the butter, shortening, peanut butter, white and brown sugars, eggs, and vanilla until well blended.
2. In a separate bowl, mix together the flour, baking soda, and salt. Stir into the peanut butter mixture, using a spoon or your hands, until well mixed.
3. Preheat oven to 375°F. Take 1 to 2 tablespoons of dough and use your hands to form it into a ball about 1" in diameter. Repeat with remaining dough and place balls about 2" to 3" apart on an ungreased cookie sheet in 3 rows of 4.
4. Dip a fork into flour and push down on each ball to partly flatten the cookie. Repeat to form a crisscross pattern. Bake for 10 to 12 minutes. Use a spatula to remove from the cookie sheet. Let cool on a wire rack.

You don't even need a mixing bowl for this easy cake you make from scratch. Just mix everything together and bake. And you don't need eggs or frosting, either. It's an almost-instant snack or dessert.

QUICK CHOCOLATE CAKE v

What You Need:

1½ cups all-purpose flour

1 cup granulated sugar

6 tablespoons vegetable oil

3 tablespoons cocoa

1 teaspoon salt

1 teaspoon baking soda

1 tablespoon vinegar

1 cup cold water

1 teaspoon vanilla extract (or imitation)

1 tablespoon confectioners' sugar

What You Do:

1. Preheat oven to 350°F. In an ungreased 9" × 12" baking pan, stir together all the ingredients except the confectioners' sugar until well blended. Bake for 25 minutes.
2. Let cool. Sprinkle with confectioners' sugar.

YELLOW CAKE v

Here's a quick and easy cake you can make from scratch. Top with Chocolate Butter Frosting (see recipe in this chapter) or your favorite canned or packaged frosting.

What You Need:

⅓ cup solid shortening, plus extra for greasing

½ cup all-purpose flour, plus extra for dusting

¾ cup white granulated sugar

2½ teaspoons baking powder

½ teaspoon salt

1 egg

1½ teaspoons vanilla extract (or imitation)

¾ cup milk

What You Do:

1. Preheat oven to 375°F. Grease a round or square baking pan with shortening and dust lightly with flour.
2. Place ⅓ cup shortening, ½ cup flour, sugar, baking powder, salt, egg, vanilla, and ½ of the milk in a large mixing bowl. Beat with an electric mixer or by hand for about 2 minutes. Pour in the remaining milk and beat for another 2 minutes. Pour the batter into the prepared baking pan.
3. Bake for 30 minutes. Test for doneness by inserting a toothpick into the center of the cake. The cake is done when the toothpick comes out clean. Remove from the oven and let cool on a wire rack. Let the cake cool completely before frosting.

Chocolate, caramel, and pecan flavors make this cake taste like everyone's favorite turtle candies. Delightful served warm topped with whipped cream or frozen nondairy whipped topping.

TURTLE CAKE v

What You Need:

1 tablespoon solid vegetable shortening

1 (18.25-ounce) box German chocolate cake mix

1 (14-ounce) package caramels

½ cup (1 stick) butter

1½ cups evaporated milk

1 cup chopped pecans

1 cup semisweet chocolate chips

What You Do:

1. Preheat oven to 350°F. Use a paper towel to grease a 9" × 13" baking pan with the shortening. Dust with about 2 teaspoons of the dry cake mix. Return "extra" dry mix to the package.
2. Mix the cake batter in a large mixing bowl, according to package directions. (Check the box for egg, oil, and water requirements to be sure you have the ingredients on hand.) Pour ½ of the batter into the prepared baking pan. Bake for 15 minutes. Remove from oven.
3. While the cake is baking, stir together the caramels, butter, and milk in a medium saucepan over low heat. Stir constantly until the caramels melt. Be careful not to let the milk scorch the bottom of the pan. After removing the cake from the oven, pour the caramel mixture over the cake. Top with a layer of pecans and a layer of chocolate chips. Cover with remaining batter. Return to oven and bake for 15 to 20 minutes, until a toothpick inserted in the center comes out clean.

POUND CAKE v

What You Need:

½ pound butter, plus 1 tablespoon for greasing the pan

2 cups all-purpose flour

1½ teaspoon baking powder

⅛ teaspoon salt

1 cup granulated sugar, divided

5 eggs

2 teaspoons vanilla extract

What You Do:

1. Unwrap the butter and set it out in a large mixing bowl to soften for 15 to 20 minutes. Preheat the oven to 325°F. Generously grease a loaf pan with 1 tablespoon of the butter. Set aside.
2. In a medium mixing bowl stir together the flour, baking powder, and salt. Set aside.
3. Beat the butter with an electric mixer until smooth. Add ¾ cup of the sugar, and beat until well blended. Add the rest of the sugar and beat until fluffy. One at a time, crack the eggs into the bowl and beat. Add the vanilla and beat some more until well blended.
4. Use a spoon—not the mixer—to stir in the flour mixture until smooth. Do not overstir. Pour the batter into the loaf pan and smooth the top. Bake for 1¼ hours.
5. After the first hour, test for doneness with a wooden toothpick. It should come out clean when inserted into the middle of the cake. If not, bake for 15 minutes more. Remove from the oven. Let sit in the pan for 5 to 10 minutes. Turn upside down so the cake falls out onto a wire rack. Turn the cake right-side up to cool before slicing.

LEVEL **M**

SERVINGS **6**

Sweet and meaty, this pie tastes so delicious, your friends will never guess how easy it is to make. And they'll be back for more. Top with whipped cream if you like.

PECAN PIE v

What You Need:

1½ cups maple syrup

¼ cup granulated sugar

¼ cup butter or margarine

1½ cups pecan halves

1 unbaked 9" pie crust

3 eggs

1 teaspoon vanilla extract (or imitation)

⅛ teaspoon salt

What You Do:

1. In a medium saucepan over medium-high heat, stir together the syrup, sugar, and butter (or margarine) until the mixture boils. Continue cooking for 5 minutes, stirring occasionally. Remove from heat.
2. Place the pecan halves in an even layer in the bottom of the pie crust. Preheat oven to 375°F.
3. In a medium mixing bowl, slightly beat the eggs with a fork. Stir in the vanilla and salt. Be sure the syrup mixture has slightly cooled (so it won't cook the eggs). Spoon a little at a time into the egg mixture, stirring until well mixed. Drizzle over the pecans.
4. Bake for 35 to 40 minutes. Test for doneness. A knife inserted in the center should come out clean.

FRESH STRAWBERRY PIE v

When luscious, fat strawberries come into season in the spring, use some of them to create this popular pie. If strawberries are out of season, you can substitute frozen ones. Thaw them first. Instead of frozen topping, you can make homemade whipped cream (see the "How Do I Whip Cream?" sidebar with this recipe).

What You Need:

1 frozen 9" pie crust

2 cups fresh strawberries

1 cup granulated sugar

2 tablespoons cornstarch

1 cup water

¼ cup strawberry-flavored gelatin (powdered mix)

1 (8-ounce) carton frozen nondairy whipped topping

What You Do:

1. Bake the pie crust according to package instructions. Set aside. Clean the strawberries (see the "How Should I Clean Strawberries?" sidebar with the Fruit Pizza recipe in this chapter). Slice about ½ of the strawberries into halves. Set aside.

2. In a large frying pan over medium heat, stir together the sugar, cornstarch, and water until the sauce is clear and thick. Remove from heat. Stir in the gelatin mix until well blended. Let cool.

3. Gently stir in the sliced and whole strawberries until well coated. Pour the mixture into the pie shell. Chill in the refrigerator. When ready to serve, top with whipped topping.

How Do I Whip Cream?

Before whipping cream, place the mixing bowl and wire whisk or beaters for your electric mixer in the freezer to chill for about 30 minutes. Pour whipping cream into the bowl. Use a wire whisk or electric mixer to whip the cream until it is stiff enough to hold a stiff peak when you lift the whisk or beater out of the bowl. Be careful not to beat too long or you'll have fresh butter! Cover and refrigerate until ready to use. If the whipped cream starts to separate while sitting in the refrigerator, whip again for 1 minute.

Here's an easy recipe for the traditional Thanksgiving dessert. Top with whipped cream, nondairy frozen whipped topping, or whipped cream in a pressurized can.

EASY PUMPKIN PIE v

What You Need:

2 eggs

1 (30-ounce) can pumpkin pie filling

1 (5-ounce) can evaporated milk

1 frozen 9" deep-dish pie crust

What You Do:

1. Preheat oven to 425°F. Beat eggs in a large mixing bowl. Stir in pumpkin pie filling and evaporated milk until well blended. Pour into frozen pie crust.
2. Bake 15 minutes. Reduce heat to 350°F. Bake for another 50 to 60 minutes. Test for doneness by inserting a knife into the center of the pie. Pie is done when knife comes out clean. Remove from oven and place on a wire cooling rack. Cool at room temperature for 2 hours. Refrigerate at least 1 hour until thoroughly chilled.

FRESH PEACH PIE v

The filling for this pie cooks into a creamy custard. You can slice the peaches instead of cutting them in half, if you like. A "rounded" tablespoon has a small "hill" that extends above the spoon. If you scrape off the "hill," you get a "level" tablespoon.

What You Need:

6 ripe peaches

1 unbaked 9" pie crust

2 rounded tablespoons cornstarch

1 cup granulated sugar

1 cup heavy cream

What You Do:

1. Peel the peaches and cut in half horizontally. Remove the pit, then place the peach halves in the pie crust, flat-side up.
2. Preheat the oven to 425°F. In a small mixing bowl, stir the cornstarch and sugar until well mixed. Sprinkle over the peaches.
3. Pour the heavy cream over the top.
4. Bake 15 minutes. Reduce heat to 375°F. Bake 40 to 45 minutes until peaches are tender and the filling bubbles.

Good enough for royalty, a trifle is a typical dessert following traditional meals in the British Isles. It may well have been enjoyed by kings and queens.

STRAWBERRY TRIFLE v

What You Need:

1 (16-ounce) package frozen, prepared pound cake

About 1 cup orange juice

1 quart fresh strawberries

2 (3.9-ounce) packages instant vanilla pudding

2 cups milk (for pudding)

1 (12-ounce) container frozen nondairy whipped topping

What You Do:

1. Cut cake into thirds horizontally, then into 1" cubes. Pour enough orange juice over the cake to soak it. (Pour a little at a time so you don't drench the cake.)
2. Clean the strawberries. Thinly slice all but 3 strawberries. Prepare pudding using milk according to package directions.
3. In a deep, glass serving bowl, repeat layers of cake, strawberries, pudding, and nondairy frozen whipped topping until mixture reaches the top of the bowl. Regardless of the last layer, end with a layer of nondairy frozen whipped topping. Use 3 whole strawberries to decorate the top. Place in the center with points facing inward and touching. Cover and refrigerate overnight before serving.

Honey cake recipes abound. Here's a recipe to get you started. Look for other variations—or ask your mother or grandmother. Before you begin, let all the ingredients stand on the counter until they reach room temperature (about 70°F).

HONEY CAKE v

What You Need:

Shortening, as needed

2 cups plus 2 tablespoons all-purpose flour, divided

½ cup butter

½ cup granulated sugar

2 eggs

½ teaspoon baking soda

1 teaspoon double-acting baking powder

½ teaspoon cinnamon

¼ teaspoon ground ginger

¼ teaspoon salt

½ cup honey

½ cup strong coffee, cooled

½ teaspoon vanilla extract (or imitation)

¾ cup chopped walnuts

1 tablespoon grated orange zest (grated orange rind)

1–2 tablespoons confectioners' sugar

What You Do:

1. Preheat oven to 350°F. Grease a 9" × 12" ovenproof baking pan. Place the 2 tablespoons flour into the pan. Tip, tilt, and gently tap the pan until the flour dusts the sides and bottom.
2. In a large mixing bowl, use a spoon or electric mixer to blend the butter and sugar until soft and smooth. Add the eggs and continue blending until the mixture is light and fluffy. Set aside.

(continued on next page)

HONEY CAKE — CONTINUED

3. Place a piece of waxed paper on the counter. Sift together the 2 cups flour, baking soda, baking powder, cinnamon, ginger, and salt onto the waxed paper. Set aside. In a separate, medium mixing bowl, stir together the honey and coffee until well blended. Stir in the vanilla extract, walnuts, and orange zest until well mixed.

4. Scoop about ⅓ of the sifted ingredients into the egg mixture. Stir. Scoop about ⅓ of the honey mixture into the egg mixture. Stir. Continue alternating ⅓ of each mixture until all the ingredients are well blended. Pour the batter into the baking pan.

5. Bake for 30 minutes. Let cool. Sprinkle with confectioners' sugar.

How Do I Sift Flour?

Sifting flour adds air to a recipe. To sift, place a small amount of flour into the top of the sifter. Hold device over a mixing bowl and pull on handle several times until all of the flour passes through the screen. One way to mix dry ingredients is to sift them together. Simply place all the ingredients into the top of the sifter at the same time. Sift. If you don't have a sifter, you can create the same effect by placing flour and other dry ingredients in a strainer. Gently shake strainer until all ingredients have passed through.

CARROT CAKE v

This well-loved dessert is best topped with Cream Cheese Frosting (see recipe in this chapter). You can substitute raisins or dried cranberries for the nuts, or combine your choices for a total of 1 cup.

What You Need:

3 cups all-purpose flour
2 cups granulated sugar
1 tablespoon baking soda
2 teaspoons cinnamon
1 teaspoon salt
1 cup vegetable oil
4 large eggs
1 teaspoon vanilla extract
3–4 fresh carrots
1 cup applesauce (sweetened or unsweetened)
1 cup chopped walnuts or pecans

What You Do:

1. Preheat the oven to 325°F. Spray 2 (9") round cake pans with nonstick cooking spray.
2. In a large mixing bowl, combine the flour, sugar, baking soda, cinnamon, and salt.
3. Place the vegetable oil, eggs, and vanilla extract in a medium mixing bowl. Stir with a fork until well-blended.
4. Use a grater to grate enough carrots to make 2 tightly packed cups. Add to the flour mixture, along with the egg mixture, and applesauce. Stir until almost blended. Add the nuts. Briefly stir just until blended.
5. Pour half of the batter into each cake pan. Bake 40 to 45 minutes. Cake is done when the top cracks and feels springy to the touch and the edges pull away from the sides of the pan.
6. Remove from the oven and cool in the pans for 15 minutes. Use a knife to loosen the cakes from the sides of the pans. Flip over cake layers onto a wire rack. Cool to room temperature before frosting.
7. Place the bottom layer on a cake plate. Slip pieces of waxed paper halfway under the cake. Frost the top of the layer. Place the second layer on top. Frost the top and sides.

LEVEL **H**

SERVINGS **8**

Tangy, sweet pineapple flavor and attractive presentation make this dessert a crowd-pleaser. Hint: 1 (8-ounce) tub of frozen whipped topping contains 2 cups; use only ½ tub in this recipe.

PINEAPPLE ANGEL FOOD CAKE v

What You Need:

1 (3.4-ounce) package instant vanilla pudding mix

1 (20-ounce) can crushed pineapple with juice

1 cup nondairy frozen whipped topping, thawed

1 (10-ounce) prepared angel food cake

10 whole fresh strawberries with stems attached

What You Do:

1. Stir together the pudding mix and crushed pineapple with juice. Slowly add the whipped topping. Set aside for five minutes.
2. Cut the cake into three horizontal layers. With the cut side up, place the bottom layer on a serving plate. Spread 1⅓ cups of the filling on top and replace the second layer. Spread 1 cup of the filling and replace the cake top.
3. Use the remaining filling to frost the top and sides of the cake. Arrange strawberries point-side out in a circle on top of the cake. Chill at least 1 hour.

LEVEL **H**

SERVINGS **8**

VARIATION:
STRAWBERRY ANGEL FOOD CAKE v

Follow recipe for Pineapple Angel Food Cake, but omit the pineapple and use strawberry-flavored prepared angel food cake and strawberry-flavored nondairy frozen whipped topping.

PARADISE ANGEL FOOD CAKE v

What You Need:

1 (2.25-ounce) package sliced almonds

1 prepared angel food cake

1 pint heavy cream

⅓ cup confectioners' sugar

2 tablespoons dry hot chocolate drink mix

What You Do:

1. Preheat oven to 375°F. Place sliced almonds on an ungreased cookie sheet. Roast for 3 to 5 minutes until golden brown. Remove from oven. Set aside. Place angel food cake on a serving plate, set aside.

2. In a small mixing bowl, whip the heavy cream (see the "How Do I Whip Cream?" sidebar with the Fresh Strawberry Pie recipe in this chapter).

3. As it starts to look fluffy, add confectioners' sugar and hot chocolate drink mix. Continue whipping until whipped cream is stiff.

4. Spread whipped cream on the top and around the side of the cake. Sprinkle almonds on top of the cake. Keep refrigerated until ready to serve.

APPENDIX A

Equipping the Kitchen

If you're new to the kitchen, you may not have the essentials you need to cook for yourself. Here's a list of basic utensils, herbs, spices, and other ingredients you'll want to have on hand. Those marked with an asterisk are recommended for all kitchens. Purchase other items as needed.

- Aluminum foil
- Appliances:
    Coffee pot
    2-quart slow cooker
    Electric blender
    Electric mixer
    *Electric (or manual) can opener
    Electric popcorn popper
    Electric skillet
    *Toaster or toaster oven
- *Colander
- *Cutting board
- Gadgets:
    Apple corer
    Bagel slicer
    *Egg slicer
    *Kitchen scissors
    *Kitchen timer
    Meat thermometer
    Sifter
    Steamer basket
- Hand Utensils:
    Cheese slicer
    Grater

Huller
Ice cream scoop
*Long-handled fork
Pizza cutter
*Potato masher
Rolling pin
*Slotted spoon
Soup ladle
Spaghetti server
*Spatula (one that's flexible and one that's firm)
*Spoon (large)
Tongs
Wooden spoon
- Knives:
    Bread knife
    *Paring knife
    *Potato peeler
    *Roast slicer
- Measuring Cups (Ovenproof Glass):
    1 cup
    *2 cup
- *Measuring spoon set
    ⅛ teaspoon to 1 tablespoon
- *Mixing bowls (set of 3)
- Muffin tin
- Ovenproof Pans:
    Baking pans (2)
    9" × 13" × 2"
    *9" × 9" × 1¾"
    *Baking sheets (2)
    Covered baking dishes (3)
    1-quart

1½-quart

*2-quart

Loaf pans

9½" × 5¼" × 2¾" or 8½" × 4½" × 2½"

Pie pan

8" or 9" diameter, 1½" deep

Roasting pan

*9" × 13" × 2"

Tube pan or bundt pan

- *Paper towels
- Plastic wrap
- Popcorn popper
- *Potholders (4)
- Stovetop Pots and Pans (with Lids):

  Double boiler, 1½-quart

  Frying pans (2)

  *9" to 10" diameter

  6" to 7" diameter

  1-quart saucepan

  *2-quart saucepan

  *4-quart Dutch oven or stew pot

- Trivet (1 or more)
- Waxed paper
- Wire whisk
- Herbs, Spices, and Other Ingredients:

  Baking soda

  Basil

  Bay leaves

  Bouillon cubes (beef, chicken, and vegetable)

  Brown sugar

  Cayenne pepper

  Cayenne pepper hot sauce

  Celery salt

  Celery seed

  Chili powder

  *Cinnamon

  Confectioners' sugar

  Cumin, ground

Curry powder

Double-acting baking powder

Dry mustard

*Flour, all-purpose

Garlic, minced

Garlic powder

*Garlic salt

Ginger, ground

*Granulated sugar

Honey

Hot pepper sauce (like Tabasco)

Ketchup

Lemon juice

Maple syrup

Mayonnaise

Mustard, prepared

Nonstick cooking spray

Nutmeg

*Olive oil

*Onion flakes, chopped

Onion, minced

Onion powder

Onion salt

Oregano

Paprika

*Parsley flakes, dried

*Pepper

Poultry seasoning

Rosemary

*Salt

Seasoned salt (like Lawry's)

Sesame seed

*Solid shortening

Tarragon

*Vanilla extract (or imitation vanilla extract)

*Vegetable oil

Vinegar, red wine

Vinegar, white

Worcestershire sauce

Glossary of Cooking Terms

à la mode: The direct translation from French is "in the fashion." Most often, this term refers to a scoop of ice cream served with a piece of pie.

al dente: Tender but still firm. Usually applies to pasta or vegetables.

au gratin: Topped with browned bread crumbs, usually blended with butter or cheese before baking.

bake: Cook in an oven with dry heat.

barbecue: Cook on a grill over hot charcoal.

baste: Spoon liquid or fat over food during cooking.

beat: Stir vigorously to add air.

blanch: Briefly cook in boiling water or fat.

blend: Mix together.

boil: Cook in steaming water or other liquid. Boiling water has large bubbles that break at the surface.

broil: Like barbecuing, broiling is cooking directly over a fire or directly under the heating element. Heat for broiling is more intense than for baking or roasting.

chill: Cool in the refrigerator until cold.

chop: Cut into small pieces.

coat: Cover with another ingredient, such as coating lettuce with salad dressing or coating a strawberry with chocolate.

colander: A bowl-like pan with holes in the bottom for draining such foods as pasta and steamed vegetables.

confectioners' sugar: Powdered sugar.

cool: No longer warm, but not yet chilled.

corer: A utensil used to remove apple cores.

cream: Stir or beat together two or more ingredients until the mixture is soft and smooth. This term usually refers to mixing fat and sugar.

crisp-tender: Food—usually vegetables or pasta—that is tender but still firm.

cube: Cut into little boxes, usually with about ½"-long sides.

dash: An imprecise measurement that means a small amount; about ⅛ teaspoon.

deep-fry: Cook by submersing in hot fat.

defrost: Thaw.

dice: Cut into little, bitty cubes, usually with sides less than ¼" long.

dilute: Add liquid to make an ingredient thinner or less strong.

drain: Remove liquid or fat; usually done by using a sieve or colander.

dust: Lightly sprinkle, usually with flour or confectioners' sugar.

entrée: The main dish of a meal—usually meat, fish, or poultry, but may be a meat substitute or a casserole.

evaporated milk: Whole milk that has been heated to remove 60 percent of its water; no sugar is added; do not substitute for sweetened condensed milk.

fillet: Meat or fish with the bones removed.

firmly packed: A way to measure an ingredient, like brown sugar, by tightly pressing it into the measuring cup or measuring spoon. This method results in more of the ingredient than using the usual measuring method.

flake: Separate into small pieces, often by using a fork; for example, you may want to flake tuna or salmon when you remove it from a can.

fold: A method of stirring from the bottom of the bowl to the top, rather than around in a horizontal circle; start with the spoon in the center of the bowl, then plunge it down to the bottom, and back toward you up the side to the top; turn the bowl and repeat until the ingredients are well mixed together.

freeze: Chill at a cold enough temperature (32°F for water) to turn solid.

fry: Cook in hot fat.

garnish: Decorate one food with another. Parsley is a frequently used garnish that improves the appearance of food.

grate: Rub a food against the small holes of a grater.

grater: A utensil with sharp-edged holes used to shred such foods as cheese, carrots, and lettuce.

grease: Coat a baking pan with solid shortening, vegetable oil, or nonstick cooking spray to prevent sticking.

heat: Make food warmer.

hull: Remove stems from fruit.

huller: A utensil used to remove the stem and leaves from strawberries.

invert: Turn upside down.

julienne: Cut into sticks similar in shape to wooden matches. Julienne strips are like long cubes.

marinade: A liquid mixture that contains an acid, seasonings, and, often, oil. Used to add flavor to meats or vegetables before cooking.

marinate: Soak food in a marinade.

melt: Change from solid form to liquid.

mince: Cut into teeny-weeny pieces.

mix: Combine foods, usually by stirring.

mull: Heat, sweeten, and add spices.

pare: Cut off the peel of such foods as apples and potatoes.

peel: The outer skin of a fruit or vegetable; also refers to removing the outer skin of a fruit or vegetable.

pinch: An imprecise measurement term that means the amount you can hold between your thumb and forefinger.

pit: A stone that contains the seed of such fruits as avocados and cherries; also refers to removing such a stone.

poach: Slowly simmer in liquid.

powdered sugar: Confectioners' sugar.

preheat: Heat an oven, frying pan, griddle, broiler, or other cooking appliance to a specific temperature prior to cooking.

rest: Let meat sit at room temperature for a while after cooking before slicing.

rinse: Clean something with water. (Never wash food with soap.)

roast: Cook uncovered using dry heat, usually in an oven. "Roast" usually applies to meat; "bake," which also means to cook with dry heat, usually applies to such foods as breads, desserts, and casseroles.

sauté: Cook in a small amount of fat in a frying pan, stirring frequently.

shortening: A fat used in baking or frying; often refers to fat in solid form.

shred: Cut into long, narrow pieces; or, rub food across the large holes of a grater.

sift: Add air to a recipe by passing such ingredients as flour through a sieve.

sifter: A utensil used to sift ingredients.

simmer: Cook in water or other liquid that is not quite as hot as boiling; water that is simmering has small bubbles below the surface.

slice: Cut a thin, flat piece of such foods as tomatoes and onions; also refers to cutting meat the same way.

soufflé: A fluffy, baked egg dish with a wide variety of other ingredients.

spoon: Scoop using a spoon.

steam: Cook in steam from boiling water rather than cooking in the water.

stew: Cook slowly in liquid over low temperature.

stir: Move a spoon or other utensil in a circle to combine ingredients.

stir-fry: Cook in a small amount of fat in a frying pan or wok over high heat, stirring constantly to prevent sticking or burning.

strainer: A sieve used for straining foods; can also be used to sift such ingredients as flour.

sweetened condensed milk: Whole milk that has been heated to remove 60 percent of its water and has been commercially sweetened; not a substitute for evaporated milk.

tent: A piece of aluminum foil folded in half and propped open like the roof of a house over such food as turkey to keep the food from getting too brown when baking or roasting in the oven.

thaw: Let warm up from a frozen state to an unfrozen one.

toss: Gently mix such ingredients as lettuce and other vegetables by scooping and lifting them with hands, spoons, or other utensils.

undiluted: Without added liquid; for recipes that include condensed soup, undiluted means not to add milk or water to the soup.

whip: Beat rapidly; like beating, whipping adds air.

whisk: A kitchen utensil usually made of wire used to blend such ingredients as eggs, milk, and cream; also used as a verb meaning "to whip."

wok: A large, deep frying pan used to stir-fry vegetables.

zest: The outer skin of such citrus fruits as lemons, limes, and oranges. Grated zest is sometimes used as a flavoring.

APPENDIX C
Cooking Vegetables

If you want to cook fresh vegetables by themselves instead of in a casserole or a fancy side dish, you can boil or steam them. Generally, steaming or boiling in a small amount of water in a covered saucepan works best for cut or small vegetables, while boiling uncovered is preferred for large or whole vegetables. Here are a few tips:

1. For most vegetables, figure about 2 servings per cup.
2. Before cooking, rinse vegetables under cold, running water. Drain. Cut off inedible stems or leaves.
3. You can boil vegetables with about ½" of water in a saucepan. Bring to a boil over high heat. Cover the saucepan. Reduce heat to medium for the prescribed cooking time.
4. Steaming is easy if you use a steamer insert that keeps the vegetables up out of the water. Or, use a pot designed as a steamer.
5. For boiling green vegetables, cook uncovered for the first 5 minutes; then cover for the remaining cooking time. For other vegetables, cover as soon as the water boils. Reduce heat to medium. Cook until tender, yet still firm.

Asparagus

You can enjoy dark green asparagus spears topped with butter, lemon pepper, cheese, or special sauces. Although it is available year-round, many people associate slender new spears with spring. In fact, peak seasons stretch from January to June and August to October, depending on the growing area. Before cooking, remove the tough bottom inch or so of the stems by cutting or breaking off as if they were sticks.

Cooking time: Tips, 5 to 8 minutes; 1" pieces, 10 to 15 minutes; whole, 10 to 20 minutes

Yields 1 serving per 5 spears

Broccoli

Choose broccoli with a firm cluster of small flower buds with dark green or sage color. A purplish tone is okay. So is a yellowish tint on the sides of the floret. However, avoid broccoli that has open clusters with greenish yellow color. Before cooking, trim off the bottom of the main stem. Serve with butter, lemon juice, and oregano, or canned cheese sauce.

Cooking time: 10 to 15 minutes

Yields 1 serving per stalk

Brussels Sprouts

Brussels sprouts look like tiny cabbages. Serve with butter or margarine and salt and pepper. Herbs and spices that enhance their flavor include garlic, basil, dill, caraway seed, or cumin. Before cooking, remove any discolored leaves. Trim stem ends.

Cooking time: 8 to 10 minutes

Yields 1 serving per 4 sprouts

Carrots

Carrots are good for your eyes, but they won't correct your vision. Carrots are high in vitamin A, which promotes good eye health and helps prevent night blindness. Packaged baby carrots that have already been cleaned may also be steamed.

Cooking time: Sliced, 10 to 20 minutes; small (whole), 15 to 20 minutes; large (whole), 20 to 30 minutes

Yields 1 serving per medium whole carrot

Cauliflower

Serve cauliflower alone or in combination with broccoli and/or carrots. Tasty toppings include melted cheese, diluted lemon juice, or bottled tartar sauce. Before cooking, cut away leaves and the center core. Cut off any discolored spots. If not cooking whole, separate the florets (the "treetops") with the stems attached.

Cooking time: Florets, 8 to 15 minutes; whole, 20 to 30 minutes

Yields 5 servings per head

Corn on the Cob

Fresh corn on the cob is a midwestern favorite. Do not add salt during cooking, as it will toughen the corn. Serve with butter or margarine and salt and pepper. Before cooking, remove husks and corn silks from the corn. For the best flavor ever, if you live on a farm or have a home garden, wait until the water is boiling before you pick the corn.

Cooking time: 5 to 8 minutes

Yields 1 serving per ear

Green Beans

Green beans are fat-free and a good source of fiber. They also are low in calories, with just 25 calories per serving. When purchasing, look for clean, tender beans with uniform shape. For added flavor, toss with butter or bacon fat after cooking. Or, season with basil, marjoram, dill weed, or thyme. Before cooking, cut or snap off the ends. Leave whole, or cut crosswise into 1"-long pieces or cut lengthwise (known as French cut).

Cooking time: Cut, 15 to 20 minutes; French cut, 10 minutes; whole, 15 to 20 minutes

Yields 1 serving per ¾ cup

Peas

Finding fresh peas in the pod is rare, so most people use frozen. Cook according to package instructions. If you want to shell your own, remove from the pods immediately before cooking. For either frozen or fresh, add 1 teaspoon sugar to the cooking water. You can also use thawed frozen peas in cold salads.

Cooking time: 8 to 15 minutes

1 cup yields 2 servings

Potatoes

The potato is the most popular vegetable in the United States. The easiest way to cook potatoes is to bake them. You can boil them for use in mashed potatoes, potato salads, or potato casseroles. You can use any variety, but red and russet potatoes work especially well for boiling.

Cooking time: Bake at 375°F for 1 hour or at 350°F for 1½ hours; boil, cut, 20 to 25 minutes; whole, 30 to 35 minutes

Yields 1 serving per medium potato

APPENDIX D

U.S. / Metric Conversion Charts

VOLUME CONVERSIONS

U.S. Volume Measure	Metric Equivalent
⅛ teaspoon	0.5 milliliters
¼ teaspoon	1 milliliters
½ teaspoon	2 milliliters
1 teaspoon	5 milliliters
½ tablespoon	7 milliliters
1 tablespoon (3 teaspoons)	15 milliliters
2 tablespoons (1 fluid ounce)	30 milliliters
¼ cup (4 tablespoons)	60 milliliters
⅓ cup	90 milliliters
½ cup (4 fluid ounces)	125 milliliters
⅔ cup	160 milliliters
¾ cup (6 fluid ounces)	180 milliliters
1 cup (16 tablespoons)	250 milliliters
1 pint (2 cups)	500 milliliters
1 quart (4 cups)	1 liter (about)

WEIGHT CONVERSIONS

U.S. Weight Measure	Metric Equivalent
½ ounce	15 grams
1 ounce	30 grams
2 ounces	60 grams
3 ounces	85 grams
¼ pound (4 ounces)	115 grams
½ pound (8 ounces)	225 grams
¾ pound (12 ounces)	340 grams
1 pound (16 ounces)	454 grams

OVEN TEMPERATURE CONVERSIONS

Degrees Fahrenheit	Degrees Celsius
200 degrees F	95 degrees C
250 degrees F	120 degrees C
275 degrees F	135 degrees C
300 degrees F	150 degrees C
325 degrees F	160 degrees C
350 degrees F	180 degrees C
375 degrees F	190 degrees C
400 degrees F	205 degrees C
425 degrees F	220 degrees C
450 degrees F	230 degrees C

BAKING PAN SIZES

American	Metric
8 × 1½ inch round baking pan	20 × 4 cm cake tin
9 × 1½ inch round baking pan	23 × 3.5 cm cake tin
11 × 7 x 1½ inch baking pan	28 × 18 × 4 cm baking tin
13 × 9 × 2 inch baking pan	30 × 20 × 5 cm baking tin
2 quart rectangular baking dish	30 × 20 × 3 cm baking tin
15 × 10 × 2 inch baking pan	30 × 25 × 2 cm baking tin (Swiss roll tin)
9 inch pie plate	22 × 4 or 23 × 4 cm pie plate
7 or 8 inch springform pan	18 or 20 cm springform or loose bottom cake tin
9 × 5 × 3 inch loaf pan	23 × 13 × 7 cm or 2 lb narrow loaf or pate tin
1½ quart casserole	1.5 liter casserole
2 quart casserole	2 liter casserole

Index